SIXTEENTH ANNUAL REPORT

OF THE

Regents of the University of the State of New-York,

ON THE CONDITION OF THE

STATE CABINET OF NATURAL HISTORY,

AND THE

HISTORICAL AND ANTIQUARIAN COLLECTION ANNEXED THERETO.

Made to the Legislature, April 15, 1863.

ALBANY:
COMSTOCK & CASSIDY, PRINTERS.
1863.

State of New York.

No. 115.

IN SENATE,

April 16, 1863.

SIXTEENTH ANNUAL REPORT

OF THE REGENTS OF THE UNIVERSITY OF THE STATE OF NEW-YORK, ON THE CONDITION OF THE STATE CABINET OF NATURAL HISTORY, AND THE HISTORICAL AND ANTIQUARIAN COLLECTION ANNEXED THERETO.

UNIVERSITY OF THE STATE OF NEW-YORK :

OFFICE OF THE REGENTS,
ALBANY, April 15, 1863.

TO THE HON. DAVID R. FLOYD JONES,
Lieutenant-Governor and President of the Senate.

SIR :

I HAVE the honor to transmit the Sixteenth Annual Report of the Regents of the University, on the State Cabinet of Natural History and the Historical and Antiquarian Collection annexed thereto.

I remain, very respectfully,
Your obedient servant,
JOHN V. L. PRUYN,
Chancellor of the University.

REPORT.

To the Legislature of the State of New-York.

The Regents of the University respectfully report :

The collections of the Cabinet continue in the same excellent condition of preservation, as at the date of the last report. Those in zoology, particularly liable to the depredations of insects, have been thoroughly examined, and were found to be entirely uninjured. It has been deemed important, as far as practicable, to procure skeletons, or at least the skulls of the animals represented in the Collection. This work has been commenced, and every opportunity of carrying it forward will be embraced. Among the skeletons already obtained is that of the Moose, an animal which is nearly extinct in this State.

The arrangement of the specimens in palæontology has been completed, and the labelling has been extended as far as the descriptions have been made and the names fixed.

The expectations of considerable additions to the collections in economic geology, from the voluntary contributions of persons engaged in converting rocks and minerals to the uses of life, have not been realized ; and the Regents have become convinced that this object can be accomplished only by the earnest efforts of a person fully comprehending and appreciating what is wanted, and acting on a well-formed and fully developed plan. Such a plan in regard to the size and form of specimens, and their collection, is already formed ; and it is intended vigorously to prosecute it, with the hope and expectation of realizing, to some considerable extent, during the present year, the objects proposed.

The printing of the grammatical and lexicographical treatise on the language of the Mohawks, communicated with the last report, has not been completed, owing to a difficulty of obtaining suitable type for some of the characters. It will be resumed and attached to the present report.

The contributions of Professor Hall to the Palæontology of the State are continued, and herewith submitted.

A list of contributions and collections made by the Curator is annexed.

Respectfully submitted,

By order of the Regents.

JOHN V. L. PRUYN,

Chancellor of the University.

Albany, April, 1863.

ACCOUNT CURRENT.

THE Secretary of the Regents of the University, in account current with the appropriation for preserving and increasing the State Cabinet of Natural History,

DR.

1862–63.	To balance to new account (See Senate Document No. 116, 1862, p. 9)....	$710 96
	To amount received from the Comptroller, on account of the appropriation for 1861–62	400 00
	To interest on bank deposit to January 1862	18 94
		$1129 90

CR.

1861–62.	By cash paid an assistant	$46 88
	.. specimens of natural history	83 75
	.. books	12 00
	.. freight	4 58
	.. postage and stationery....	31 25
	.. chemicals	48 93
	.. contingent expenses....	44 60
	[*Vouchers Nos.* 1 – 6.]	$271 99
	By balance	857 91
		$1129 90

IN BEHALF of the Standing Committee on the State Cabinet, I have examined the above account, and find it correct. The payments have been made by order of the Standing Committee, and are accompanied with proper vouchers. J. N. CAMPBELL.

ALBANY, April 14, 1863.

CONTENTS OF THE APPENDIX.

A. Donations to the State Cabinet during 1862.

B. Catalogue of the Collections made by the Curator during 1862.

C. Birds of New-York in Maine. H. A. DANKER.

D. Contributions to the Palæontology of New-York, by Professor JAMES HALL.

E. Radical Words of the Mohawk Language, with their derivatives : By Rev. JAMES BRUYAS S. J. (Omitted in the report of last year). .

APPENDIX.

(A.)

DONATIONS TO THE STATE CABINET DURING 1862.

From S. S. WHITMAN, Littlefalls, N.Y.

Two specimens of SANDSTONE from the Calciferous sandrock.

Four specimens of ANTHRACITE COAL, one with crystals of quartz, from the Calciferous sandrock.

Dr. J. H. SALISBURY, Newark, Ohio.

Part of a TREE petrified; ANTHRACITE and CHERT from the Coal measures near Falmouth, Ohio.

Mr. HOWE, of Schoharie county, N.Y.

Two large STALACTITES, from Howe's Cave.

C. V. R. HORTON, Chaumont, Jefferson county, N.Y.

Six STONE ARROWHEADS, and a STONE CHISEL.

Lieut. FISK, 66th Regiment New-York Volunteers.

A FLINT ARROWHEAD from the Battle-field of Malvern Hill.

PETER TEN EYCK.

A large COPPERHEAD SNAKE.

CHARLES H. PECK, Albany.

Fifty species of MOSSES, collected in the vicinity of Albany.

GEORGE T. HALL, Normal School.

Specimens of INDURATED CLAY, from Ballston, Saratoga county, N.Y.

E. JEWETT.

Three EURYPTERUS REMIPES; and a slab of beautiful CRINOIDS, seven in number.

HENRY A. HOMES.

FOSSILS from the Hamilton group.

FOSSILS from the Pleistocene formation, Brandon, Vermont.

GEORGE E. GRAVES, Albany.

LIZARDS, FISHES and INSECTS in alcohol, from South America.

JOSEPH HENRY, LL.D., Washington.

Catalogue of North-American Birds, by S. F. Baird.
Classification of the Coleoptera of North America, by J. L. Leconte.
The Coleoptera of Kansas and Eastern New-Mexico, by J.L.Leconte.
Synopsis of the Neuroptera of North America, by Hermann Hugen.
Synopsis of the Lepidoptera of North America, by John G. Morris.
Monograph of the Diptera of North America, by H.
Catalogue of the described Diptera of N. America, by R. Osten Sacken.
A box of Tertiary fossils.

Dr. E. W. HUBBARD, Taltonville, Staten island.

Three species of Serpents.
Six species of Crustaceans.
Four species of Fishes. Coleopterous insects.
Three species of Salamanders.
Two species of Star-fishes.
Two specimens of Phrynosome orbicularis (Horned frogs), Texas.
Specimen of Scarabæus hercules, from South America.

HENRY RADCLIFF, Albany.

A collection of Esquimaux dresses, etc.

Jumper, or Coat for male.
Pants and Boots for male.
Jumper, or Coat for female.
Pants and Boots for female.
Spear for killing Bear.
Spear for killing Walrus and Seal.
Lance, Harpoon-line, Dog-trace, Whip-lash, Lamp, Lamp-wick, Matches, Knife, Sleigh equipments.

(B.)

COLLECTED BY THE CURATOR.

From the Chemung group [Catskill of the Reports], Franklin, Delaware county.

TEETH and PLATES of several species of FISHES. Also MOLLUSKS and PLANTS.

Three specimens of EURYPTERUS REMIPES.

A Slab of MARIACRINUS PACHYDACTYLUS, seven in number.
Jerusalem Hill, Herkimer county.

(C.)

A LIST OF THE BIRDS OF NEW-YORK,

Noticed in Maine during June 1862.

BY HENRY A. DANKER.

AQUILA CHRYSÆTOS,	Golden Eagle.
HALIÆTOS LEUCOCEPHALUS,	Bald Eagle.
PANDION CAROLINENSIS,	Fish-Hawk.
ASTUR COOPERI,	Cooper's Hawk.
CHORDEILES AMERICANUS,	Nighthawk.
CHÆTURA PELASGIA,	Chimney Swallow.
HIRUNDO PURPUREA,	Martin.

Hirundo bicolor,	Whitebellied Swallow.
Hirundo riparia,	Bank Swallow.
Hirundo rufa,	Barn Swallow.
Hirundo lunifrons,	Cliff Swallow.
Alcedo alcyon,	Belted Kingfisher.
Trochilus colubris,	Hummingbird.
Sitta carolinensis,	Whitebreasted Nuthatch.
Troglodytes hyemalis,	Winter Wren.
Parus atricapillus,	Chicadee.
Sialia wilsoni,	Bluebird.
Turdus migratorius,	Robin.
Turdus mustelinus,	Wood Thrush.
Turdus solitarius,	Hermit Thrush.
Turdus wilsoni,	Wilson's Thrush.
Seiurus aurocapillus,	Oven-bird.
Trichas marilandica,	Yellow Thrush.
Vermivora peregrina,	Tennessee Warbler.
Vermivora rubricapilla,	Nashville Warbler.
Sylvicola coronata,	Myrtle-bird.
Sylvicola maculosa,	Spotted Warbler.
Sylvicola pardalina,	Canada Flycatcher.
Sylvicola canadensis,	Blackthroated Warbler.
Sylvicola icterocephalus,	Chestnutsided Warbler.
Muscicapa ruticilla,	Redstart.
Muscicapa pusilla,	Least Flycatcher.
Muscicapa fusca,	Phœbe-bird.
Tyrannus intrepidus,	Kingbird.
Tyrannus cooperi,	Olivesided Kingbird.
Vireo gilvus,	Warbling Vireo.
Vireo olivaceus,	Redeyed Vireo.
Garrulus cristatus,	Blue Jay.
Garrulus canadensis,	Whiskey-jack, Canada Jay.
Corvus americanus,	Crow.
Quiscalus versicolor,	Blackbird.
Quiscalus ferrugineus,	Rusty Grakle.
Struthus hyemalis,	Common Snowbird.
Fringilla melodia,	Song Sparrow.
Fringilla pennsylvanica,	Whitethroated Finch.
Fringilla leucophrys,	Whitecrowned Finch.
Emberiza socialis,	Chipping Sparrow.
Ammodramus palustris,	Swamp Finch.
Carduelis tristis,	Yellowbird.
Picus pileatus,	Crested Woodpecker.
Picus villosus,	Hairy Woodpecker.
Picus pubescens,	Downy Woodpecker.
Picus varius,	Yellowbellied Woodpecker.
Tetrao umbellus,	Ruffed Grouse.
Tetrao canadensis,	Spruce Grouse.
Totanus macularius,	Sandlark.
Larus zonorhyncus	American Gull.
Mergus serrator,	Redbreasted Sheldrake.
Anas obscura,	Black Duck.
Anas sponsa,	Wood Duck.

(E.)

RADICAL WORDS

OF THE

MOHAWK LANGUAGE,

WITH THEIR DERIVATIVES.

BY REV. JAMES BRUYAS S. J.

MISSIONARY ON THE MOHAWK.

Published from the Original Manuscript.

PREFACE.

THIS volume contains undoubtedly the oldest grammatical or lexicographical treatise on the language of the Mohawks; and although but few of that tribe now reside in the State, the Mohawks occupy a most important place in our early history, and undoubtedly decided the sovereignty of New-York, and with it of most of North America. The History of the Five Nations, Hotinonsionni as they called themselves, has been imperfectly written by COLDEN, and will hereafter afford a subject for a noble work.

The Iroquois left no monuments on our soil : their language is their real monument. The Jesuit missionaries, who, from the days of the devoted Jogues to the close of the seventeenth century, when the cruel act of Bellomont prohibited any further attempts to christianise them, labored among the tribes, studied the various dialects with the care and ability of educated men. Chaumonot wrote a Huron grammar and works in Onondaga, Carheil in Cayuga, and Bruyas in Mohawk.

The present volume is one of the works of the last named, and was written evidently in the latter part of the seventeenth century, and most probably on the banks of the Mohawk. It is a closely written manuscript of 146 pages, which has been long preserved in the Mission House at Caughnawaga or Sault St.Louis near Montreal, adding to the interest of the room where Charlevoix and Lafitau wrote.

The grammatical sketch is rather a series of notes. The main work, the RACINES AGNIERES, or Mohawk Radical Words, comprises the primitive words of the language, arranged in five conjugations, with derivatives from each word, and examples in many cases of great importance as explaining the manners, habits and ideas of the people. Except in strict alphabetical arrangement, it is a very full Mohawk Dictionary, written in Latin, but with the meaning of the words in French.

The word taken as a root is a supposed infinitive; and in subsequent revisions of this work, the present indicative was adopted, but the present is the book as prepared by its author.

This clergyman, Father Jacques Bruyas, of the Society of Jesus, a native of Lyons, came to Canada in 1666, arriving at Quebec on the third of August. From the fourteenth of July 1767, when he set out for the Mohawk, down to his death at the Mohawk mission of Sault St.Louis, subsequent to 1700, he was constantly connected with the missions among the Five Nations; spoke the Mohawk as well as he did French; and was regarded as the Master of the language, in which he composed several works, besides the present and other treatises on it. His abilities were admitted by all, not only the writers of his order, but by Hennepin (who seems to have perused this very manuscript), Earl Bellomont and Cotton Mather. His knowledge of the various dialects of the Iroquois must have been great indeed; for after a short stay among the Mohawks in 1667, he was at Oneida from September 1667 to 1671; then among the Mohawks till 1679, except in 1673, when he was in the Seneca tribe. After this, he was chiefly at the Mission of Sault St.Louis on the St.Lawrence. He was Superior of the Iroquois missions for several years, and Superior of all the missions in Canada from 1693 to 1700. In the negotiations between the French and Iroquois from 1699 to 1701, he took an active part, and visited New-York with a letter announcing the termination of hostilities. His last appearance in New-York was in 1700 and 1701, at Onondaga.

PROEMIUM.

DE FORMATIONE VERBORUM.

Quatuor sunt tempora primitiva, ex quibus alia formantur, scil. : Infinitivus, præsens indicativi, futurum affirmationis et negativum.

A præsenti formatur imperfectum addendo aliquid in fine, ut Geθeθakȣe, *je pilais*, à geθeθa, *je pile.*

Præteritum quod habet eamdem finalem cum infinitivo, Plusquam perfectum, Futurum præterito mixtum, cognata sunt tempora quia ejusdem sunt paradigmatis.

Plusquam perfectum addit *nen* finali præteriti : ȣagatentionnen, *j'étois parti*, à præterito ȣagatention, *je suis party.*

Futurum affirmationis, Aoristus præsens Modi Potentialis et Imperativus sunt ejusdem terminationis, ut : egiθet, ȣageθet, seθet.

Futurum negationis duplex est aliud quod idem est cum præt. indic. : Iaten ȣagatention, *je ne partirai pas ;* aliud quod formatur a præsenti indicativi addita aliqua ex particulis motus localibus *nde*, ***he***, *χe*, ***se***, ***θe***, ***sere*** *:* Iaten gatentionhe, *je ne partirai pas ;* Iaten geθeθanne o teram.

Potentialis modus vocatur ille qui respondet voci gallicæ *j'aurois :* Aongȣatentiong, *je serois parti.*

Imperativus formatur a 2da pers. singul. fut. affirm. sublato initiali E : seθet, *pile*, a eseθet, *tu pileras.*

Si post S sequitur I, præfigendum est T ante S ; v. g. Tsien .. netsi, ab Esien ; Tsiagenne, *sors*, ab esiagenne, *tu sortiras.*

Optativi tempora non differunt a potentiali modo nisi per postpositam voti expressivam *sen* vel *señȣen :* Aongȣatentiong señȣen, *utinam profectus essem.*

Subjunctivi tempora non sunt diversa a potentialis modi temporibus. Hactenus de initialibus verborum ; nunc agendum de finalibus ipsorum, et inflexionibus verborum.

DE TEMPORUM FINALIBUS ET INFLEXIONIBUS VERBORUM.

A.

Verba quorum infinitiv. desinit in A habent ut plurimum *præsens* terminatum in ȣ, *imp.* in akȣe, *fut.* in en, *neg.* in anne, quod est potius in usu ad significandum motum quam negationem subjunctivis, v. g. :

Kagannra, *voir*, P. Ch. *pr.* Tekkan-re, *imp.* Tekkansakȣe, nren, ranne; gahra, *mettre dessus*, gahre, hakȣe, hren, hranne.

Gentskȣahra, *mettre* v. g. *sur un siege*; Gaiatara, *peindre.* Iis omnibus additur *tie* ad significandam continuationem actionis vel actio æ. exercitur proficiscendo, v. g. Raθaratie, *il va parlant*, *il parle en marchant.*

Excipe Gaienna, *prendre*, quod habet *pr.* terminatum in as, *aff.* in χa, *neg.* nasere.

Gaiatara, neutr. *estre present ;* giatare, giatarakȣe, giatarag vel giatarann.

Onterita dicitur potius Ontentaon, *bruler la terre pour l'ensemencer ; pr.* tas, *f*, taȣe, *n.* tasere.

E.

Verba in E habent communiter *pr.* in e, *imp.* in ekȣe, *f.* in eg, *neg.* in sere, vel seg v. θe.

Gentagre, *estre gisant*, *couché*, *malade ; p.* gitagre, *I.* gitagrekȣe, *f.* ȣgitagreg, *n.* egitagrensere.

Onnhe, *vivre; p.* gonnha, *imp.* gonnhekȣe, *f.* egonnheg, *n.* egonnheseg.

Sic Ioθore, *il fait froid ;* Ioθarekȣe, eiȣθoreg.

Hogete, *il porte;* tekȣe, P. S.

Hoθonte, *il est attentif;* hoθontekȣe, P. S.

Hannagre, *il demeure;* grekȣe, greg, P. Ch.

Hæc verba sumunt alia tempora a verbis : Aθontaton, atketaton, ennagraton, aθoraton.

Ita Hajatate, *il y est present;* hajatatekȣe, tateg.

Onhȣentsiase, *il y a une teste;* tekȣe, teg.

Garonhiate, *il y a un ciel;* P. Ch. tet, ȣe, teg.

Iȣkste, *cela peze;* 2ae conj. P. S. tekȣe, teg.

Excipe 1° :

Gagȣanne, *estre grand;* P. Ch. *imp.* gȣannenne, *f.* gȣannha, *n.* nhasere.

Gahȣae, *frapper sur quelque chose; f.* eg.

Ohare, *laver; imp.* rehakȣe, renne.

Gaiote, *estre empeché:* S. agiote, *f.* eȣagioten, *n.* eȣagiotensere.

Teiosȣaθe, *lucet;* θekȣe, *f.* θenne vel θeg.

Excipe 2. Numeralia desinentia in age, quæ sic inflectuntur age, agennen, agehag. Tegni, te ȣenniserage, *il y a deux jours que* .. te ȣenniseragennen, *il y avait; f.* te ȣenniseragehag.

Excipe 3. Relativa in se, v. g. Gasȣense, *hayr* quelqu'un; *imp.* schakȣe, *f.* eȣakȣenseg.

I.

Verba in I significantia plenitudinem habent *pr.* in i, *imp.* innen, *f.* ig vel isere.

Gannonsi, *la cabane est pleine ;* gannonsinnen, gannonsig.

Sic omnia relativa in i habent *pr.* isk, *imp.* iskȣe, *f.* nien, *n.* nire. Aχerihonniannisk, *j'enseigne;* nihakȣe, nien, nire.

Sic Atsori, *manger la sagamité ; pr.* gatsorisk, *imp.* rihakȣe, *f.* ri, *n.* rianne.

Onni et composita sic inflectes : nisk, nihakȣe, ni, nianne.

Sic ori et composita : Gannonhȣarori, *pr.* s, *dire sa chanson de mort ;* Atati, tisk, tali, tahianne v. tatiasere.

AON.

Verba in AON habent *pr.* in as, *imp.* askȣe, *f.* anne, *f. motus*, asere.

Gannhaon, *louer*, *commander;* nhas, nhaskȣe, nhanne, nhasere.
Gaȣejentataon, *sçavoir;* tas, tanne, tasere.
Gannontraon, *rencontrer*, *atteindre;* tras, traskȣe, tranne, trasere.
Gaientaon, tas, taskȣe, tanne, tasere, *tomber.*
Gannontaraon, *scandere montem;* taras, taranne, tarasere.

Excipe 1°. Gaiatajesion, *ne trouver pas une personne qu'on cherche;* P. Ch. sas, saskȣe, sa, sasere.
Gentaon, *dormir; pr.* tas, taskȣe, taȣe, taseg.

EñON,

habent *pr.* in ens, *imp.* enskȣe, *f.* enne, *n.* ensere.

Gaiageñon, *sortir;* P. Ch. ens, enskȣe, enne, ensere.
Gaiateñon, *tomber;* P. Ch. Gannagreñon, *avoir abondance*, quod in aoristo habet Ongnagren, P. S.
Garheñon, *le jour venir;* ens, enskȣe, enne, enrhensere.

Excipe Gasȣeñon, *haïr;* P. Ch. *pr.* gasȣense, *imp.* sehakȣe, *f.* se, *n.* sere.

Gannaχȣeñon, P. S. *être en colere, se dépiter; pr.* ens, *imp.* enskȣe, *f.* en, *n.* ioreseg.

Sic composita a verbo eñon, *arriver*, habent en in futuro.
Gateñon, *n'obeir pas;* tens, ten, tensere.

ION PRO INDICATIVO HURONICO.

Gahoña^{c}rion, *canot verser;* ris, riskȣe, rinne, risere.
Ka^{c}rion, *s'user;* " " " "
Ga^{c}rion, *verser de liquore;* " " rire, "
Gannontakȣion, *estre saoul*, *detêter.*

ONON VEL *OON* PRO *ONDI.*

Gaskoon, *tomber dans l'eau;* P. Ch. os, oskȣe, onne, osere.
Ateroñon, *avair peur;* P. S. ons, onskȣe, onne, onsere.
Gasoñon, *pr.* sas, *f.* sa, *n.* saanne, *achever.* Atsoñon, *estre achevé.*

VERBA IN *GON*,

habent *pr.* in ks, *imp.* kskȣe, *f.* ag, *n.* aχe.

Garihȣanderaχon, *pecher;* P. Ch. raks, raksȣe, rag, raχe.
Gaiagon, *couper;* P. Ch.
Ennitiagon, *porter au col quelque chose.*
Esagon, *chercher;* saks, sag, saχe.
Excipe : Gagȣegon, *estre ensemble*, quod habet in fut. aff. et neg. gonhag.
Gennhongon, *aller chercher*, P. S. quod habet *f. n.* in kse.

VERBA IN *RON*.

Alia habent in *præsenti* rhe, in *fut.* r, in *f. n.* anne.

Gentenron, *avoir pitié de quelqu'un;* P. S. gitenrhe, egitenr, egitenrhanne.
Enron, P. S. *laisser;* ensk, enr, enranne. Et
Arihȣenron, *laisser, emettre une affaire.*
Garonhiahenron, *apeller;* rhe, r, ranne.

Alia habent *præsens* in onsk, *f.* on, *n.* ronne : sic Atonriaron, P. Ch. *arroser d'eau medicinale.*

Alia habent *præsens* in ons, *f.* in re, *n.* in reseg : sic Gannon[c]karon, *tondre quelqu'un; pr.* ons, *f.* re, *n.* reseg.

Gannogaron, *estre malheureux, haïr;* res, re, rese.
Oron et composita Ennonhȣaroron, *avoir un bonnet.*
Iondiron et composita habent in *fut.* rha :
Orihȣandiron, *chose affermie; s.* ejorihȣandirha.

RION.

Atsenrion, *avouer;* P. Ch. ries, rieskȣe, ri, risere.
Gaiataterion, P. S. *faire une bonne rencontre; pr.* teres, *f.* teri v. terenne, *n.* teresere.

VERBA IN *SE*,

tam relativa quam non, habent in *præsenti* et *fut.* se, in *n.* sere.

Asense, *tomber à quelq.*
Garihȣaȣase, P. S. *prendre le soin des affaires de quelq.*
Gaiennaȣase, *aider quelqu'un.*

AON.

Atkaon, *cesser;* kaȣas, askȣe, *f.* kao, *n.* ȣasere.
Ateȣhaon, cum redup. *guerir.* Tsisateȣhaon, *tu t'es gueri;* sesateȣha, *tu gueriras; n.* te sesateȣhasere.
Entoraon, *se lasser; pr.* torha, *f.* toren, *n.* toranne.

ȣAN.

Tȣatrakiȣan, *mettre des nippes à ses jambes, souliers;* ras, *f.* kiȣe.
Garageȣan, *effacer;* ȣas, *f.* eo, *n.* ȣasere.

Destructivum, gȣan vel kȣan.
Ategȣan, *s'enfuir;* gȣas, go, gȣasere.
Oseragȣan, *passer l'hyver;* gȣas, go, gȣasere.
Onhȣentsiagȣatagȣan, *redresser la terre,* cum redupl., v. gȣatongȣan.
Ogȣan, *tirer de l'eau;* ab O, *il y a de la liqueur.*
Gata^{c}kȣan, *tirer dehors;* kȣas, ko, kohe ; ab Ataa, *mettre dedans.*
Atitakȣan, *se debarquer;* ab Atit, *s'embarquer.*

SION DESTRUCTIVUM.

Atseronnia^{c}sion, *se deshabiller ; pr.* sionst, *f.* si, *n.* sionnhe ; ab verbo Atseronni.
Ara^{c}ta^{c}sion, *se dechausser ses souliers.*
Atrataȣita^{c}sion, *oster son capot.*
Tȣatrakiȣa^{c}sion, *oster ses bas.* Ganneren^{c}sion, *deslier.*

EN.

Ex iis multa sunt irregularia.
Gaien, *possidere;* P. S. *imp.* takȣe, *f.* tag, *n.* tanne ; reliquis significationibus e P. A.
Gaien, *y avoir;* takȣe, *f.* tag.
Quædam composita a gaien addunt *t* in fine infinitivi.
Atient, *s'asseoir;* ensk, en, enne. Atrendajent, *prier.*
Gahasent, *tenir conseil; pr.* et *f.* en, *n.* tag, tanne.

IN *GEN,*

faciunt præsens in χa, *fut.* in g, *f. n.* ganne.

A^{c}rongen, *entendre;* P. C. Ga^{c}ronχa, ega^{c}rong, tegaronganne.
Attogen, *se sentir mal;* P. S. χa, g, ganne.
Excipe Gandigon^{c}ratogen, v. gandigon^{c}ratogeñon, S. gens, genskȣa, genne, gensere, ogen, *un canot faire eau; pr.* igogas, *f.* egoχa, *n.* tegogasere.

IN *GANNEN* v. *GENNEN,*

habent *pr.* gennha, *f.* genn, *n.* gennande.

Aseragennen, *disputer pour avoir une hache:* Gaseragennha, egaseragenn, te gaseragennanne.
Onhȣentsiagannen, *debattre à qui aura une terre;* nha, nn, nanne.
Atȣagannen, *parler une langue étrangère.* Atsagannen, idem.
Atiatoχȣannen, *engloutir un animal.*
Gaieren, *faire, dire;* gierha, engiere, gieranne. Sic Atieren, *faire.*

IEN.

In ien sunt irregularia :
Gagarien, *manger;* riask, ri, rihe.
Kaien, *jouer;* jensk, *f.* en, *n.* enne.
Gannien, *abboyer; pr.* et *f.* niha, *n.* nianne.
Kaχen, *estre jumeaux :* Te hieχen, *ils sont 2 jumeaux.*

In compositione, sic inflectes :

Kannehȣaχen, *joindre* 2 *peaux* : Te gnehȣaχes, χa, χase.
Gannesen, *lier;* rensk, ren, renχe.

Et alia pro quibus nulla potest dari regula generalis.

Aterijen, *se chauffer;* P. Ch. ens, en, enne.

IN *HON* PRO *HȣI* HURONICO, ET *AON* PRO ȣ*I*.

In hon pro hȣi, habent *pr.* ask, *f.* hȣe, *n.* hosere.

Gaserhon, *verser de l'eau; pr.* rast, rehȣe. Gannigoserhon, *baptiser.*
Okaon pro Okaȣi, *mattachier;* kask, ka, te sokaȣhe.
Otarhon pro Otrahȣi, hosk, ho, hosere. Ontarhon, *mettre dedans.*
Tagendigon^{c}rontarho, *infunde nobis animum.*

Excipe :

Gannaȣi, S. *pescher abondamment;* ȣisk, ȣi, ȣisere.
Gaiageñon pro gaiagenhȣi, *mettre dehors quelque chose;* ensk, enȣe, ensere.
Asohon pro asohȣi, *teindre de quelque couleur;* ons, on, onne.

T.

In at, habent *pr.* at, *imp.* atakȣe.

Gandigonrat, *avoir de l'esprit* : S. agendigonrat, *j'en ay.*
Iȣat, *il y a dedans quelque chose* : Iȣatakȣe, *il y avoit.*

In et, habent θa, ten, tanne.

Endet, *fovere in sinu;* χenneθa, eχenneten. Iaten te χennetanne.
Gasȣannet, *couvrir de plusieurs habits.*

In ȣt, Gahonrȣt, θa, ten, tanne.

In ent, habent *pr.* ent, *imp.* entakȣe, *f.* tag, *n.* tanne.

Kaga^{c}karent, *avoir deux yeux.*

Nota verba fere omnia in at, et, it, ȣt, ont, habere duplex præsens, pro duplici ratione ; quando res actu significatur, habent pro finale t ; quando habitus, habent θa, v. g.

Atsat, *montrer :* Ihotsat, *ostendit actu;* hatsaθa, *solet ostendere.* Primum est Parad. S ; 2, Parad. Ch.

Sic Atit, *s'embarquer;* Ihotet, *il embarque;* Hatiθa, *il a coutume de s'embarquer;* Gaiatit, *être embarqué,* vel *embarquer quelque chose.*

Nota 2. Pro diversa præsentis significatione variari in futura :

Gaientȣt, *il y a un baston planté :* Egatentȣtanne, *il y aura;* hajentȣθa, *il plante un baton,* ehajentȣten.

Ergo pro actu dices in illis verbis in præsenti t, in *f.* tanne, *n.* tasere ; pro habitu, dices in *pr.* θa, in *f.* ten, *n.* tanne.

Sic Atiront, *tirer :*

Gatiront, *je tire actu;* egatirontanne, tegatirontasere.
Gatironθa, *je tire habitu;* egatironten, tegatirontanne.
Gaskont, *rostir; pr.* gaskont vel gaskonθa, *f.* egaskontanne v. egaskonten, *n.* jaten tegaskontasere v. tegaskontanne.
Gaȣennont, Atȣennont, Ch. θa, ten.

TE PRO *TA*.

Okte, *finir, abboutir; pr.* ta, *imp.* takȣe, *f.* ten, *n.* tanne.
Ennisrokte, *jour finir.*

TI.

Gannagȣati, *semer pour quelqu'un; pr.* tisk, *f.* tars, *n.* tire.
Gaiotati, *empecher quelqu'un;* tisk, ts, tire.
Aθontati, *obeir à quelqu'un;* tisk, ts, tire.
Excipe Atati, *parler;* tisk, ti, tianne.

TION,

habent *præsens* ties, *f.* ti, *n.* tiesere.
Ation, *jetter, abandonner.* Gaiatontion.

STON,

habent *præsens* θa, *f.* t, *n.* tanne.
Garihȣioston, *croire;* grihȣiosθa, egrihȣiost, egrihȣiostanne.
Gagonnienston, *estimer, priser.*

θ*ON*.

Gaienθon, *avoir des champs;* Ch. *p.* θosk, θo, θosere.
Gannhonθon, *donner quelque chose dans la bouche de quelqu'un.*
Gaskonθon, *mettre quelqu'un au feu;* θosk, θo, θosere.

Verba in O sunt omnia fere irregularia.
Gario, *tuer, blesser;* rios, rioske. rio, riosere.
Gan^{c}dio, *germer;* nios, nio, niohe vel niosere. Non constat t.
Gan^{c}nio, *passer quelqu'un en canot;* R. jungitur semper particula motus.
Ganniohon, *pr.* he, henn, ha, hase.
Igo, *il y a liqueur; f.* egoha.
Gaȣendio, *estre maitre;* geȣendio, egennen ; *j'estois le maistre,* geȣendio, egenhag vel eȣaton, *je seray le maistre.*

Verba in ton, quorum particula ton signat causalitatem, faciunt *pr.* in θa, *f.* t, *n.* in tanne, v. g.:

Ategaton, *faire du feu,* P. Ch.
Gatsienton, *guerir,* cum reduplic. θa, t, tanne.
Gannaȣenton, *descendre la rivière.*
Gannonȣireχton, *tomber dans un abysme,* P. S.

Quando vero ton non significat causalitatem, habent *pr.* s, *f.* t, *n.* θe.
Atketaton, *porter;* Ch. *pr.* tats, tat, taθe.
Gannagȣaton, *fouyr,* Ch.
Ennograton, *s'habituer,* S.
Aθoraton, *avoir froid,* P. S.
Aθontaton, *escoutter,* Ch.
Oseraton, *l'hyver venir,* S.
Tȣatonton, *se mettre plusieurs ensemble.*
Tehontons, *ils sont à un même plat.*

IN *ON*,

non habent certam terminationem præsentis et futuri, quare nulla regula generalis dari potest.

Gandoron, *estre important;* S. *pr.* on, *f.* on, *n.* onne.
Garihȣannonton, *interroger;* Ch. onsk, on, onsere.
Aton, *estre possible;* S. ton, ton, tonre.
Gasennion, R. nies, ni, nionhe.
Gagarennion, Ch. nies, ni, nionhe. Sic Kandigon[c]kennion, *tromper.*
Onharon, *sarcler;* onsk, on, onne.
Genteron, *estre;* P. ron, *f.* tag.
Genheioñ, *mourir;* onsk, heie, hejonsere.

Verba in on, significantia motum, præsens et aoristum eodem modo se habent, terminant in es vel e, *imp.* enn vel eskȣe, *f.* a, *n.* ese.

E quidem ad significandum actum, *es* habitum.

Hon : Gagohon, *aller querir;* kkohe, *je vais querir;* kkohes, pro habitu ; *f.* ekkohe ; *n.* ten, tekkohese.

Ron : Gannaθaron, *aller visiter.*

Non : Anendajennon, *aller prier; pr.* et *aor.* nne, *f.* nna, *n.* nese.
Gaien[c]non, *aller mettre, porter.*
Genteronnon, *aller conduire quelqu'un.*

Son : Ennihason, *aller emprunter.*

Xon : Garontiaχon, *aller couper un arbre;* χe, χa, χese.

Θon : Aθontaton, *aller ecouter.*

REGULÆ COMMUNES PRO OMNIBUS VERBIS.

PRO IMPERFECTO.

Præsens in A, E, O, habent *imp.* in kȣe ; ut,

Gnegirha, *je bois de l'eau :* Gnegirhakȣe, *je buvois.*
Gonnhe, *je vis ;* gonnhekȣe, *je vivois.*
Garonto, *il y a un arbre dans l'eau ;* garontokȣe, *il y avoit.*

Excipe ea vocabula quæ numeralibus junguntur :

Te ȣennisrage, *il y a deux jours ;* te ȣenniseragennen, *il y avoit.*
Te garihȣage, *il y avoit* 2 *affaires ;* garihȣagennen.

Verba in t addunt nnen :

Gienteri, *je connois ;* gienterinnen, *je connoissois.*
Tegni, *deux ;* tegninnen, *il y en avoit deux.*

Sic quædam infinitiva quæ usurpantur ad significandam 3[am] personam passivam :

Gaserondi, *cela est accommodé ;* gaseronninnen, *cela estoit.*
Ia neθo te gaieren, gaierennen, *cela n'etoit pas ainsi.*

Præsens in ask, ensk, osk, onsk, habet imperfectum addendo ȣe :
Grihȣanderask, *je peche;* grihȣanderaskȣe, *je pechois.*
Ratrendaiensk, *il prie;* ratrendajenskȣe.
Gnaarhosk, *j'ecris;* gnaarhoskȣe, *j'ecrivois.*
Gienseronsk, *j'escorche;* gienseronskȣe.

Præsens in isk habet imperfectum in akȣe :
Raseronnisk, *il fait des haches;* raseronnihakȣe.

Præsens in s habet imperfectum in skȣe :
Ronnȣseras, *il est galleux;* ronnȣseraskȣe.

Præsens in t habet imperfectum in takȣe :
Iȣat, *il y a dedans;* isatakȣe.

REGULÆ PRO VARIIS TEMPORIBUS ET MODIS.

Quando nescis futurum negativum, utere præterito cum negatione, v. g. Iaten te rotention, *il ne partira pas.*

Quando actio continuata jungitur motui, exprimitur per hatie vel atie additum finali infinitivi :
Gatrendajentatie, *je vais priant.*
Gatrorihatie, *je vais racontant.*
Assen nihatihatie, *ils vont etant trois.*

Additur s huic hatie, ad exprimendum habitum :
Hatigȣegonhaties, *ils sont toujours ensemble.*

Ex activis fiunt passiva præfigendo at 1^{ae} personæ præsentis indicat. ablato g. :
Gaseθa, *je cache;* gataseθa, *je suis caché.*
Otennoronkon, *res est factu difficilis;* a Gandoronkon.
Hotonnheton, *il est mis au monde;* ab Onheton, *donner la vie.*

Excipe 1° verba 2^{ae} conjug. inchoata a gag :
Satkonsagetȣten, *montre ton visage;* pro sategonsagetȣten.

2° inchoata a gah, habent eamdem crasim :
Aχȣendori pro Atchȣendori, ab Gahȣendori, *battre une isle pour tuer les bêtes qui y sont.*
Atkoñannegen, *canots être près l'un de l'autre;* pro Atchoñannegen a Gahoñannegen, *mettre les canots aupres l'un de l'autre.*

3° inchoata a gaȣ :
Atȣennarakon, *etre obei,* pro Ateȣennarakon.
Atȣendioston, *se rendre maistre;* pro Ateȣendioston, a Gaȣendioston.

Nota quod 2ª conjug. transeunte in jam, fit passivum verbum ex activo ; v. g. : Aserondi, *s'accommoder,* a Gaseronni, *accommoder.*

Ex his passivis fiunt reciproca per additionem alterius at, v. g. :
Atatase^{c}ton, *se cacher soymême,* ou *s'entrecacher l'un l'autre;* ab Atase^{c}ton, *estre caché.*
Atatrihonnianni, *s'entreseigner;* ab Atrihonnianni.

Hæc verba reciproca sunt frequentissima in verbis relativis ad significandum infinitivum, v. g. :

ȣatiesen, atatriaahose, *facile est sibi mutuo scribere.*

Item ad significanda substantiva, ut :

Gandoron atatrihonnianni, ***instructio difficilis est***, seu ***difficile est alios docere.***

Nota hæc réciproca usurpare fere in omnibus relativis ad significandum infinitivum, vel nomen verbale quod pro infinitivo exprimitur, v. g. :

Agȣegon jennonhȣes atatronhioenton, ***tous aiment d'estre caressés;*** pro Garonhiaenton.

Verba deponentia sunt quæ licet habeant initiale at, quod est nota passivæ vocis, active tamen sonant :

Hatennhas, *il commande;* a relativo Gannhaon.

Hatetsiens, *il guerit, est medecin;* a rel. Gatsienton.

Hatrios, *il combat;* a rel. Gario, *battre.*

DE POSTPOSITIONIBUS *KON*, *STON* & *TON*.

Tres istæ particulæ adduntur verbis ad significandum causalitatem, vel formalem vel materialem vel efficientem aut finalem.

VERBA QUÆ ADDUNT ^{c}*KON*.

1° Ea quorum infinitivus desinit in A; v. g. Garakon, ***mettre quelque chose***, a gara, ***mettre dessus.***

2° Ea quorum infinitivus et præsens desinunt in E, v. g. Onnhekon, ***vivre de quelque chose;*** ab onnhe, ***vivre.***

3° Ea quorum infinitivus desinit in on et præsens in onsk, v. g. Gahiatonkon, *escrire avec quelque chose;* ab Gahieton, *escrire.*

Excipe Aton, ***perdre***, et Aton, ***devenir***, quæ addunt particulam ton, non vero kon. Sic dices Atonton, ***perdre, egarer quelq.*** non atonkon.

4° Finita in T addunt akon, v. g. Gahasen^{c}takon, ***tenir conseil de quelque chose;*** a Gahasent, ***tenir conseil.***

5° Verbis quorum præsens terminatur in θa vel sta, v. g. :

Gaθeθakon, ***piler avec quelque chose;*** a præsenti geθeθa, ***je pile.***

Garihȣiostakon, a præsenti Grihȣiosta, ***j'escris.***

His adde Genteron, ***estre;*** gageron, ***estre plusieurs;*** gaien, ***avoir***, quorum futuris in tag additur kon, sublato g, v. g. :

Gaientakon, *cela est pour cela.* Θennon esitronta^{c}kon, ***pourquoy es tu là?***

VERBA QUÆ POSTPONUNT *STON*.

1° Composita ab jo, quod significat magnitudinem, addunt ston; ut,

Garihȣioston, *faire estat de quelque chose;* a Garihȣa, ***chose***, et io, ***grand, important.***

2° Verba quorum præsens desinit in ens, ut :

Gandigon^{c}ratogenston, *scavoir par le moyen de quelque chose* ou ***personne.***

Gannhatenston, ***faire regretter quelqu'un :*** Gannhaten, ***regretter.***

Tonsaȣatogenston, ***se demarier pour quelque chose;*** naie tetsiontogensθa, *on se.*

3° Finita in ton, quorum præsens desinit in ts, v. g. :

Gannagȣaston, ***fouyr avec quelque chose;*** a Gannagȣaton, gnagȣats.

RELIQUIS VERBIS POSTPONITUR *TON*, MODO SEQUENTI.

1° Terminata in aon, eñon, oon, mutant has finales in ton, v. g. :
Gannhaton, *faire louer ;* a Gannhaon.
Garonhiagenton, *faire souffrir ;* a Garonhiageñon.
Gaskóton, *faire noyer ;* a Gaskóon.

Excipe A^c^taston, *se saouler de quelque chose :* ab A^c^taon, *se saouler ; pr.* agatas.
Kataston, *se lever debout pour quelque chose ;* a Kataon, *pr.* tektas.

2° Desinentia in on, gon, ȣi, hon et ron, mutant finalem syllabam in ton, v. g. : Gasaton, *achever tout ;* a Gason, *accomplir.*
Garihȣanderaton, *faire pescher ;* a Garihȣanderogon, *peccare.*
Gaserhaton, *arroser avec quelque chose ;* a Gaserhon.
Ganniraton, *affermir ;* ab Jondiron, *cela est ferme.*
Asohe^c^ton, *teindre avec quelque chose ;* ab Osohon, *teindre.*

3° Terminata in en, gen, hen, mutant illud in aton, v. g. :
Askannaton, *faire desirer ;* a Gaskannhen, *desirer.*
Arongaton, *faire entendre quelque chose ;* ab Arongen, *entendre.*
Atehaton, *hontoyer quelqu'un ;* ab Atehen v. Ateheñon, *avoir honte.*
Garihȣaksaton, *rendre mauvaise quelque chose ;* a Garihȣaksen, *res mala.*
Gaieraton, *faire avec quelque chose ;* a Gaieren.

Excipe Katenston, *faire prendre l'essor ;* a Katen, *s'envoler.*
Kajatorenston, *findere aliquod animale en* 2 ; a Kajatoren.

4° Desinentia in O addunt ton, v. g. :
Garioton, *tuer avec quelque chose ;* a Gario, *tuer.*

5° Finita in ȣan, kon, χon, mutant an et t in ati, v. g. :
Ategȣaton, *faire fuir ;* ab Ategȣan, *fuir.*
Gannoronkȣaton, a Gannoronkon, *estimer, priser.*
Gaienθoton, a Gaienθon, *avoir des champs.*

6° Terminata in on, quorum præsens est es v. onsk, mutant illud in aton, v. g. : Gagarenniaton, *eloigner avec quelque chose ;* a Gagarennion, *pr.* es.
Genheiaton, *faire mourir ;* a Genheion.

7° Desinentia in e, quorum præsens est ek, addunt ton, v. g. :
Gagaȣeton, *nager avec quelque chose ;* a Gagaȣe, *nager.*
Gaieton, *suscitare ;* a Gaie, *susciter.*

At dices Gannistiageston, *faire uriner ;* a Gannistiage, *uriner.*

8° Onni, ori cum compositis, et atatri, sumunt aton, v. g. :
Gaseronniaton, *faire avec cela ;* a Gaseronni.
Atoriaton, *chasser avec ch. ;* ab Atori.
Gandigonroriaton, *divertir avec quelque chose ;* a Gandigonrori.
Atatiaton, *parler avec cela ;* ab Atati.

NOTA Illas particulas significare in locum :

θo hatientakȣa, *il demeure là.*
ka θojenta^c^kon, *d'où vient il?*
ken etiontaȣiatakȣa, *c'est par là qu'on entre.*
θo hajenθoθa, *c'est là où il fait ses champs.*

Sic dices Nongati igandaȣatekon, *de l'autre coté de la rivière.*
Θo hereθa, *c'est le lieu où il va.*

Ton et kon significant etiam tempus, v. g. :
Onnaie isro sinni ongȣatentiaton, *rediit quando profecti sumus.*
Naie hondatikakon, *le jour qu'ils se sont embarqués.*

Significant etiam materiam ex qua fit aliquid, et instrumentum quo fit :
Tsonnito hatinnonȣaroseronniaθa, *ils font des chapeaux avec le castor.*
Naie esakonserakȣa, *tu te serviras de chevet.*

Causam finalem : Naie gakonθa, *ideo dico hoc.*
Naie goñjarontonkȣa, *ideo te interrogo.*

Formalem : Naie tionnhe^ckon nongȣatonnheston, *notre ame nous fait vivre.*

DE FORMATIONE VERBORUM RELATIVORUM.

Verborum alia sunt simpliciter, et per se relativa ; alia fiunt relativa, additione aliquarum syllabarum vel litterarum.

1° Verba ex absolutis possunt fieri relativa additione particularum causalitatis ton, ston, kon ; ut,
Ategȣaton, *fugare aliquem;* ab Ategȣan, *fuir.*
Akhaton, *hontoyer quelqu'un;* ab Ataheñon, *estre honteux.*
Gaiataksaton, *rendre laid quelqu'un;* a Gaiatakseñon, *estre laid.*

Ab A fiunt relativa in Anni v. Enni :
Garanni, *donner à manger à quelqu'un;* a Gara, *f.* rhas.
Gaθaranni, *quereller quelq.* Asongȣatarhas, *il nous a.*

Excipe Garaȣi, *couvrir quelqu'un;* hakraȣi, *il m'a couvert;* ehakrase, *il me couvrira;* a Gahra, *mettre dessus.*

Ab Eñon, fiunt relativa in Ase :
Gannaχȣase, *irasci alicui;* a Gannaχȣeñon.
Atehase, *etre honteux pour quelq.;* ab Atehenon.
Garihase, *bouillir pour quelq.;* ab Orihen.

A ton, cujus præsens in ts :
Gannagȣati, *semer pour quelq.;* tisk, ts, tire, a Gannakȣaton, *semer.*
Arati, *coucher aupres de quelq.;* tisk, ts, tire, ab Araten, ts, t, θi.
Ennonhȣeti, *coucher avec quelq.* (in malam partem) ; ab Ennohȣeton.
Aθontati, *obeir à quelq.*; ab Aθonti, *estre attentif.*
Aθorati, *chasser pour quelq.;* ab Aθoraton, rats, rat, raθe.

Verba in Gȣan fiunt relativa addendo ni in infinitivo, et mutando n in s pro futuro affirmativo :
Garagȣanni, *oster de dessus pour quelq.;* a Garagȣan, esaragȣas, *on te.*
Garontageskȣanni, *lever un arbre à quelq.; f.* kȣas.

A verbis in gon fiunt relativa in gi :
A Garontiagon, *couper un arbre;* Garontiagi, *scindere alicui.*
Ab Esagon, *chercher;* Esagi, *chercher à quelq.*
Tagȣasaks, *cherche moi,* v. g. *des pommes.*

NEUTRO ACQUISITIVA.

Atonse, *estre possible à quelq.;* ab Aton, *estre possible. Fut.* Esatonse, ken. *Poterisne?*

Asensa, *tomber à quelq.;* ab Aseñon, *tomber.*

RELATIVA FIUNT AB ABSOLUTIS.

Ateȣejentonni, *garder à quelq.; f.* tonhas, ab Ateȣejenton.

Arontatse, *souffler pour quelq.; f,* ts, ab Arontaton.

Aratȣe, *conter pour quelq.; f.* ts, ab Araton.

Gannagȣatse, *semer pour quelq.;* a Gannagȣaton.

Garontiakse, *couper un arbre pour quelq.* a Garontiagon.

Gaiennaȣase, *aider quelqu'un.*

Tȣatontonse, *se jetter sur quelq.; f.* onsen, a Tȣatonton.

Garihȣagaratatse, *reciter à quelq.;* a Gariȣagaraton.

En mutatur in ATON :

Kasterihaton, *presser quelq.;* a Kasterihen.

Garihaton, *faire bouillir à quelq.;* ab Orihen.

Ategaton, ab Ategen, *il y a du feu.*

Kagasaiatanni, *retarder quelqu'un en chemin;* a Kagasaien.

Gaieraton, *servir de quelque chose;* a Gaieren.

Excipe Atsinnhaston, *se lier avec quelque chose;* pro Atsinnhaton, ab Atsinnhen.

Gon finale mutatur in KTON, v. g. :

Gaiatannentagon, *estre attaché;* Gaiatannentakton, *attacher.*

Tȣenron, *laisser quelque chose,* v. g. *de son discours,* relativum entsi.

Niahoθennon te skȣentse, *tu ne m'as rien laissé.*

Gatagȣentse, *laisse moi.*

RELATIVA AB *EN*.

Kaχenni, *joindre pour quelq.; f.* χas, a Kaχen.

Gaienni, *mettre pour quelq.; f.* enhas, a Gaien.

Verba finita per HASE particulas fieri possunt relativa mutando EN finale in ANNI pro *prœter.*, et in EN pro *fut. affirm.:*

Gaθeθanni, *piler à quelq.;* a Gaθeθon.

Garakȣanni, *mettre dans un plat à manger à quelqu'un;* a Garakon.

Verba in A fiunt relativa addendo NI *prœter.*, et *fut.* rhas :

Garanni, *mettre dessus dedans à quelq.; f.* tagerhas, a Gara.

Verba in ȣAN addunt NI pro *prœterito,* et pro *futuro* S ; ut,

Garagȣanni, *oster dessus à quelq.;* a Garagȣan, *f.* tagragȣas.

Verba in GON fiunt relativa mutando GON in ASE vel AKSE :

Garihȣanderase, *faire pecher quelq.;* a Garihȣanderagon.

Garontiakse, *couper un arbre à quelq.;* a Garontiagon.

Finita in HON mutant N in SE :

Gannaarhose, *escrire pour quelq.; f.* a Gannaarhon, *escrire.*

Composita ab ONNI et ORI addunt ANNI in *prœt.*, et in *fut.* EN :

Gaseronnianni, *faire pour quelq.;* a Gaseronni.

Garihonnianni, *troubler quelq.;* a Garihori, askrihorien, *tu me.*

Finita in T fiunt relativa addendo ANNI v. SE, *f.* S :

Gaskontanni vel Gaskontase, *faire rostir à quelq.;* a Gaskont.

Atsatanni, *montrer à quelq.; f.* Egatsaθas, ab Atsat.

Ab ATION, *jetter*, et ONTION in compos. :

Atiense, *jetter à quelq.; f.* tiens.

Kagasiase, *separer à quelq.; f.* kaχasion.

Atriose, *se battre pour quelq.;* ab Atrio.

Oskaranni, *f.* oskaras, ab Oskaron, tagrenhosχaras, *esbranche moi des arbres.*

Atentiase, *partir pour quelq.; f.* egonjatenties, *je partiray pour toi.*

Finita in θON mutant illud in θOSE pro relativo :

Askȣaserenθos, *tu as usé ma hache;* ab Aserenθose, *user une hache à q.*

PRO NOMINIBUS.

Nomina non inflectuntur per casus, atque adeo non patiuntur ab alio nomine, neque ab ullo verbo vel præeunte vel sequente ullam mutationem, nisi cum illo intrent in compositionem, v. g. :

Ontak, *chaudière*, sive præponatur sive postponatur verbo ȣagiehȣas, *j'ai besoin*, idem prorsus manet dicesque : Ontak ȣagiehȣas vel ȣagiehȣas ontak.

Duo substantiva simul juncta, sic exprimas :

Le livre d' Orite, Orite aorihȣa.

La maison d'Asendase, Asendase ronnonsto.

Appellativa sic exprimunt pro verbo :

Le Capitaine des Iroquois, Hotinnonsionni θoaȣennagan^{c}nere ; id est, *Iroquois habent illum in Dominum.*

Le neveu de Garihȣatiron, Garihȣatiron haȣenhȣaten, seu *il l'a pour neveu.*

Le frere d'Orite, Orite hiatatageña; id est, *Orite et luy sont frères.*

Nomina nationalia formantur a nomine proprio nationis, addendo illis RONNON vel HAGA, sic : Ganniegeronnon vel Ganniegehaga, a Ganniege.

Nomina verbalia qualia sunt *l'amour*, *le peché*, *la crainte*, exprimuntur vel per infinitivum, ut : *Dieu hait le peché*, Diȣ rasȣense ne garihȣanderon; vel per impersonale, Diȣ rasȣense njeriȣanderask; vel per personale, Diȣ rasȣense niagȣarihȣanderase.

Nomina derivativa ab adjectivo, v. g. *la beauté*, *la laideur*, sic efferuntur: Jaχinnonste njontχenniata, id est, *nous aimons les beaux;* Jaχesȣense nieiatakseña, *nous haissons les laids*, quæ per adjectivum exprimuntur; vel per nomina significantia actionem et passionem, v. g. a Gannaarhon, *escrire*, fit Gannaarhontsera, *escriture;* a Gannenskȣan, *desrober*, fit Gannenskȣatsera, *larcin;* vel etiam aliquando formant hujusmodi substantiva ab appellativis, v. g. ab Onnhetien, *femme*, Onnhetiensera, quasi diceres *feminin.*

SYNTAXIS SUBSTANTIVI CUM ADJECTIVO.

Quoniam substantiva quædam subeunt compositionem, quædam vero non subeunt, diversa est etiam earum syntaxis.

Substantiva quæ componuntur, in eo conveniunt cum adjectivis quibus junguntur quod induant naturam eorum paradigmatis, v. g. Gannonsagatste, *cabane de durée*, Parad. Chi, quia gagatste est illius paradig. Si vero Gannonsa componatur cum adjectivo Iondiron, *fort*, dices Onnonsondiron, *cabane forte*, quia Iondiron est Paradigmatis S.

Substantiva quæ non componuntur conveniunt genere, numero et perr sonâ cum suo adjectivo, v. g. Ratsinn, *mas.*, si adjectivo Gatsatste, *fort*, adhærent, dices Ratsatste cum initiali R, quæ est nota 3[ae] personæ masculinæ. Si vero Onnhetien sit subjectiva, illius prædicti dices Gatsatste.

Nota Componi tantum nomina generica et specifica, non autem nomina individuæ contenta sub genere et .. ne, v. g. :

Garonta, *arbre;* Garontio, *bel arbre.* ...ariton, *chesne* non componitur.

RADICES VERBORUM

1ae CONJUGATIONIS.

A, significans *grandeur : imp.* asaȣa, *f.* egaska.

Sing. Kenniga, *ie suis grand comme cela ;* isa, ita, iaga, iȣa de rebus inanim.

Dual. Sateiagna, satetna, satesna, satehna, sategna.

Plur. Sateiagȣas, etȣas, esȣas, ehonnas, egonnas.

Θo niaga neksaa, *combien grand sont les enfants.*

Egajas dicitur de hominibus ; sed de rebus inanimatis et aliis, dicitur eȣas.

De duobus tantum dices Satenna vel Sateȣa, *aussi grand l'un que l'autre.*

Tegni ȣatario okȣari kennasateȣa, *il a tué deux ours d'égale grandeur.*

A impersonale, *y avoir en telle quantité ou grandeur.*

Iaten neθo teȣa, *il n'y a pas tant que cela.*

Niθo nisȣa sinni θaskȣa jesannonten, *il y en a encore autant qu'on t'en a donné.*

Ne θo sinn iȣa, *il y en a assez : cela est assez grand.*

Sȣaska, diminutivum.

A in compositione. Nigannatsia, *grande chaudière;* Nigannatsaa, *petite chaudière ;* Nigannatsias, *de plusieurs chaudières.* Kennigannatsias : *imp.* Gannatsiaskȣa, *f.* Kennigannatsiaska.

Nihaȣenda, *grosse voix;* Nihaȣendaa, *petite voix.*

A in comp., *prendre :* ȣagonnetsa, *je te prens par le bras;* ȣagonhoña, *je prends ton canot.*

Aga, *ramasser des fesoles, pommes de terre :* inusitatum nisi in præsenti; *imp.* son : Jonχas, *on en cherche.*

A significans *arriver,* v. Conjugationes.

A significans *prix, valeur.* Sategna gasire ne isonnito, *une couverte vaut un castor.*

Agannon, *en aller chercher :* ne *pr.* et *fut.* gaganne, *je vais chercher;* hondagannon, *ils en sont alles chercher.*

Agaraon, S. *estre nuit; en estre surpris,* ras, rahȣe, raseg.

Etiogaras, *il fait nuit.* Onne ȣaogaraȣe, *il se fait nuit.*

Agoraton, *causer la nuit.*

Agaratanni, *oster le jour à quelqu'un;* R. *f.* ten.

Satonnek eskȣatagaraten, *retire toi, tu m'otes le jour.*

Agaraon, S. cum reiter : *voir encore la nuit, passer encore le jour*

Tsiongȣagaraon, *nous sejournerons encore aujourd'hui.*

Agarion, *faire des trappes aux lievres.*

Age, particula numeralis subjunctiva quæ numerum indicat :

Θo nioserage, *Combien d'hyvers?*

Præponitur particula TE in num. duali : Te joserage, 2 *hivers;* Te gaiatage, 2 *hommes* ou *autres animaux;* Asen nigannehȣage, *trois peaux.*

In *imp.* habet gennen ; in *f.* gehag : Asen nagandegorhage has, *qu'il y ait* 8 *grains de pourcelaine.*

Agenron, *manquer,* Ch. *imp.* Jogenron si renteron, *comme s'il luy.* ȣagenresnon, *en manque-t-il.*

Ogenra, *cendre, poudre;* P. S. Raogenra, *sa poudre;* Honnagenra, *leur poudre.* Jaten te ȣagagenraien, *je n'ai point de poudre,* 1ae conj.

Gagenronni, *mépriser;* R. nisk, ni, nianne.

Gagenronseronni, idem.

Atagenronnion, Ch. nisk, ni, nianne, *estre reduit en cendres, à neant.*

Agenrata, Ch. *charger un fusil.* Agenrat, *il y a de la poudre dedans.*

Agenratacksan, *la tirer de dedans.*

Atagenrotagȣan, *se decharger, le feu se prendre à la poudre.*

Atagenrotagȣanni, *R.* steg, *f.* gȣas : Ongȣatagenrotagȣas, *le feu s'est pris à ma poudre.*

Atragenrion, Ch. *se rouler, vautrer dans les cendres;* ries, ri.

Agon, *dedans,* in comp.; nagon, *extra,* comp.

Gannatagon, *dans le village.* Gannonskon pro Gannonsagon, *dans la maison.* Dicunt potius ongie.

Asatagon, *en secret,* comme qui diroit *jetter dans l'obscurité ce qu'on dit;* nam osata significat *nuée, fumée.*

Agon, P. O. *estre nud, vuide :* vid. in 4a conj.

Agoennagon te jennonniakȣe; gagogon, jges onnatogon, *le bourg est vuide.*

Rossitagon, *il a des pieds nuds.*

Inde P. P. Recollectos vocant Hondasitagon, *ils ont les pieds nuds.*

Agraon, P. rha, ranne, rasere, *flotter.*

Jogerha, *cela flotte.* Hoiatagranne, *il va flottant.*

Hatiȣendogerha, *Les Hurons* (*quia in insula habitabant*).

Gahoñog-raon, Ch. rha, ranne, *canot flotter.*

Agrakon, P. A. *ce qui fait flotter; pr.* et *f.* kȣa, kȣanne.

A....n, S. *sentir des rapports, provoquer a vomir.*

Agoren, *un autre,* de hominibus.

Ogra, *neige; imp.* vide in fine Ogrigon.

Agreñon, Ch. *neiger, tomber de la neige;* grenns, gren, grensere.

Agratarakon, *s'etre surpris de la neige en voyage*; ks, g, χe.

Agrogȣan, cum nota local. Onneiȣt, gȣas, go, gohe.

Atagrogȣan, Ch. *cesser de neiger.* Tȣagriagon, *idem.*

Agȣaton, *fouir;* Ch. θa, t, θe. Onhȣentsiagȣaton, *fodere terram.*

Aha v. **Ahaha,** *chemin,* extra et intra compos.

Johahio, *beau chemin.* Johahȣanne, vel kenn Johaha, *grand chemin.*

Ahate Johate, *il y a un chemin;* vel Johahonte, *imp.* tekȣe, *f.* teg, *n.* tekse.

Ahahogen, cum nota dualit. te, *chemin fourchu;* te sohahogen v. johahogen, *chemin fourchu.*

Aθahagȣegon, S. *le chemin estre bouché.*

Aθahagȣarision, S. *le chemin estre droit;* v. Tiahonnihare.

Aθahakton, *chemin qui va de biais.*

Gahahonni, Ch. *faire un chemin.*

Gahahonnianni, R. *f.* nien ; vel Gahahisaanni, R. *f.* sas. Iesȣs songȣahahisaanni ne garonhiage ionθa, *Jésus nous a fait le chemin pour aller au ciel.*

Gahaθotkaon, Ch. *faire le chemin sur les neiges.*

Aθahiton, Ch. θa, t, tanne ; vel Aθahonton, Ch. *prendre, suivre le chemin.*

Aθahitackon, Ch. *le lieu où l'on prend le chemin.*

Aθaharagȣan, Ch. gȣas, go, gohe; *couper chemin.*

Gahahenton, Ch. *suivre le chemin.*

Ohio, in comp.; kahik, extra comp. *fruit ;* Ohiagon, *bon fruit.*

Ahisari, Ch. ris, ri, risere, *fruit mur;* vel etiam P. O. Ahiariseron.

Ahientaon, Ch. tas, tanne, tasere; *le saison de fruits se passer.*

Aθahionni, S. *y avoir quantité de fruits.*

Ahiannionten, S. *fruit estre attaché à l'arbre, pendre.*

Gahianniontagȣan, Ch. gȣas, go, gohe; *detacher le fruit de l'arbre.*

Gahianniontagȣanni, R. *f.* gȣas.

Gahiennonten, R. *donner des fruits.*

Ahiaχon, Ch. χe, χa, χese; *aller, cueiller des fruits.*

Ahiaχonse, R. tagȣahiaχonseha, *va moy cueiller des fruits.*

Ohioge, *à la rivière :* Ohioge son, *le long de la rivière;* ohioge kȣann.

Ahonta, *oreille.* Tȣahontiagon, S ks. g ke; *avoir l'oreille coupée.*

Tȣahontiagi, R. Ahonsori, R. *rompre les oreilles à quelqu'un.*

Gahonsnoren, R. *faire prendre une chose pour une autre, empecher d'estre attentif.*

Aθahonsneren, P. A. *n'estre pas attentif.*

Gahonsatogeñon, S. *estre assuré, savoir au vrai une nouvelle.*

Gahonsatogaton vel Gahontogaton, *esclaircir de la verité d'une nouvelle.*

Tȣahontagȣegon, s. gȣeks, gȣek, gȣeχe; *estre sourd.*

Tȣatahontagȣegon, *se faire sourd.*

Kahontararágon, Ch. *percer l'oreille.* Kahontararagi, R.

Ohonti, *herbe dont la feuille est un peu grande.*

Joθontonni si gonnes agosatensk, *il y a bien de l'herbe où sont les chevaux.*

Akararen, S. *estre sensible à la douleur.* Akarienni s.

Gandigonckararen, s. *avoir l'esprit tendre et delicat.*

Okȣari, *ours.* Ganniagȣari, *grande ourse.* Okȣarita in comp.

Akȣari v. Akȣarigon, Ch. *empaqueter,* ris, ri; non est in usu, sed ejus loco Atakȣari, Ch. *faire son paquet.* Atakȣarise, R.

Atakȣarision, Ch. sions, si, sionné, *depaqueter;* v. Atakȣarisiongȣan.
Atakȣarisionse, R. vel Atakȣarisiongȣanni, f. gȣas.
Akȣerit, *embarquer paquet;* v. Atit.

Akȣason, Ch. *s'habiller, se vestir;* pr. et f. kȣes, n, kȣasere.
Ch. *se vestir de quelque chose;* θa, t, tanne.

Akte, *ailleurs, autrement.*

Akton, Ch. tons, ton, tonne; *aller faire un tour.*

Akta, *au bord;* Aktahe.

Okte, *bout, achever;* ȣagokten, ȣasokten.
Atokte, S. θa, ten; *estre achevé.* Atoktanni, f. θas.
Garihokte, garihoktanni.
Aterientokte, Ch. *desesperer.*

Akȣiseron, Ch. *s'efforcer;* rons, ron, ronne.
Atakȣeseron, idem a Gahȣisera, *force.*

Anno, *froid,* in comp. 2ae conj. Gaiatanno, *avoir froid.*
Gaiatannoston, S. *devenir froid;* θa, t, tanne.
Gannonȣanno, *cabane froide.* Oncneganno, *eau froide.*

Annonton, inusitat; *chercher, fouiller.* 2ae conj. Garihȣannonton, Ch. *demander des nouvelles* est etiam R.; tons, ton, tonre.
Harihȣannontonskon, *importun à interroger.*

Aogon, *pur, simple.* Aogon jongȣatkaston, *nous avons fait de la sagamité sans assaissonment.*
Aogonge, *il n'y a personne; grande solitude au village, a la cabane.*

Aȣagon, Ch. ks, g, χe; *cribler, secouer.*
Aȣakton, Ch. *cribler avec q. c.* Onnaȣak, *crible.*

Aȣen, *eau,* extra comp. Oncnega, in comp.
Aȣenge, *dans l'eau.* Aȣen ȣatkaston, *ta bouillié n'est que de l'eau claire.*

Aȣenrion, Ch. ries, rie, riese; *remuer, mouvoir.*
Saȣenrie, seθaseraȣenrie, *remue la farine.*
JeθeseraȣenrieΘa, *spatule.*

Tiȣenrioston, *temps sombre, couvert.*

Tȣtennagarȣt, S. *s'asseoir sur son derriere en ecartant les jambes.*
Tȣatotkȣaienneton, Ch. *s'asseoir commes les femmes q. elles jouent.*

Aȣenha, *fleur.* Aȣenhararagon, Ch. *fleurs etre épanouies.*
Aȣenhet, *fraise,* dimin.; v. Niohontesa, *petite feuille.*
Aȣenhagenrat, *chataigne.*

Aȣenrion, *mesler;* Ch. ries, rie, riese.
Erientaȣenrion, *troubler l'esprit,* R.
Aterientaȣenrion, Ch. *s'oublier;* ries, ri, ries.
Gaserentaȣenrion, *avoir eu un mauvais songe suivi d'un facheux accident.* P. O.

Aȣentaon, Ch. tas, tanne, tasere, *mourir,* de plurib; Aȣentaseron.
Aȣenθon, R. *tuer;* θosk, θo, θosere, *tuer plus.*
Ataȣenθon, *neut.* ch.

Aȣente, Ch. *joindre quelque chose; estre avec ou au dessus du principal.*
Onnonraȣente ne gaionni, *il y a une chevelure attaché au collier.*
Asare ejaȣentek, *qu'il y ayt un couteau avec.*

Aȣentaton, *accroitre à quelqu'un.*

Aȣetarontsi, *la piece est bien mise.*

Aȣetarhon, *mettre entre deux, y avoir.*
Ganniataraȣetarhon, *un lac est entre deux.*
Gannonsaȣetarhon, *cabane est entre deux.*

Aȣenron, in comp.: Gaiataȣenron, ganonaȣenron.
Aȣenraton, *passer par dessus;* Ch. θa, t, θa, sæpius in comp. quam Aȣenron.
Gannonsaȣenraton, *sauter par dessus la cabane.*
Atenraȣenraton, Ch. *passer sur la palisade.*
Tȣataȣenron, *tour à tour;* rons, re, ronne.

Aȣeron, *vuider,* Ch. rons, ron, ronne.

Aȣerontaon, *renverser de fonds en comble.*
Gannonsaȣeronton, Ch. *renverser, ruiner la cabane.*
Atrihȣaȣeron, Ch. *se disputer.*

Tȣaȣeston, *percer.*
Atȣeston, *passer;* θa, t, θe, Ch.
Atȣestanni, R. *f.* ten.
Atȣestakon, *lieu où l'on passe.*

Aȣi, R. *donner;* ȣisk, ȣi, ȣisere.
Aȣihon, *donner à plusieurs.*
Atataȣihon, Ch. *s'entredonner,* v. conj.

Aȣiaton, *faire entrer;* Ch. θa, t, tanne; *inde* Onnisnonsaȣiat, *bague.*
Atiataȣit, *capot.*
Ataȣiaton, Ch. *entrer.*
Ataȣiatanni, R. *f.* ten.
Ataȣiata^{c}kon, *pr.* et *f.* kȣa.

Arase, caret sing. Agiarase, tiarase, tsiar, hiar, giarase, agȣarase, tȣarase, &c.
Tȣarasenθon, R. *donner des coups de pied;* θosk, θo, θosere.
ȣrata, *talon.*

Arata, intra comp. *mettre ses souliers,* Ch.
Aratasion, Ch. v. Aratasiongȣan, *les oster.*
Aratasionse v. Aratasiongȣanni, R.
Karatie^{c}ton, Ch. θa, t; *estre las, fatigué du chemin ou du travail.*
Tȣara^{c}taton, *courir;* Ch. tats, tat, taθe. Est etiam relativum : te songȣara^{c}taton, *il courut sur nous.*

Araton, *coucher;* Ch. rats, rat, raθe.
Araston, Ch. *lieu où l'on couche.*
Arasta^{c}kon, *le lieu, la natte où l'on couche.*
Arati, R. *coucher aupres de quelqu'un;* tisk, ti, tire.

Araton, Ch. *compter.* Aratse, R. tagȣarats, *compte pour moy.*

Aregȣan, Ch. gȣas, go, gohe; *aller en guerre.*
N. Roregȣan, *N. est allé en guerre; est le chef de la bande.*
Jaten haregȣas, *il ne va pas en guerre* (grande injure).
Aregȣatsera, *bande de guerriers.*
Aregohaton, *diverses bandes aller en guerre.*

Areko, *pas encore.*

Tȣareron, Ch. *courir* 2 *ensemble à qui et.*

Aresen, S. *être gras.*
Aresenseronni, Ch. *engraisser cochons, &c.*
Aresenton, Ch. *s'engraisser de quelque chose.*
Kenniondaresen oskennonton, *les cerfs sont gras,* etc.

Gari, *meur, cuit;* utriusq. parad. 2ae conj. Onne jori, *cela est cuit.*
Egarig niari, *attends qu'il soit cuit.*
Subit etiam comp. Onne onnenhari, *le blé, la sagamité est cuitte.*
Joritsihȣen, *très cuit.*

Arkȣan, Ch. kȣas, ko, kohe; *coucher en chemin, gister.*

Arongen, Ch. χa, g, ganne; *entendre, écouter, concevoir.*
Arongaton, Ch. *entendre par ou pour quelque chose.*
Est etiam R. tagȣarongat, *escoute moy.*
Arongen in comp. Hoñaȣendaronχa, *on entend sa voix.*
Arongannion, Ch.
Garihȣacrongen, Ch. *entendre, apprendre quelque nouvelle.*

Oronckara, S. *palme.*
Tsioronckarat, *une seule palme.*
Atronckarare, Ch. *f.* re, ren; *mesurer par palmes.*
Garonckaron, R. *donner une palme.*
Garonkaratise, R. Θentenhaȣiθa hoñaronckaratisa, *on a donné à,* etc. Ainsi dit on quand les Agoianders s'entredonnent de la porcelaine.

Arontaton, Ch. *souffler, tirer le fusil et arroser d'eau medicinale.* Est R. in omnibus ts, t, θe.
Atatarontaton, Ch. *se tirer à soimême.*
Arontetsera, *un coup de mousquet.*
Arontason, Ch. tons, ton, tonne: multipliciter significat.
Arontatston, Ch. *ce avec quoi l'on tire.*

Arosen, *escureuil.*

Asaga, Ch. ga, g; *avoir la toux.*
Asagaton, *ce qui fait avoir la toux.*
Asaganna agrios, *la toux me tue.*

Asara, *corde à lier, collier.*
Asarinnon, Ch. *traisner avec une corde,* est etiam R.
Asaront, S. *estre lié comme sont les esclaves.*
Asaronniontatie, *aller traisnant son licol.*
Atasaront, Ch. cum te affir. *lier, attacher une collier à une manne;* θa, ten, tanne ; Ti satosaronten, *attache ton collier.*

Atasarontakon, Ch. *se servir de quelque chose pour attacher*, ainsi : Hoθennon te gatasarontak? *Qu'attacherai je à mon panier?*

Quand le fardeau est envelloppé de toile, on dans un sac, on dit : Satakȣari, et non pas Satasaronten.

Asara, *anse de chaudière.*

Asaront, Ch. θa, ten, tanne; *en mettre une.*

Asarontanni, R. *f.* θas.

Tontagȣasaronθas, *remets moi l'anse de ma chaudière.*

Asarontagȣan, *l'oster*, Ch. neut.

Asarontagȣanni, Neut. acq. *l'anse s'oster à quelq.*

Asarakȣa, *dessus de soulier.*

Asare, *couteau.* Agȣasare, sasare, raosare; mon, ton, son.

Asare onȣe, *couteau simple a 1 vaine.*

Atasaraseθa, *jambette,* seu *couteau qui se ferme qui se cache.*

Te ȣatasarisa^c^ks, *ciseau,* quasi diceres *couteaux qui se cherchent.*

Eθo si Johiȣθie, *le tranchant.*

Gasonne, *le dos d'un couteau.*

Asatagon, *en secret.*

Asatagon onȣati gaionni, *je donne un colier en secret.*

Ase, neuf. gannonsase, *cabanne neuve.*

Asegȣe, *epée, halebarde.* Asegȣare in comp.

Hatisegȣarenhaȣinnontie, *ils vont portant la hallebarde.*

Asen, *trois.* Satius esset ut significaret *dix*, sicuti significat apud Iroquaos superiores.

Inde autem fiunt Te ȣasen, 20, quasi 2 fois dix; Asen niȣasen, *trente.*

Porro Asen conjugat. est que Parad. Ch. Te iagȣasen, te sȣasen, te honsen, te gonsen, *imp.* sennen, *fut.* senhag : Tsiatak niaȣenre asen niaonsenhag, 27.

Subit etiam compositionem, Te jagȣajatasen, *nous sommes* 20; Asen nigastarokȣasen, 30 *grains de rassade.*

Asensera, *dixaine.* Asenseratagȣan, Ch. gȣas, go, gohe; *reciter la dixaine de son chaplet.*

Asenserȣannen, Ch. *vendre cher.*

Asenserȣt, Ch. *dix par dessus;* ch, θa, takȣe, tag.

Skat te ȣenniaȣe tegni te josenserot, 120.

Asennonte, *petit sac que les femmes attachent à leur ceinture dans lequel est leur blé de semence.*

Aseñon, extra comp. Ch. sens, senne, sensere; *tomber.* Assumit notam localitatis, tonsenne, *cela tombe.*

Asense, neut. acq. *laisser tomber, tomber à quelq.*

Asen^c^ton, Ch. *faire tomber;* θa, t, tanne.

Asentanni, R. *f.* ten, *faire tomber quelque chose à quelq.*

Asenθa, *dossier de la natte, l'entredeux d'une cabane.*

Te gasentȣte, *il y a un dossier.*

Gasentonni, Ch. *en faire un.*

Gasentonnianni, R. *f.* nien.

Tȣasenθa, *sault d'eau,* seu *où l'eau tombe.*

Tȣasenθon, Ch. θos, θo, θosere; *gemir, se plaindre.*
Tȣasenθoseron, Ch. de multis.

Asera, *hache,* in comp.
Aserio, *bonne hache.* Aseraksen, *mechante.*
Aseragaraon, R. *tenir la hache levée pour frapper quelq.*
Aserense, *la faire tomber sur quelqu'un.*
Aserȣθion, Ch. *l'aiguiser;* pr. et f. θie.
Aserȣtionse, R. *f.* ons. Tȣaseriagi, R. *f.* ks.
ȣateskȣaseriaks, *tu m'as rompu ma hache.* Tȣataseriagi, R. recip.
Tȣaseriakton, R. *rompre une hache par ou sur quelque chose.*
Tȣaserakȣan, Ch. P. kȣa, f. kȣa, n. kȣanne.
Onne tontajonserakȣe ganniege onsahoñajent ne ratsagannha, *L'Agnier reprend la hache pour frapper le Mahingan.*
Aseragannennaton, Ch. θa, t, tanne; *faire divers coups, casser quantité de testes.*
Aserȣtagȣan, Ch. *satisfaire pour quelque coup.*
Tȣaseragȣanni, R. *oster la hache à quelqu'un.*
Ateserenton, Ch. *donner un coup.*
Aserȣton, *hache d'armes.*
Onteseronti, *la foudre est tombé.*

Aserahon, R. serask, ra; *donner de la pourcelaine pour remercier de quelque esclave donné.*

ȣasere, *il y a de l'eau dans le ruisseau, fontaine,* &c.

Asecton, Ch. θa, t, tanne; *cacher.* Rariȣaseθa, *il cache l'affaire.*
Jotrihȣaseton, *l'affaire est cachée.*
Ataseton, *se cacher, se mettre à couvert de quelque mauvais temps.*
Atasetonkon, *se cacher avec quelque chose.*
Gaiataseton, *cacher quelqu'un.* Gaiatasetanni, R.
Asetanni, R. *f.* ten. ȣahagrihȣaseten, *il m'a caché l'affaire.*
Atasetanni, *se cacher à quelqu'un;* R. acq.
Atatasetanni, R. recip. *s'entrecacher.*

Aseton, R. *tuer en cachette, assassiner.*

Aseton, *compter;* Ch. tas, t, tanne.
Ionsetas ondegorha onnontageronnons, *les Onnontagués comptent la porcelaine.*
Ionsetasθa, *ce avec quoy l'on compte;* sic etiam vocant *un livre.*

Asisat, *pilon,* extra comp. Asisata in comp. est 2ae conj.

Askahon, Ch. ȣas, ȣe, ȣasere; *mascher.*
Askaȣanni, R. f. kaȣas; *mascher à quelqu'un.*

Asi, *pied,* S. Raosige, *à son pied.*
Osita v. Arasita, in comp. S.
Tȣarasitagarhaθon, *tourner le pied.*
Tȣasinnitagon, Ch. *avoir froid aux pieds;* ks, g, χe.
Tȣasinnitontagȣan, S. gȣas, go, gohe; *se geler les pieds.*
Tȣasiteñon, *avoir les pieds engourdis.*
Tȣatsinniagon, S.

Askaȣe, *aller pieds nuds*, s. Gainaskaȣe, idem.
Gariskaȣe, *aller sans bas*, s.

Askannegon, Ch. ks, g, kseg, χe; *desirer quelque chose.*
Askannegon, R. *desirer de bonheur d'un autre.*

Askati, *d'un costé.* Skannatati, *de l'autre costé.*

Askȣa, *eschaffaut.*
Askȣage, *sur l'eschaffaut; θo* si etȣaskȣah-re, *la où est l'eschaffaut.*
Askȣaȣeron, R. *le vuider, renvoyer le prisonier.*

Askȣannonte, *l'avant d'une cabane.*

Tȣaskȣaseron, *marcher dessus;* Ch. rons, re, ronne.
Tȣaskȣaserakȣan, R. kȣa, kȣe, kȣanne.

Askôton. Ch. θa, t, tanne; *avoir, faire des trappes au castor, ours,* &c.
Hondatskotonnon, *ils sont allés faire des trappes.*
Askȣentannon, *tendre des colets.*

Asneragon, *blesser sans dessein, par mégarde.*

Asnenton, Ch. *descendre; θa*, t, tanne.

Asȣan, *s'esteindre le feu;* sȣas, sȣa, sȣasere.
Asȣan, neut. acq. *le feu s'esteindre à quelq.*
Ongȣasȣa, *mon feu s'esteint.*
Asȣaton, Ch. θa, t, tanne; *l'esteindre.*
Asȣatanni, *l'esteindre à quelq.*
Asȣennonnianni, R. *f.* nien; *donner à fumer à quelq.*
Osȣen, *charbon.* Osȣenta, *noir.*

Asohon, Ch. sohos, soho, sohose; *teindre.*
Asohoton, Ch. *teindre avec quelque chose.*
Asohot, *racine rouge qui teint en escarlatte que les Agniers nomment* Onnonkȣat.

Ason, *encore.* Asonsi giatase, *quand j'etais encore jeune.*

Asonnionkon, Ch. *pr.* et *f.* kȣa, *n.* kȣanne; *estre deffendu.*
Naie ȣasonnionkȣa, *cela est defendu*; est etiam 2ae conj. et frequentius.
Asonnionkon, neut. acq. Naie ongsonnionkȣe, *cela m'est deffendu.*
Asonnionkon, *avoir ses mois.*
Asonnionkȣanni, R. *f.* kȣen.

Asonratsi, *gros canard.*

Asonta, *nuit.* Asontes, *longue nuit.* Kenniȣasontesa, *courte nuit.*
Asonθenna, *pendant la nuit*, v. Asontage.
Asonθen, *minuit.* Kenȣasonte, *cette nuit.*
Oia tsi tiogaras, *la nuit d'avant hier.*
Tȣasontison, Ch. *estre nuit close.*
Asontagȣan, *passer la nuit*, s.
Asontanniron, S. *avoir peine à passer la nuit.*
Asontongoton, *passer la nuit*, ch.
Asontonni, S. *marquer tant de nuits.*
Asontenhaȣi, Ch. *idem.*

Asontajenni, *idem*, R. *f.* enhas.
Tȣasontraon, Ch. terha, tren, tranne; *mettre bout à bout.*
Tȣasontranni, R. *f.* terhas.

Astaȣen, *tortue que le jongleur tient en main en chantant.*
Astaȣeñon, *chanter l'ayant en main;* ens, en, eusere.

Ostara, *goutte d'eau.*
Astaren, *pleurer;* Ch. rha, ren, ranne.
Astaron, *de multis flentibus.*
Astarha^{c}kon, Ch. *pleurer pour quelque chose.*
Astarontion, Ch. ties, ti, tiese; *pleuvoir.*

Aste, *dehors.* Asteon, S. tes, teg; *estre à sec.*
Astese, neut. acq. Onne tsiondastese tsonnito, *les castors sont à sec.*

Astenniaron, R. rons, ron, ronne; *donner du courage.*
Astenniaron, neut. Ch. *s'encourager.*

Ostenra, *rocher.* Ostenrio, *beau rocher.*
Osten^{c}rionni, *point du rocher qui advance.*
Ostenragȣarionni, *lieu de pesche des Onneionts.*
Si etiostenrahre, *village des Agniers.*
Osten^{c}ragȣentare, *rocher plat.*

Asteriston, Ch. *garder, se soucier, avoir soin;* θa, t, tanne.
Tagȣasterist, *aye soin de nous,* est etiam 2^{ae} conj.
ȣaksterast, tsinni, raiatȣten; *je considere, fais cas, aye egard à sa façon d'agir.*
Iosterest, *chose belle, agreable, pretieuse à la veue.*
Asterista^{c}kon, Ch. *se mettre en peine de quelque chose pour raison.*

Asti, S. *estre pris au gozier d'une areste.*
Ongȣasti, *je suis pris au gozier.*
Astigahon, Ch. ȣas, ȣa; *passer souvent par un même lieu.*
Tȣastigon, Ch. gons, g; *vomir.*
Tȣastigaton, *provoquer à vomir,* est etiam R.

Aston, Ch. θa, st, stanne; *se servir.*
Θennon esastanne? *A quoi t'en veux tu servir?*

Astoron, *viste,* Ch.; melius Gasnoron.

At, *il y a dedans quelque chose;* jȣat, *imp.* jȣatakȣe, *f.* eȣatak.
Iȣatarion, *il y a quantité de choses;* vel Itȣat, ab Atarion. inde
Atariongȣan, Ch. *tirer dedans quantité de choses.*
Iaten te sȣat, *il ny a plus rien dedans.*
Gaïatate, *chose vivante être dedans.*
Ata, *mettre dedans;* tas v. ta, taanne, *enterrer.*
Atase, R. Tageθas, *mets moi cela dedans.*
Garihȣatare, R. *mettre l'affaire dans quelqu'un.*
Atrihȣata, neut. acq. *se mettre l'affaire.*
ȣagatrihȣataθe, *je vais escoutter.*
Gaiatata, R. *enterrer quelqu'un.*
Atiatata, Ch. *se mettre dedans quelque chose.*
Atiatataani, R. *se mettre dans quelqu'un; f.* tas.

Atakon, *ce dans quoy il y a*, in comp.
Gan^enegatakon, *où l'on met de l'eau.*
Gatakȣan, Ch. *tirer de dedans;* kȣas, ko, kohe.
Gatakȣanni, R. *f.* kȣas.
Gatakȣaton, *tirer de dedans avec quelque chose.*

Ata, *soulier*, extra comp.; Atakȣa, in comp. Te jotarion.
Ata, R. *mettre les souliers à quelqu'un.*
ȣagoñjata, *que je te met les souliers.*
ȣagoñjata^ekon, *je te donne des souliers.*

Ata, extra comp.; Atatsera, in comp., *cheville, petit baton.*
Atatserat, *il y a une cheville dedans.*
Atatserȣt, *y en avoir; f.* tak: quando autem significat active, *y en mettre* habet in *præsenti* θa, in *f.* ten, *n.* tanne.
Atatserȣton, *y avoir plusieurs chevilles.*
Atatserȣtagȣan, Ch. *l'oster;* gȣas, go, gohe : vel
Atatserotsion, Ch. sions, si, sionha.

Onta, *nuit*, extra comp. *f.* tag.
θo nonta rotention? *Combien y a-t-il de nuits qu'il est parti?*
θo gati neȣata ensraȣe? *En combien de nuits sera-t-il de retour?*

Ataon, S. tas, tanne, tasere; *estre rassassié.*
Jaten te rotas, *il ne se saoule point.*
Ataston, S. *se saouler de quelque chose;* θa, t, tanne.
Ataston, R. *saouler quelq.*

Atageronte, *quarré*, S. Gannatageronte, *village quarré.*

Atagariton, S. cum reit. *se porter mieux;* θa, te.

Atagȣarision, *developper, dresser;* Ch. sions, si, sionhe.
Aontagȣarisi sandigon^era, *aye l'esprit droit.*

Atagȣan, *estre refusé;* S. gȣas, go, gohe.
Gatagȣentaron, Ch. *estre gisant;* 2^{ae} conj.

Atagȣenton, S. θas, t, tanne; *estre large.*
Gaionni ken niotagȣente, *un colier de cette largeur.*
Atagȣententenston, Act. ch. *eslargir.*

Atanniharon, Ch. rons, ron, ronne; *enfiler.*
Ganniharon, 2^{ae} conj. inusitat.
Atanniharono^e, R.
Atanniharongȣan, Ch. *desenfiler.*
Atanniharongȣanni, R. *f.* gȣas.
Atanniharon^ekon, Ch. *p.* et *f.* kȣa, kȣanne; *enfiler avec quelque chose :* forté derivatur a Gannihare, *jusques* aqh.

Ataȣa, Ch. *garder pour peu de tems.*
Ataȣase, R. Tagȣataȣas agosa, *garde moi ma robe.*

Ataȣen, Ch. ens, en, ensere; *se baigner :* forte ab Aȣen, *de l'eau.*
Ataȣensera, *bain.*
Ataȣenhon, Ch. *s'aller baigner.*
Ataȣenston, Ch. θa, t, tanne; *se baigner, se laver avec quelque chose.*

Atasaȣen, Ch. cum notâ local., *commencer.*
Neθo tontasaȣen, *l'affaire a commencé par là.*
Atasaȣakon, *commencer par là.*

Otara, *argile, terre grasse.*
Ataragȣaronton, S. *terre elevée, bosse de terre.*
Ota^c^ragȣara, *fezoles de terre.*

Ata, Atasera in comp., *petit escorce ou bois sec pour servir de flambeaux à la chasse des tourtes pendant la nuit.*
Ataseront, Ch. θa, ten, tanne; *chasser en cette façon.*
Ataserontanni, R. *f.* θas; *chasser pour quelqu'un.*
Ataserontannon, Ch. *y aller.*
Tagȣataserontanniha, *Va chasser pour moy.*

Atatsense, Ch. *imp.* schakȣé, *f.* seg, *n.* sere; *n'en pouvoir plus.*

Atati, Ch. tisk, ti, tianne; *parler:*
Atatiase, R. *parler à quelqu'un et pour quelqu'un.*
Atatiaton, Ch. θa, t, tanne; *parler avec quelque chose.*

Ategen, neut. S. *y avoir du feu;* χa, teg, tekse, teganne.
Iȣteχa, *il y a du feu;* ajoteg, *qu'il y ait du feu.*
Hoiatateχa, *il brusle;* hotiatategannon Jonhȣentsiagon, *ardent in inferis.*
Ategase, neut. acq. S. *ardere alicui.*
Ategaton, Ch. θa, t, tanne; *allumer du feu.*
Ategatanni, R. *f.* ten; *allumer du feu à quelqu'un.*
Ategata^c^kon, Ch. *pr.* et *f.* kȣa, kȣanne; *allumer avec quelq. chose.*
Gannongȣategen, *cabane se bruler.*

Ategon, *diverses choses.* Jategon soñа, *quantité de choses de diverse façon.*

Ategȣan, Ch. gȣas, go, gohe; *s'enfuir.*
Ategȣaton, R. θa, t, tanne; *donner la fuite à quelqu'un.*
Ategȣata^c^kon, Ch. *chasser avec quelque chose.*
Ategȣasen *vel* Ategȣasenton, *lieu de fuitte; imp.* takȣe, *f.* tak.

Ateheñon, Ch. ens, en, ensere; *avoir honte.*
Atehaton, Ch. *être honteux pour quelque chose.*
Atehaton, R. θa, t, tanne, *hontoyer quelqu'un;* vel
Atehatanni, *f.* ten.
Atehase, neut. R. *estre honteux à cause de quelque chose.*
Iotehat, *celà est honteux.*
Atehensera, *honte.*
Atehenserageȣen, Ch. *essuyer sa honte.*
Atehenseraratie, *aller estant honteux.*
Aongȣatehenseragasteg, *je serai bien effronté.*

Atehȣaon, cum reit. ȣas, ȣa, ȣasere; *guerir.*

Atehȣat, Ch. θa, ten, tanne; *garder, mettre en reserve.*
Atehȣatanni, R. *f.* θas; *garder à quelqu'un.*

Atekȣagȣan, Ch. *enlever un morceau;* gȣas, go, gohe.
Atekȣison, Ch. sas, sa, saanne; *manger tout.*

Atennaton, Ch. θa, t, tanne; *prendre pour provisions.*
Atennatsera, S. *provision :* Raotennatsera hondat.
Atennatseronni, Ch. nisk, ni, nianne; *faire des provisions.*
Atennatseronnianni, R. *f.* nien.
Atennatseratson, Ch. *consommer ses provisions.*
Atennatserokten, Ch. θa, ten; *estre à bout de ses provisions.*

Atengehȣen, R. hȣas, hȣa, hȣasere; *estre jaloux.*

Atenjen, Ch. *p.* en, *f.* en, *n.* anne; *se chauffer.*
Ateñiase, R. *se chauffer chez quelqu'un.*

Atennraon, utriusq. parad. ons, on, onne; *estre fort, robuste.*
Atennraonston, R. *rendre quelq. fort;* θa, t, tanne.
Taktenneraonst Iesȣs, *Donne moy des forces, O Jesus!*

Atennȣsen, cum notâ dual. *être frère et sœur :* caret sing.

Atennienten, Ch. tens, ten, tensere; *marquer.*
Atennientenseron, multip.
Atennientenston, Ch. θa, t, tanne; *marquer avec quelque chose.*
Atennientensθa, *marque.*
Naie Iontennientensθa ne Jagorihȣioston Iaten te Jerihȣanderen, *On distingue les Chrétiens en ce qu'ils ne pechent point.*

Atennise, *baston sur lequel s'appuye;* S. Raotennhis *son.*
Atenniserenhaȣi, Ch. *aller avec un baston.*
Satenniserȣten, *appuye-toi sur son baston.*

Atennohȣajen, Ch. ens, en, ensere; *se baisser de peur de frapper.*

Atencra, *palissade.*
Atenrȣt, *y avoir palissade;* takȣe, tak, utriusq. parad. dicunt enim Hondatenhrȣt, *ils ont palissade;* Sȣatencrati, *hors la palissade.*
ȣatencrannoron, *palissade forte.*
ȣatencratsannit, Onneia.
Atenrȣtakon,
Atenrienneñon, Ch. *palissade tomber.*
Atenrogaton, Ch. *entrer dans la palissade.*
Atenronni, Ch. *en faire une.* Atenronnianni, R.
Atenraȣeraton, Ch. *passer pas dessus.*
Atenrion, Ch. *entrer dedans;* rion, rio, rionne.
ȣaontencrio, *on entre dans la palissade.*
Atenrionse, R. *f.* rions; *entrer dans la palissade par.*
Eθo si etȣatencragarent, *à la porte de la palissade.*
Tagȣatencrionnsenniha, *venez nous secourir.*

Ateȣasaron, S. *pendant d'oreilles.*
Ateȣasaront, *en mettre;* Ch. θa, ten, tanne.
Ateȣasarontanni, R. *f.* θas.

Ateȣaton, cum reiter. Ch. *manquer son coup;* θa, t, tanne. Il se dit de toute sorte d'occasion qu'on a perdue, aussi bien que d'un mechant tireur. Sȣatrihȣateȣaton, Ch.

Ateȣiat, *brasse.* Sȣateȣiat, *une brasse;* te ȣateȣiage, 2 *brasses.*
Tȣateȣiaren, Ch. *brasser;* v. Tȣatnensaren.

Ateȣejennonni, S. *faire avec addresse.*
Ateȣejennonnianni, R. *f.* nien.

Ateȣejenton, Ch. tonsk, ton, tonne; *garder, faire bien.*
Ateȣejentonni, R. *f.* has.
Tagȣateȣejentonhas, *fais moy bien cela, garde moy cela.*

Atention, *partir;* Ch. ties, ti, tionhe.
Atentiaton, *partir pour quelque chose,* Ch.
Atentiaton, R. *faire partir;* θa, t, tanne.
Atentiase, R. acq. *partir pour quelqu'un.*

Atentonni, *estre anneanti;* Ch. tonnisk, ni, nianne.
Jotentonni go, *il n'y a personne dans la cabane ou au village, grande silence et solitude.*
Ronneron hatigaionton Jaten teȣatentonnianne ongȣarihȣa, *Les ancestres ont voulu que leur affaire ne se perdit pas.*
Atentonniaton, R. θa, t, tanne; *faire partir.*
ȣasongȣatentonniat ronnontio, N. *nous a anneantis, ruinés.*

Atentoriaton, Ch. θa, t, tanne; *se desennuyer, divertir.*
Atentoriata°kon, Ch. kȣa, kȣag, kȣanne; *se desennuyer avec q. c.*

Tȣaterakiȣan, Ch. ȣas, ȣe, ȣasere; *se chausser, mettre ses mitasses.*
Tȣaterakiȣasion, Ch. *se les oster.*
Aterakiȣitsera, *mitasses ou autres nippes dont on se couvre les jambés.*

Aterannonte, S. *y avoir de l'espace, du jour entre deux choses qui ne sont bien jointes.*

Atenriennentons, Ch. *Convoquer les Agoianders de chaque bourg des Agniers dans un, pour tenir conseil.*

Aterasȣan, Ch. *rever en dormant;* sȣas, sȣa, sȣasere.
Aterasȣaton, Ch. *songer à quelque chose.*

Atera, *manne.*
Ateraȣiriens, aterȣannen, *grande manne.*
Ateronni, Ch. *en faire une.*
Ateronniaton, Ch. *bois dont on fait les mannes :* Onnonna.
Ateragete, S. *la porter.*

Aterhenton, Ch. θa, t, tanne; *muer, quitter son poil.*

Ateriaθa, Ch. *estre hardy, vaillant.*

Ateronkȣaronni, S. *estre rude, mal poli.*

Ateronkȣaton, Ch. θa, t, tanne; *employer mal, gater quelque chose.*
Ateronkȣatanni, R. *f.* ten; *gaster quelque chose à quelqu'un.*

Ateronni, S. *estre poltron.*
Ateroñon, S. rons, ron, ronsera; *avoir peur.*
Ateronton, S. *craindre pour quelque chose.*
Aterontanni, *f.* ten; *faire peur à quelq.*
Ateronse, R. acq. *craindre pour quelqu'un.*
ȣateronge eȣaton, *il y a à craindre.*
Ateroñon, S. *estre faché;* rons, ron, ronsere.
ȣagateronse, *je suis faché.*

Atetseñon, S. ens, en, ensere; *estre effrayé en dormant.*
Ongȣatetsen, *j'ai eu un mauvais songe.*
Atetsatanni, R. *f.* ten; *causer un mauvais songe à quelqu'un.*
Ateχonni, utriusq. parad. nisk, ni, nianne; *manger quelque chose de bon.*
Ateχonniaton, Ch. forte a Gakȣa, *morceau;* in comp. Gakȣio, *bon morceau.*
Atenro, *estre camarade*, Ch.
Agiatenro, tiatenro, tsiat, hiat.
Atenrotsera, *camaradise.*
Atenrotseragateñon, S. *avoir beaucoup d'amis.*
Atenrosen, *avoir un camarade;* R. takȣe, tag.
Ateton, in comp. *fort.*
Gaiatatéton, S. *homme laborieux.*
Jonnaȣatet, *rapide courant.* Ojengȣatet, *petun fort.*
Atkaon, *cesser;* Ch. ȣas, ȣe, ȣasere.
Atkaon, pass. cum reit. Ch. *se desdire.*
Atkaȣanni, R. *f.* ȣas.
Atkarioñ, Ch. rions, rion, rionne; *aller viste.*
Ratkariontie, *il va viste.*
Atkariseronni, Ch. *jouer, se divertir comme font les enfants.*
Atkariseronniaton, Ch. θa, t, tanne.
Atkatokȣisaon, Ch. as, sa, sanne; *pescher avec un pannier.*
Atkaθon, Ch. θos, θo, θosere; *regarder:* est etiam R. Tagȣatkaθo, *respice me.*
Atatkaθon, *se regarder*, Ch.
Atkaθóton, *regarder avec quelque chose.*
Jontatkaθota, *un miroir.*
Atkennaton, Ch. θa, t, tanne; *avoir fait coup.*
Jagotkennatonhatie, *on va ayant fait coup, victorieux.*
Atkennatatsera, *victoire*, S.
Raotkennatatsera,
Atkennison, Ch. sas, sa, saanne; *estre assemblé.*
Atkennisáton, Ch. *s'assembler pour ou par quelque chose.*
Atkeñon, S. ens, en, ensere; *estre pourry.*
Onnataratken, *pain pourry.*
Atkense, neut. acq. S. *se pourrir à quelqu'un.*
Otkenseri, extra comp. *pourriture.*
Onnitkenseri, in comp.
Jonnitkenseronni, *il s'est formé de la pourriture.*
Atkenserinnigeñon, S. ens, en, ensere; *pourriture sortir.*
Atkenȣaton, Ch. θa, t, tanne; *gouster.*
Atkenráton, Ch. θas, t, tanne; *cesser:* Onneiȣt.
Atkenratanni, R. *f.* ten.
Atkerȣθie, *peigne.* Atkerȣθion, Ch. *se peigner.* Gakerȣθionse, R.
Atkeᶜtaton, Ch. ts, t, taθe; *porter.*
Atkeᶜtati, R. *f.* ts; *porter pour quelq.*

Atkȣente, S. *estre mattachié.*

Atkȣenteeston, Ch. *se mattachier avec quelque chose.*

Atkon, *demon*, S. Il se dit aussi d'un homme hardy, &c. à qui rien n'est difficile.

Hondatkon nahontrio ganniegeronnon, *Les Agniers sont des demons en guerre.*

Hotkon rotatonni, *il est devenu demon, intrepide.*

Ati, *costé.* Skati, *d'un côté.* Kennongati, *de ce côté là.*

Skannátati, *d'un costé du village.*

Skiatarati, *un costé de la beste.*

Skannaatagarati, *un seul plat costé.*

Atkonskenniaton, Ch. *faire signe avec la teste;* θa, t, tanne.

Atkonskenniatanni, R. *f.* ten.

Atianneron, S. *avoir des visions, estre effrayé*; rons, ron, ronne.

Atianneronkon, S. *p.* et *f.* kȣa, *ce qui cause ces frayers.*

Atianneronkȣanni, R. *f.* kȣen.

Ataȣanre, Impson. rek, reg : *Cela ne peut pas entrer*, v. g. *par la porte ou ailleurs; cela est deffendu.*

Atraȣenre, neutre S.

Ongȣatiaȣenre, *Nous n'osons faire celà, de peur que quelque malheur n'arrive.* Dicunt potius Ongȣasonnionkȣe.

Atiaȣenraton, Ch. rats, rat, raθe; *defendre.*

Otiarenta, *fleur de citrouille.*

Otiarenta niot, otiarentage nigoserȣten, *couverte, étoffe jaune.*

Atiarentiaχon, Ch. χes, χo; *aller cueiller de fleurs de citrouille.*

Atiarentiaχonse, R.

Atiatagetaton, R. ts, t, θa; *renverser, jetter par terre.*

Atiatennion, de Gatennion, 2 C. *se changer*; nions, tenni, nionha.

Onneia eȣatiatenni gannatarok eȣaton, *lapides mutabuntur in panem.*

Atiaktanni, neut. S. *f.* ten; *estre arreté.*

Ongȣatiakten, *je suis arretté.*

Gaiaktanni, S. *idem.*

Atiaktanni, R. *arrester, retarder quelqu'un.*

Naie jongȣatiaktanni nyoθore, *le froid nous a retardés.*

Atiataȣit, S. *capot.* Raotiataȣit, *son capot.*

Atiataȣiton, S. θa, t, *avoir son capot* est etiam R.

Atiataȣitasion, S. *l'oster*, sion, si, sionhe.

Tȣatierenton, cum notâ local. θa, t, *le* 1er *commencer.*

Igi eskatierent, *je commencerai le premier.*

Etiotierenton v. tontierent, *ab initio.*

Atiarentakon, Ch. *p.* & *f.* kȣa, kȣanne.

Atient, Ch. ensk, en, enne; *s'asseoir.*

Atienni, R. *f.* enhas.

Atientakon, Ch. *p.* & *f.* kȣa; *s'asseoir là.*

Otienni, *quelque chose qui repond beaucoup.*

Ajotiennik ostarokȣa okti agȣegon aχeiaȣiseg : *Il faudrait que la rassade repondit beaucoup pour que j'en donnasse à tous.*

Jotenni ohiegaront : *Il faut peu de saumon pour assaisonnement, il repond beaucoup.*

Jotennisoten, *ce qui repond peu.*

Atiesen, *liberal,* S. Aontiesenha onnonkȣat, *Comme si l'on devoit prodiguer les médecines.*

Atihen, cum notâ local.: 2 *choses inégalement mises, comme ces deux lignes* ═══──, *l'une deborde plus que l'autre.*

Te giaθihen, 2 *choses inégales.*

Atihenton, Ch. cum notâ local. θos, θo, θosere; *tirer par force.*

Atihenton, R. Gaiatatihenton, R.

Atio, sing. *no.* caret : *estre beau-frère.*

Agiatio, tiatio, tsiatio, hiatio.

Ation, S. ties, ti, tiese; in comp. ontion, *jetter.*

Sati, *jette cela.* Ogont ȣagoti, *jetter, laisser pour moy.*

Atiense, R. *f.* tiens; *jetter à quelqu'un.*

Tagȣatiens, *jette moy cela.*

Atieton, S. θa, t, tanne; *jetter en arrière.*

Ontion, in comp. Gaiatontion, R. *abandonner q.*

Gaiatontieton, *abandonner entièrement quelqu'un.*

Garihontion, *jetter l'affaire,* S.

Garihontiense, R. Jontatrihontiens te jagoȣennaraon.

Atiogont, v. tiôtkont, *toujours.*

Atiȣen, S. ens, en, ensere; *estre maigre.*

Atiȣaon, S. θas, θa, θasere; *le devenir.*

Atiȣaton, Ch. *s'amaigrer pour quelque chose.*

Atiront, Ch. θa, ten, tanne; *attirer, tirer, allonger.*

Sennhohatironten, *tire la porte.*

Atiront, R. ȣahiatatironten, *il t'a attiré.*

Atirontanni, R. acq. *f.* θas.

Gatagȣatironθas, *tire moy celà.*

Atisaien, S. *tardif à croistre.*

Atisnore, S. *prompt à croire.*

Atiskȣentaron, R. ron, re, ronne; *se coucher sur le ventre.*

Gaiatiskȣentaron, R. *coucher.* Tȣatoren, *se moderer.*

Atenneha, *du plantin.*

Atnenha, *noyau.*

Tȣatnenhaȣinneton, Ch. θa, t, tanne : *jouer avec des noyaux comme font les femmes, en les jettant avec la main.*

Tȣatennaȣeron, Ch. rons, ron, ronne : *y jouer au plat.*

Tonsaȣatógen, S. *se démarier,* ab Ogen, quod significat divisionem.

Te tsiongiatogen nondȣtagete, *j'ai quitté la guerre.*

Tonsaȣatogeston, Ch. θa, t, tanne: *se démarier pour quelque raison.*

Naie te tsiontogesθa jaten te jagonhȣioston, *on se démarie parceque on n'est pas heureux.*

Atogȣat, *cueillière.* Atogȣatsera, in comp.

Atohara, *bout de flèche pointu,* Huron. Tagȣatoharonnien.

Atsoθen (dicitur de pisce), θosk, θo, θosere : *sauter, se plonger.*

Tȣatsoθon, Ch. *le soleil se coucher.* V. infra.

Aton, *devenir, etre fait;* onk, on, onre. Eȣatonre v. Eȣatonsere.

Onhȣentsia señȣen aonton, *terra fiat.*

Nota quod verbum hoc concordat aliquando numero et genere cum substantivo, v. g. Jesȣs ongȣe rotoñon, *Jesus s'est fait homme.*

Aliquando non concordat quando nimirum sumitur impersonaliter, v. g. Ise satsihenstatsi eȣaton, *tu fies religiosus.* Otkon etȣaton netsitȣatonnhet, *vel* ongȣatkon eȣaton nïentsitȣatonnhet; *nous deviendrons esprits quand nous resusciterons.*

Ation, impersonalitur jungitur verbis quorum finalis non inflectitur. Ita seȣendio eȣaton, aonton, ajotonong.

Aton, *estre possible.*

Eȣaton ken asa^{c}tenti, *possibile ne erit proficiscaris.* Aonton gatigen; *quasi vero possibile foret.*

Atonse, neutr. acq. S. *devenir à quelqu'un.*

Aȣen ongȣtons nagatkaston, *la sagamité que je fais devient de l'eau.*

Atonse, neutr. acq. S. *possibile esse alicui.*

Jaten te ȣagatonse, *non mihi est possibile.*

Atoñon, cum reit. Ch. *guerir; p. & f.* ton, n, tonne.

Onne onsagaton, *je suis gueri.*

Aonsaiontonon gaion^{e}negiren onnonkȣat, *elle eut été guerie si elle eut pris médecine.*

Aton, *apparaitre en figure.*

Onniare jotonhatienn notkon, *le démon prit la figure d'un serpent.*

Atonni, R. in comp. cum Garata, passivi vocis.

Songȣatiatatonni, *il nous est apparu.*

Atoon, impers. S. *y avoir beaucoup de productions de la terre.*

Jotoon aȣenhagenrat, *il y a beaucoup de chataignes.*

Taonχen jotoon ne gontisk okȣari! *O qu'il y a bien de ce que les ours mangent!*

Atonton, Ch. θa, t, tanne; *faire le tantieme,* jungitur numeris ordinalibus.

Ise gaieri nesatont, *tu seras le* 4eme.

Gaieri aesatontong, *tu fuisses* 4us.

I. ȣisk gatonθa, *je suis le* 5eme.

Tȣatonton, Ch. *se mettre deux au même plat ou à faire même chose.*

Te tsiatont nhetsegeña notsiatsori, *manges ensemble toy et ton cadet.*

Tȣatontonse, R. acq. *se mettre 2 ou 3 pour ou contre quelqu'un.*

ȣaθoñatontons ahoñario, *ils se mirent 2 pour le battre.*

Atonton, sine te dual. *se mettre plusieurs pour faire une même chose.*

Gaieri natsiatonte, *soyes 4 ensemble.*

Ojeri nahontonte, *ils se mirent dix.*

Aton, Ch. θa, t, tanne; *se servir.*

Θennen ensat? *A quoy t'en serviras tu?*

Ason gaθa, *je m'en sers encore.* Ontagaton.

Tȣaton, S. impers. *estre de manque.*
Niahoθennon te tio^{c}ton garonhiage, *il ne manque de rien au ciel.*
Etȣagaton, *j'y manque.* N. joton, *N. y manque.*
Ontagaiataton, *la lune manquer.*
Tegni tetkaiataton, *d'icy à deux mois.*

Atoñon, Ch. *se perdre, s'egarer q. ch.;* tonk, ton, tonne.
Niahoθennon te ȣatonk si etiongȣannonsȣte, *rien ne se perd dans notre maison.*
Onne agarihȣaton, *voilà l'affaire perdue.*
Atoñon, *se perdre, s'égarer* (de re vivente).
Asiataton v. Saiataton, *tu t'es trompé, égaré.*
Atonni, neutr. S. tonnisk, ton, tonnire; *estre perdu à quelqu'un.*
Agatonni v. Ongȣaton, *hoc mihi periit.*
Agiatatonni v. Ongiataton nagetsennen enhas, *j'ai perdu mon chien.*
Aton^{c}ton, θa, t, t, tanne; *faire perdre, égarer.*
Horihȣa^{c}tonton, *il a fait perdre cette chose.*
ȣahagiatatont, *il m'a deceu, fait perdre.*
Atiatatontȣn, *s'évader.*
Atontanni, R. acq. *perdre à quelqu'un.*
ȣahagȣa^{c}tonten, *il m'a perdu quelque chose.*
ȣahagrihȣatonten, *il m'a esgaré mon livre.*
Atatontanni, neutr. acq.
Asongȣatiatatonten, *il s'est enfuy de nous.*

Atoñaronnion, Ch. ni, nianne; *estre ruiné de fonds en comble, ne rien rester.*
Jatonaronnion nȣagientakȣe, *tout ce que j'avais est perdu.*
Atoñaronniaton, Ch. *perdre, dissiper, gaster tout,* est etiam relativum.

Atonhȣajen, *se baisser, se tourner d'un autre costé.*
Tȣatonharenron, *estre en crainte pour quelque malheur advenir.* S.
Tȣatonharenron^{c}kon, S. *estre en crainte pour quelque chose.*

Atonkariagon, Ch. *avoir faim;* ks, g, χe.
Atonkariakton, Ch. *ce qui cause la faim;* est etiam rel.

Tȣatonnhakarien, Ch. riaste, ri, rihe; *estre misérable, souffrir beaucoup.* Vide Gagarien.
Tȣatonnhakariakton, Ch. *estre malheureux pour q. c.,* est etiam rel.
Tenskȣatonnhakariakte, *tu nous rends misérables.*

Otonkȣa, *flamme, fièvre.*
Gatonkȣarhoon, S. hos, ho, hosere; *avoir la fièvre.*
Gatonkȣarhoston, S. *causer la fièvre.*
Atetonkȣaragȣan, Ch. *la chaleur de la fièvre s'en aller.*
Te gatonkȣare, Ch. *avoir grand chaud.*
Atetonkogȣan, *la flamme s'eslever.*

Atonnhien, Ch. nhiha, nhie, nianne; *nier, s'excuser.*
Atonnhianni, R. acq. *f.* nhien.
Eskȣatonnhien, *tu mihi vel pro me negabis.*

Atonrion, Ch. ries, ri, riese; *respirer.* V. aonria, *halitus.*
Atonrieθon, Ch. θa, t, tanne; *respirer par quelque chose.*
Atonriajen, *faire le hé hé au chant des guerriers.*
Atonriajenni, R. *f.* enhas; *le faire pour quelq.*
Atonriokte, Ch. θa, ten, tanne; *perdre haleine.*
Atonrianneron, Ch. ons, on, onre.
Atonrianneronkon, Ch. kȣa.

Atonriaron, Ch. rons, ron, ronne; *médiciner.* Est etiam rel.
Atonriaronkon, Ch. *médiciner avec q. c.*

Atonranni, R. *f.*, *rien remercier.*
Atonraseron, Ch. rons, ron, ronne, est etiam rel.
Atonraseronkon, *remercier par q. ch.; p. & f.* kȣa, kȣanne.

Atonriate^c^ton, Ch. θa, t; *un chien gronder.*

Atonnotsion, Ch. *laver la gale.*

Atonȣaraien, Ch. *s'abbaisser de peur de heurter.*
Tȣatonȣesaon, Ch. sas; *danse des femmes.*

Atonrohon, Ch. ros, rohȣe, rohese; *plonger.*
Atenrohose, R. *f.* ros; *plonger pour honorer, saluer quelqu'un.*

Atonront, Ch. θa, ten, tanne; *chanter un air auquel on repond par des hen hen.* Satonronten, *chante.*
Atonrontakon, Ch. kȣa, kȣag, kȣanne; *chanter pour cause.*
Atonrontanni, R. *f.* θas; *canere alicui.*
Tȣatontarikton, Ch. θas, t, tanne; *faire huée* est etiam R.

Atontarion, *les varangues du canot.*

Atoon, S. tos, to, tosere; *vouloir, consentir.* Atose, R. *f.* tos.

Atȣagannen, Ch. nha; *parler une langue étrangère.*
Atȣagannhannion, multip.
Atȣagannhase, R. *parler à quelq. un langue differente.*

Atȣannha, S. *brasselet.*
Atȣannhen, S. nha, nhag; *en avoir, en mettre.*
Atȣannhaston, S. *en faire de q. chose.*

Atȣendȣtakȣaton, R. θa, θ, tanne; *demander q. chose à quelqu'un, s'en prier.*

Atȣeston, Ch. θa, t, tanne; *passer.*
Atȣestanni, R. *f.* ten; *passer quelqu'un.*
Atȣestakon, Ch. *p. & f.* kȣa, *n.* kȣanne; *le lieu par où l'on passe.*

Tȣaȣeston, *percer.* ȣationȣest, *on perce.*
Tȣaȣesta^e^kon, Ch. *percer par quelque chose.*

Atȣekon, S. *estre affable.*

Atȣenteton, Ch. *abandonner quelque chose;* θa, t, θe. Est etiam relat.
ȣahoñatȣentat, *on l'a abandonné.*

Atori, Ch. *chasser des bestes.*
Atorianni, R. *chasser à quelq. ou pour quelq.*

Ti geθa, Si seθa, &c. *je fais à dessein.*
Te ȣageθon, S. taget, taset, taret.

Aθo, S. *froid* a quo, Joθore, *il fait froid;* reksе, reg.
Aθoraton, Ch. rats, rat, raθe; *faire froid.*
Jaten te ȣaθorats garonhiage, *il ne fait pas froid au ciel.*
Nota quod quando significatur actus utendum est impersonale parad. S., v. g.: Joθore, *il fait froid.* Ejoθoreg, *il fera froid.*
Si vero significatur habitus utendum, impers. parad. Ch., v. g.:
ȣaθorats te giatontarigon, *il fait froid à Kebec.*
ȣaθoratskȣa eȣaθorat jaten te eȣaθoraθe.
Aθoraton, neut. S. *avoir froid.*
ȣagaθorats, *j'ay eu froid.* ȣesaθorat, *tu as eu froid.*
Aθoraston, *causer le froid.* Ch.
Naie ȣaθorasθa, *voilà ce qui fait le froid.*
Aθoge, *le nord, du costé du froid.*

Aθoraton, Ch. ts, t, taθe; *chasser.*
Aθoraθon, *y aller.*
Aθorati, R. *chasser pour quelqu'un.*

Aθontaton, Ch. *entendre, obeir;* ts, t, θe.
Aθontati, R. *obeir à quelqu'un; f.* tats.
Aθontasθa, Ch. *ce qui fait obeir.*

Aθonte, S. *approuver, consentir;* te, teg, tekse.

Aθotaton, Ch. *se reposer, cesser d'agir;* ts, t, θe.
Jaten te gaθotats tsinni ȣagióte, *je ne me repose point tant je suis occupé.*
Aθote, S. *demeurer en repos, ne dire plus mot.*
Stotek, *tais toy.* Gatsiaθoteg, *taisez-vous, vous* 3 *ou* 4, &c.

Tȣatotsinneᵉton, Ch. θa, t, tanne; *glisser sur la glace.*
Tȣatotsinnetakon, *glisser en un lieu marqué.*
Te jontotsinnetakȣa, *écorche ou planche sur laquelle on glisse.*

Tȣarennion, Ch. nies, ni; *eloigner, écarter.*
Tȣarenniaton, Ch. est etiam rel.

Atratitsera, *fourrure de souliers.*
Tagȣatratitseragenas, *fais moi de la paille pour garnir mes souliers.*
Atratitserata, *mettre des fourrures.*
Atratitserat, *y en avoir.*

Atrea, *avoir pour petit fils ou petite fille.*
Hiatrea, *c'est mon petit fils.* χeiatrea, *c'est ma p. f.*
In voc. kȣatri, *o mon petit fils; o ma petite fille.*
Kȣatre ogon, *o vous mes petits fils.*
Atresera, in comp.
Atreseraien, S. *en avoir.*

Atren, S. trens, trenskȣe, tren, trensere; *faire festin.*
Metaphorice, N. Hotrenskȣe nondȣtagete, *N. est la chef de la guerre.*
Atrentandi, R. *f.* ten; *donner à quelqu'un de quoi faire festin.*
Atrenton, S. θa, t, tanni; *faire festin de quelque chose.*
Atren, S. *danse des anciens, chanter.*

Jagotrens, *on chante.*

Atrendȣt, Ch. θa, ten, tanne; *chanter.*

Atrentanni, *R. chanter pour quelqu'un.*

Atreon, S. ons, on, onne; *porter le deuil, estre veuf.*

Atri, *courroye de raquette.* S. extra comp.

Atriston, *en faire de q. c.* Atritsera in comp.

Atsia, extra comp. Atsianna, in comp. *le dedans de la main.* Te ȣatsiannage, 2 *jointées.*

Atsiagȣennonni, *serrer la main.*

Atsiagȣarision, *l'ouvrir.*

Atsiohare, Ch. re, reg; *laver ses mains.*

Atsiannont, S. *avoir quelque chose en la main.*

Θennon satsannontati, *que vas tu portant à la main?*

Atsagannen, Ch. nha, nhag; *parler une langue étrangère.*

Atsagannen, S. *estre étranger, d'une langue differente.*

Atsagannhannion, Ch. *parler diverses langues differentes.*

Atsagannhenta, in comp.

Ratsagannhentaksen, *le méchant parleur.*

Atsannhon, Ch. ons, on, onhe; *degoutter, l'eau tomber goutte à goutte.*

Atsennhonnion, Ch. *quantité de gouttières.*

Atsaȣendori, S. ri; *se divertir, se moquer.*

Atsaȣendorieton, Ch. *faire son divertissement, son jeu de quelque chose,* est etiam rel.

Atsarogȣan, Ch. gȣas, go, gohe; *bruit de plusieurs qui parlent.*

Atsaton, Ch. tons, ton, tonne; *faire une cache.*

Atsatonkon, Ch. *p.* et *f.* kȣa, n, kȣane; *lieu où l'on fait cache.*

Atsatonse, R. *faire une cache à quelqu'un.*

Atsatongȣan, Ch. gȣas, go, gohe; *la decouvrir.*

Atsatongȣanni, *la decouvrir.*

ȣaonχigaronni, onχiatsongȣanni, *on nous a fait grand tort, on nous a decovert une cache.*

Atesatongȣan, neut. Ch. *cache se decouvrir.*

Otsata, *brouillard.* Atsateñon, *tomber br.*

Josateñon nagendigonra, *j'ai l'esprit brouillé d'affliction.*

Atsatajenθon, S. *y avoir brouillard.*

Atsatageȣan, *le brouillard se dissiper.*

Atsat, *montrer;* saθa, saten, saθanne. Hetsatsaten, *montre le.*

Ise ȣahiat saten, *il l'a montré, indiqué.*

Atsatanni, R. *f.* θas; *montrer à quelq.*

Atseïaron, Ch. rons, ron, ronne; *estre timide, n'oser pas, perdre courage.*

Θosa tegatsejaron nagrihȣiost, *que je ne sois pas honteux d'être chrétien.*

Atseiaronse, R. *craindre, être honteux pour quelq.*

Atȣendatseiaron, Ch. *n'oser pas parler par crainte, par timidité.*

Atsenharen, S. *perdre un bon morceau pour ne se pas trouver, ou pour n'avoir rien tué.*

Atsennonnion, Ch. v. S. nisk, ni, nianne; *estre bien aisé, estre heureux.*
Atsennonniaton, Ch. *estre heureux pour q. chose*, est etiam rel.

Atseratéron, Ch. res, ren, rese; *estre possible.*
Atseratéron, neut. S. Jaten taongȣatseraterenn, *non possem.*

Atserhaton, R. θa, t, tanne; *poursuivre quelq.*

Atsi, *camarade.* Atsisera, in comp. Ongiatsi, *nos 2 sumus.*
Atsiserajen, S. *en avoir.*

Otsiera, *ongle*, S. Gatsierarágȣan, Ch. *arracher l'ongle.*
Gatsieraragȣanni, R. *f.* gȣas.

Otsiskȣa, *boule.* Tȣatsikȣaon, *crosser.*
Tȣatsikȣaeston, Ch. θa, θ.

Tȣatsigaȣeron, *nàger.* Ch.

Atsinnaton, Ch. tons, ton, tonne; *courir la nuit, faire mal, &c.*

Atsinnaχen, S. *jongleur.*

Atsinnha, *jartière.* Atsinnhaχon, g. *mettre ses jartières.*
Atsinnhaston, Ch. *avoir des jartières.*

Tȣatsinnaȣiagon vel **Tȣannojagon**, S. aks, ag, aχe; *être bossu.*

Atsiriaȣen, Ch. *estreindre, serrer.*

Tȣatsisònχon, Ch. *trembleterre.*

Otsigre, *nuée.* Jotsigre, *il y a de nuées.*
Ontajotsigrontie v. tagotsigratie, *le ciel s'obscurcit de nuées.*

Ontsa, *genou.* Tȣatonsȣt, Ch. θa, ten, tanne; *se mettre à genoux.*

Atsogȣan, Ch. gȣas, go, gohe; *petuner.*
Atsogȣanni, R. *f.* gȣas; *donner à petuner à quelqu'un.*
Atsogȣaton, Ch. *petuner avec quelque chose.*

Atsogȣannen, S. *riche.*

Atsonnion, *coucher le long du feu.*

Atsoθon, Ch. θosk, θo, θosere; *sauter dans l'eau, d'un poisson.*
Tȣatsoθon, Ch. *se mettre dans l'eau, y entrer.*
Significat etiam *le soleil se coucher, quasi immergat se.*
Tȣatsoθoθon, Ch. *la ou l'on se met dans l'eau.*
Te ȣatseθo nongati, *du coste du soleil couchant.*

Tȣateȣasoθon, Ch. θa, t, t, tanne; *faire le devin, entrer dans la suerie pour sçavoir le passé, present et advenir.*

Atsori, C. risk, ri, rianne; *manger de la sagamité.*
Atsoriaton, Ch. *le lieu ou le temps où on mange la sagamité.*

Atsotsion, Ch. sions, si; *se brusler la bouche.*

Tȣattetaron, neut. Ch. *s'entrouvrir;* ron, re, ronne.
Etȣatonhȣentsiattetare, *la terre s'entrouvrira.*
Attetarongȣan, *idem.*
Atterigȣan, Ch. cum notâ reit. et loc. *s'enfler.*
Attetanni, R. *f.* ten; *tancer, menacer.*

Attogen, *avoir de l'esprit;* Ch. χa, g, χag.

Ogrigon, in comp. *être retiré, refroigné.*
Tȣatkonsogrigon, S. *avoir la visage refroigné.*
Te ȣagenniogri, *j'ai les doits retirés.*
Atogrigon, S. pass. Jotogri raondigon^e^ra, *il a l'esprit retreci, retiré de douleur.*

Atȣekon, S. *p.* et *f.* ek, en, eχe; *estre affable.*
Agatȣek, satȣek, rotȣek, jotȣek. Garȣten, S. *idem.*

VERBA 2^ae^ CONJUGATIONIS.

Gaason, R. *donner un coup de couteau;* sons, son, sonne.
Atataason, neut. recip. *s'en donner soymême.*

Ogakȣenta, *Pois, sorte de farine un peu grosse.*

Gagaion, S. *estre laborieux.*
Gagaieñon, ense, en, ensere; *desirer de voir son pays.*
Atkaienton, *desirer en songe.* Ch.

Gagaion, impers. *estre vieux, usé.*
Gannatagaion, *vieux village.*
Gannonsagaion, *vieille cabane.*
Gagaionton, S. *les ancetres, anciens.*
Gagaiont, Ch. *estre indisposé.*
Ragaiontes, *il est indisposé.*

Gagáon, S. gas, gaȣe; *trouver bon :* inflectitur ut verba 3^ae^.
Garihȣagáon, Ch. *aimer l'affaire, trouver bonne.*

Kagannere, *voir*, Ch. est etiam rel.
Kaganneron vel Kagannerâon, S. nre, nranne; *voir en songe.*

Gagannenton, Ch. *lescher;* θa, t.
Snatsiagannent, *leche la chaudière.* Significat etiam *baiser quelqu'un, le caresser.*
Atatgannenton, Ch. *s'entresaluer.*

Gagannonnion, non est in usu sed inde composita.
Atkannonnion, Ch. *pr.* ni; *estre bon, beau, parfait.*
Jotkannion naondigonra, *il a l'esprit bien fait.*
Gaiatagannonnion, Ch. *estre bien fait de corps.*
Garihȣagannonnion, *bonne affaire.*

Gagaȣet, *aviron.* Agaȣetsera, in comp.
Gagaȣe, Ch. *manier l'aviron, ramer.*
Hatigaȣennontie, *ils vont ramant.*
Gagaȣetseragȣetaron, Ch. *en couper un.*

Gagaȣon, Ch. ȣas ou ȣasera; *dresser la sagamité.*
Gagaȣanni, R. *f.* geȣas.

Gagara, *fable.*
Gagaraton, Ch. tons, ton, tonne; *en dire.*
Gagaratonni, R. *f.* tonhas.

Jogarate, *de cette hauteur.* K^e^n n'ahotakȣendiagarate, *il y a des meubles, un meuble de cette hauteur.*

Ogare, *escorce dont on se sert pour lier.*
Gagaron, Ch. *en lever.*
Gagaronhon, *en aller lever.*
Gagarotsion, *la detacher de la premiere peau.*
Gagariagon, Ch. *payer ses dettes;* ks, g, χe.
Gagariagi, R. acq. *payer pour quelqu'un.*
Gagarokte, Ch. *achever de tout payer.*
Gagariakton, Ch. θa, t, tanne; *payer avec q. c.*
Gagaroktanni, R. *donner à credit; f.* θas.
Gagarȣt, S. *avoir, faire ses dettes.*
Gagarennion, Ch. nies, ni, niase; *eloigner,* est etiam rel.
Gagarenniaton, Ch. *eloigner par quelque chose.*
Gagarenron, S. *pancher d'un costé.*
Onne jogarenre, *il est après midi.*
Gannatsiagarenron, Ch. *chaudière qui penche d'un costé.*
Gagarenton, S. θa, t, tag; *estre percé.*
Jonhȣentsiagarent, *un trou en terre.*
Gagareȣaton, R. θa, t, tanne; *blesser quelqu'un, ou se blesser.* Est Parad. S. ȣahogareȣat, *il s'est blessé.*
Significat etiam apud Onnejȣtos, *regretter un mort.*
N. raondigonra rogareȣat, *et en disant cela on jette la pourcelaine sur le corps.*
Significat etiam *estre la cause d'un mal arrivé.*
Θennon ȣahogareȣat, *quasi dicunt qui l'a blessé.*
Gagarhaθon, Ch. θosk, θo, θosere; *tourner, renverser.*
Onhȣentsiagarhaθon, *renverser la terre.*
Gagarhatennion, Ch. nions, ni, nionhe; *idem.*
Gaiatagarhatennion, *de re vivente.*
Atkarhatennion, *se tourner,* Ch.; ȣatkarhatennions, *une roue.*
Gandigonragarhaθon vel Gandigonragarhatennion, *renverser l'esprit à quelqu'ün.*
Iogaȣ agontak, *ma chaudiére coule.* V. ȣaoχa.
Gagarien, Ch. riask, ri, rihe; *manger, mordre.*
Gannatagarien, *manger un village,* est etiam R. Hoüagarien, *on l'a mangé.*
Gagariaton, S. *ce qui fait manger.*
Jogariat, *O qu'il mange ici à cause des puce,* etc.
Jogaratianne, *maringouins* (vel potius Jogariatanne).
Gagarien, neüt. S. rogarias tsinnon, *il a des poux.*
Tȣaterientagarien, Ch. *estre misérablement tourmenté de l'esprit pour un mal present* ou *futur.*
Tȣaterientagariakton, R. *affliger quelq.*
Atkarien, in comp.
Tȣateriaskarien, Ch. *estre pauvre.*
Tȣatonnhakarien, Ch. *souffrir beaucoup.* Fiunt relativa uti supra.
Atatkarien, Ch. *s'entremanger.*
Gagarihaton, R. *manger beaucoup,* v. g. *d'esclaves.*

Gagaronnion, R. nisk, ni; *faire tort à quelqu'un, lui causer quelque perte.*

Atkaronnion, Ch. *faire quelque perte.*

ȣaonχig'aronni, *on vous a fait un grand deplaisir.*

Gagaroon, Ch. rosk, ro, rosere; *carder du chanvre.*

Ogarȣsta, *boyaux.* Agarȣstagon, *dans les boyaux.*

Gagasera, *larme.* Gagatsia, *idem* in comp.

Gagasereñon, S. *des larmes tomber.*

Gagaserariron, Ch. *en repandre.*

Kagaseragesen, Ch. *les essuyer.*

Kagaseragesenni, P. *f.* esas.

Kagasiagenton, *repandre des larmes.* Ch.

Te sagakente, *tu as des marques d'avoir pleuré.*

Gagasaien, S. *estre lent à marcher.* Gagasaiaton.

Gagasaiatanni, R. *f.* ten; *retarder quelqu'un par sa lenteur.*

Gagaste, Ch. *aimer beaucoup;* takȣe, tak.

Kgasθa nondȣtagete, *j'aime beaucoup la guerre.*

In comp. Gannegagasθa, Ch. *aimer à boire.*

Gagatste, impers. Ch. *fort, dur.*

Onnhegatste, *vie dure, longue.* Gaiatagatste.

Gasiragatste, *étoffe forte.*

Atkatste, *estre patient à endurer.* S.

Gandigonkatste, *esprit fort.*

Atatkatste, S. *se fortifier pour endurer.*

Ataskatste, S. *être heureux, à son aise, ne manquer de rien.*

Gagaston, R. *faire sagamité à quelq.;* tons, ton, tonne.

Atkaston, Ch. *faire sagamité.*

Atkastongȣan, Ch. *l'avoir faitte.*

Atkastonkon, Ch. *la faire de q. c.;* kȣa, kȣag, kȣanne.

Gagateñon, S. *avoir abondance de q. c.* Sæpius in comp.

Gentsiagateñon, *avoir abondance de poisson.* S. te, teg, tensere.

Gagatenston, *en avoir abondance pour ou par q. c.*

Gagatenni, R. *f.* ten; *faire avoir abondance à quelq.*

Garihȣagateñon, S. *estre babillard, grand parleur.*

Garihȣagatanni, R. *f.* ten; *parler, dire beaucoup de choses à quelq.*

Atkate, *être beaucoup de monde.* S.

Jagokate ongȣe, *quantité de monde.*

Oga^{c}te, *cru.* Osaragate, *chair crue.*

Ogate, *œil,* extra comp. Kgatake, *à mes yeux;* sgate, ragate.

In comp. Okara.

Gakario, *beaux, bons yeux.*

Kaga^{c}rogaton, *pocher l'œil.*

Gakarohason, act. r.

Atkaroheson, *se borgner.* P.

Kakarotagȣan, *arracher l'œil.*

Kakarannoñagon vel Kakarahiagon, S. *avoir mal aux yeux.*

Kagakarenron, S. *estre louche.*

Ti agotkakaratihen, *on est louche.*
Tȣatkataȣeñjon, S. *estre borgne.*
Gagarateton, S. *avoir l'œil perçant.*
Kagakȣarision, Ch. *ouvrir les yeux.*
Kagakennion, R. nies, ni; *decouvrir l'ennemi sans en être vu.*

Kagaton, S. *aller viste, estre bon marcheur;* θa, t, tanne.

Gagatotsienton, Ch. θa, t, tanne; *pescher en puisant le poisson comme font les Agniers le haran.*

Gagen *ou* Gageña, *avoir pour cadet.*
Higeña, *mon cadet;* χegeña, *ma cadette.*
Hetsigeña, *ton,* rogeña, *son,* agogeña, *sa cadette.*

Gagen, *voir,* Ch. ensk, en, ensere.
Gagen, R. ȣahoñagen, *on l'a vu.*
Gȣannonsagen, *on a vu une cabane.*
Significat etiam de visu in somnis, v. g.:
ȣahagen rotsinnaχen, *le jongleur a vu.*
Atken, Ch. est etiam R. Goñjatkensere, *je te viens voir.*
Atkensennion, Ch. *voir de tous cotés.*
Atkenseron, *aller à la decouverte.*
Atatken, *s'entrevoir;* kens, ken, kensere.

Atken, *se lever sur son séant.* Satkenχio, *leve toi.*

Ogenha, *couverte.* Gagenhaksen, *mechante couv.*

Gagenia, *cheveux qui tombent sur le front, extremité.*
Gagenhiagon, *les couper,* Ch. Gagenhiagi, R.
Tȣatgenhogen, *avoir les chevaux sur le front divisés, d'où ils ont nommé les femmes;* te hondatkentiogen..

Gagenhiat, *bout, extremité de quelque chose.*
Gannontagenhiat, *a bout de la montagne.*
Gannonskenjat, *pro* Gannonsagenhiat.

Gagengȣara, *front.* Jegengȣaren, *au milieu du front.*
K'kengȣarakske, *à mon front.*

Gagengȣaton, *passer à costé.* Ch.
ȣagennatagengȣaton, *j'ai passe à coté du* B.

Gagenhorogon, *boucher,* Ch. Gagenhorokton, θa, t.

Gagennha, *esté.* Gagennhagé, *pendant l'été.*
Gagenhihen — Kenȣagennhe, *cet été.*
Oia tsi etȣgennhe, *il y a deux ans.*
Gagennhioston, *avoir un bel été.*
Kagenhokte *vel* Kagennhiagon *v.* Kagennhongon, Ch. *passer l'été.*
Gagennhagarhaθon, S. *avoir grande secheresse.*

Gagennen, in comp. *debattre à qui aura.*
Gaiatagennen, R. nhe, nhag, nhasere; *disputer à qui aura une,* &c.
Onhȣentsiagennon, Ch. *disputer d'une terre à qui l'aura.*
Tȣ-askennen, extra comp.
ȣationskennha, *on debat à qui l'emportera.*
Gagennion, in comp. *vaincre, disputer.*

Garihȣagennion, Ch. *fermer la bouche à quelqu'un, le vaincre par raison.*

Garihȣagenniaton, Ch. θa, t, tanne; *l'exces de q. c. ou de quelque, ou en bien ou en mal.*

Atrihȣagennion, Ch. *disputer par parole, se quereller.*

Garengennion, R. nies, ni; *surmontre en force, adresse.*

Atkenniaton, Ch. θa; *estre beau.*

ȣasrihȣagenniat, *tu excedes, surpasses ma pensée.*

Jorihȣagenniaton ongnaχȣen, *je suis en colere au dela de ce que je peux dire.*

Tikenha θeten onȣa ontagarihȣagenniatanne: *Ce n'etait qu'un peu dernierement, mais maintenant il passera tout.*

Tȣ–askennion, Ch. extra comp. nies, ni, niese.

ȣaθiaskenni, *ils se surmontent l'un l'autre.*

Gandigonragennion, R. *vaincre l'esprit de quelqu'un.*

Gandigonkennion, R. *tromper quelq. lui presentant q. c. et retirant le bras.* Sumit notam local.

Gagennoron, impers. *pleuvoir;* re, resere.

Onnaogennere, *voila qu'il pleut.*

Jogennoron v. Jogennoreskon, *il pleut beaucoup.*

Taonχen jogennoreserannonhȣes, *il se plait à pleuvoir.*

Gagennoron, neut. S. *avoir de la pluye.*

ȣesagennore, *tu as eu de la pluye.*

Gagenrat, in comp. *blanc.* Kragen, extra comp. Ch.

Gragen, *je suis blanc;* sragen, haragen.

Gasiragenrat, *couverte blanche.*

Gagonskenrat *pro* Gagonsagenrat, *visage blanc.*

Gaȣakenrat, *chair blanche.*

Gagenrion, Ch. ries, ri, riese; *rouler, se veautrer,* in comp.

Atragenrion, *se rouler dans le cendres.* Ch. est etiam rel.

Gagenritaon, Ch. tas, tahȣe, tasere; *faire rôtir du blé ou autre chose.* Inde Agenrita, *du petit blé.*

Gagenron, Ch. *manquer;* re, r.

ȣagenre snon? *comme s'il manquoit.*

Rogenron si renteron, *rien ne luy manque.*

Ajogenron gati gen? *Parum ne foret?*

Gagenronni, R. *mepriser.* Vid. supra Ogenra.

Gagenraton, *dedaigner;* S. θa, t, tanne.

Gagentennion, S. *estre étourdi,* in comp.

Atiengȣagentennion, S. *estre étourdi du petun.*

Aθonagentennion, S. *estre étourdi du branle du canot.*

Atnigȣensagentennion, S. *du sang qui coule de la veine.*

Gagentoranni, R. *f.* torhas; *mettre une emplatre.*

Gagentoregȣan, Ch. *l'oster.*

Gagentoragȣanni, R. *f.* gȣas.

Segon gagentore, *il y a encore un amplattre.*

Gageron, *quelque chose ou quelquesuns être ensemble, vel ponere aliquos vel aliqua alicubi.*

Θo gageron agetsennen, *voila mes prisonniers qui sont là.*

Gannenstageron, *monceau de blé, quantité de blé par terre.*

Ken ȣakkeron, *je mets là.* Eθo skeron, *mets là.*

Gageronni, R. *f.* ronhas.

ȣahoñageronhas, *on a mis devant luy,* v. g. *de la pourcelaine.*

Gaget, Ch. ts, t; *gratter, doler.* Vel Gageθon, θas, t, θaθe.

Gannohȣageθon, *gratter une peau.*

Tageȣaget gesonne, *gratte moi le dos.*

Atket vel Atkeθon, *se gratter.* Ch.

Θosa tesatket, *ne te gratte pas.*

Gagetak, S. *carquois.*

Gage^c^te, S. *porter; pr.* dumtaxat in usu.

ȣakkete, *je porte;* sagete, rogete, jogete.

Inde forte Atketaton, 1^ae^ Conj.

Gage^c^ton, S. *collier à porter;* ȣakketon, sageton, raogeton.

Asara, *le collier qui se met au front.*

Orenta, *les 2 branches.*

Atketare, *le porter sur le front.*

Gagetȣt, θa, ten, tanne, Ch. *se montrer, paroitre par dessus.* Skat te ȣenniaȣe skat iogetȣt, 101.

Atketȣt, Ch. θa, ten, tanne; *se faire voir.*

Satketȣtanni, *va te montrer, va voir.*

JonketȣθakȢa, *une fenetre, seu par où l'on se montre.*

Intrat etiam in comp. Gaiategetȣt, Ch. *rem viventem se producere.*

Gagetskȣan, Ch. *se lever*; in comp. kȣas, ko, kohe.

Garontagetskȣan gaiànderesera, *lever l'arbre de paix.*

Gagetskȣanni, R. *f.* kȣas.

Atketskȣan, Ch. *se lever;* Satketsko, *leve toi.*

Atketskȣanni, R. *f.* kȣas; *se lever pour faire place à quelqu'un.*

Gagon, Ch. heterocl. ks, g, χ; *manger.*

Igeks, iseks, iraks, iȣaks. V. conj. intrat in comp.

Gannataragon, Ch. *manger du pain.*

Gagon, *nomen* indecl. in comp. significat Bon.

Ohiagon, *bon fruit*; gannontaragon, *bonne bouillié;* ronnontagon, *il trouve le lait bon.*

Ronnegagon iotskarat, *il trouve bonne l'eau de vie.*

Iaȣagon, *cela est bon.*

Gagonhara, *le milieu ou le gros os du nez :* inde

Gagonharionni, *lieu sur le chemin des flamands, où il y a une longue montagne qui a une bosse et eminence au milieu.*

Nigagonhres, *dit on d'un long visage.*

Kagonhen, R. *donner de prisonniers.*
Te hoñagonhen, *on luy a donne un esclave.*
Tȣatkonhan, *estre donné,* Ch.
N. ȣaθiatkonhen, *il est donné pour N.*
Tȣatkonhenton, *de multis.*

Gagonnienston, Ch. *aimer, estimer;* θa, t, tanne.
Atkonnienston, S. *s'aimer, s'estimer, s'en faire accroire.*
Gagonnienston, R. *aimer quelqu'un, le caresser.*
Dicunt etiam Rogonnienst, *il estime bien sa marche.*

Gagonregon, Ch. kȣe, reg, reχe; *frappe, coigner, pousser.*
Gasgonreg, *pousse, frappe;* est etiam R.
Atatkonregon, Ch. *s'entrepousser.*
Gagonraseron, Ch. *donner quantité de coups;* est etiam R.
Atatkonreseron, Ch. Jegonreesθa, *marteau ou chose avec quoy on frappe.*

Gagonretsa, *le poignet.* Kagonretsiagon, *couper le poignet.*

Gagonsa, *visage.* Gagonsarogon, *visage balafre,* Ch.
Gagonsajagon, R. *donner un soufflet.*
Gagonsaȣenron, S. *ne rien prendre à la chasse.*
Gagonsannetarion, Ch. *foule de monde plusieurs visages joints.*
Gagonsȣtanni, R. *f.* θas.
ȣagatkonsaȣenrat, *j'ai montré le nez par dessus.*

Kagont, Ch. *ne pas retourner du lieu où l'on est allé.*
Te hatigont hondaregȣan, *ceux qui sont allés en guerre ne retournent pas.*
Iategagont, *c'est pour toujours.*
Gáiatagont, Ch. θa, ten, tanne; *demeurer, sans retourner.*
Gaiatagontakon, R. *être la cause qu'un autre ne retourne pas, ne pas le ramener.*
Atkont, Ch. *idem,* θa, ten.
Onni ȣaharkonten, *il ne retourne pas.*
Tȣatkontakon, Ch. *être la cause qu'on ne retourne pas.*
Θennon tejontkontakȣa te hotiagi, *qu'est ce qui arrête le monde à Montréal.*
ȣatisarihȣagontan garihȣanderen, *que ton peché sois sans retour.*
Ateratȣendagonten asaterientasa, *que ton propos soit pour toujours.*
Gaȣendagont, *tenir ferme dans ce que l'on a promis.*

Gagonton, *ignorer.* Garihȣagonton, Ch. *ignorer la chose.*

Gagȣan, Ch. gȣas, go, gohe; *cueillir, amasser, lever, prendre.*
Gagȣanni, R. *f.* gȣas, n, nire; intrat in comp. frequentissime.
Gaȣaragȣan, Ch. *prendre de la viande.*
Gaiatagȣanni, R. *prendre, tirer une chose vivante à quelqu'un.*

Gagohon, Ch. hes, ha, hese : *aller querir;* componitur cum omnibus fere verbis.
Gentsiagohon, *aller querir du poisson.*

Gȣannen & **Gagȣannen,** *grand l'estre*; nens, nha, nhasore : istud de rebus viventibus, hoc de inanim.

Gȣannen intrat in comp. et subditum nomini vel voci exprimit magnitudinem, v. g. Gannatȣannen, *grande ville;* Gannatsiȣannen, *grande chaudière.*

Gogȣannhaon, Ch. nhas, nha, nhasere; *devenir grand.*

Gagȣannhase, R. *être grand à quelqu'un.*

Gȣannhaton, in comp. act. Ch. *aggrandir;* θa, t, tanne.

Snatsiȣannhat, *aggrandir la chaudière.*

Gannonsȣannhaton, *aggrandir la maison.*

Atkȣannhaton, pass. Ch. θa, t, tanne; *enlever, prendre, engloutir tout.*

Atkȣannhatanni, R. *f.* ten.

Sagokȣannatanni Onnontio, *Onnontio a enlevé, s'est fait maitre de.*

Ogȣario, S. *animal domestique.*

Gagȣarion, Ch. ries, rie, riese; *quantité de monde se mettre en chemin.*

Gatke ehatigȣarie hotinnonsionni, *quand es ce que les faiseurs de cabane se mettront en chemin.*

Gagȣarieton, Ch. θa, t; *se mettre en chemin pour quelque chose.*

Sæpius assumit notam local. Onne ontajegȣarie, *voila du monde qui, &c.*

Gogȣarision, in comp. *droit.* Atagȣarision, pass. Garihȣagarision, cum red.

Kagȣaronton, S. *avoir des bosses.*

Gogȣaton, Ch. θos, θo, θosore; *aller jusqu'en quelque lieu.*

Onneiȣte ȣaskȣaθo, *tu as été à Onneiȣt.*

Gagȣaton, in comp. *courber.*

Garihȣagȣaton, Ch. *brouiller les affaires.*

Gagȣatagȣan, cum reit. *les redresser, les racommoder.*

Onsaharihȣagȣatago, *il a raccommodé les affaires.*

Tȣatkȣaton, Ch. *tuer avec l'arc ou fusil;* θa, t, θe.

ȣatekkȣat, *j'ai tué.* Te hokȣaton onte, *il a abattu une tourte.*

Atkȣatagȣan, pass. Ch. cum reit. *estre redressé.*

Esȣatkȣatago ne sandigonra, *ton esprit sera remis, rassuré, redressé.*

Tȣatentkȣaton, Ch. *redonner ailleurs un captif qu'on avait eu pour qu'il ait la vie.*

Gagȣegon, Ch. *tous :* caret sing. et duali (Senikȣekon).

Sȣagȣegonhag, *vous y soyez tous.*

Componitur etiam Gannatagȣegon, *tout le bourg.*

Agȣegon, adv. *tout.*

Gagȣegon, *être bouché, fermé,* in comp.

Gaskȣegon pro Gasagȣegon, R. *fermer la bouche à quelq.*; gȣeks, gȣeg, gȣeχe.

Ataskȣegon, pass. Ch. *l'avoir fermée.*

Aθahagȣegon, S. *le chemin être bouché.*

Atiatagȣegon, Ch. *estre constipé.*

Atrihȣagȣegon, Ch. *ne savoir rien d'une nouvelle.*

Gagȣennion, Ch. nies, nie, niese; *pouvoir.*
Askȣenni gati gen? *Le pourrais tu?*
Gagȣenniaton, neut. S.
Jaten tsi te jogȣenniat naonsahatkaȣe, *impossibile est ut desistat.*

Gagȣenraron, *être par ci par là en divers endroits.*
Jogȣenraron haronχa, *il entend par ci par là.*
Asen niagogȣenrare ganniege, *les* 3 *terres d'agnie;* imp. rarakȣe, f. rarag.
Asen niȣakȣenrare, *moy qui ay* 3 *terres différentes.*
Gagȣenraron v. Gagȣenraronnion, S. *bigarrer.*

Ogonstȣenrha, *barbe,* S. Ogonsθȣenrhes, *longue barbe.*
Te jonnhatogen raogonsθȣenrha, *a la barbe fourchue.*
Kagonsθȣenron, *en avoir,* S.
Kagonsθȣenrharanni, R. *la razer.*

Gagȣetaron, Ch. ron, re, ronne; *couper un morceau, lambeau de q. c.*
Skȣetare ne sasare, *coupe.*
Gagȣetaronse, R. *f.* ronhas.
Gasiragȣetaron, Ch. *couper un morceau d'étoffe.*
Atkȣetaron, Ch. *un lambeau se detacher.* Gagȣetarongȣan, Ch.

Ogȣentsera, *peinture rouge.*
Gagȣentserarhon, Ch. *matachier de rouge.*

Gagȣentaron, in comp. *étendu par terre.*
Gaiatagȣentaron, Ch. re; *couché, étendu par terre de re viv.*
Atagȣentaron, pass. Ch. Atiskȣentaron, pass. S. *se coucher, s'étendre sur la terre.*
Satiskȣentare, *étends, couche toi sur la terre.*

Kagonȣenton, S. tons, ton, tonsere; *être malade.*
Te jagogoñȣentons, *on est malade.*

Ogȣitsa, *genouil.*

Gahaȣak, *avoir pour enfant.* Hihaȣak, *mon fils;* Hetsahaȣak, *ton fils.*

Gaha, anomal. *emporter.* V. conj.
ȣaχa, *j'ai emporté;* jesaha, jehoha, ejoha.
Gaha, R. *emmener quelq.*
ȣaonχihas, ȣaejengȣire, *on nous emmenne à la chasse.*
Gȣatiha, *on les a emmenés.*

Gahaȣio, *la neige, poudre.*

Gahaȣi, Ch. ȣis, ȣi, ȣisere; *apporter.*
Iχaȣe, isaȣe, rahaȣe, gahaȣe : V. conj. anomal. est etiam rel.
Goñjaȣisere, *je te viens apporter.*
Gahaȣiton, Ch. θa, t, tanne; *apporter de quel lieu,* cum nota local.
Skandiatarati enagohaȣiton, *on a apporté d'Europe.*
Gahaȣiton, *eloigner.*
Atkȣiton, Ch. *se retirer;* θa, t, tanne. Atkȣiton, pass.
Gahaȣitanni, R. *f.* ten; *apporter à quelqu'un.* Intrat in comp.
Gaȣennenhaȣi, R. *apporter le voix.*

Jesȣs hoñaȣennenhaȣis hatitsihenstatsi, *Les robes noirs apportent la voix de Jésus.*

Gaiatenhaȣi, R. *apporter quelqu'un.*

Gaiatenhaȣiton, R. *apporter quelqu'un de quelque lieu.*

Sumitur étiam neut. Garihȣioston nagiatenhaȣit ganniege, *C'est la foi que m'a amene à Agnier.*

Gaheȣo, Ch. *amener.*

Atatiateȣe, Ch. *s'amener soimême.*

Oskeronge ȣagatatiateȣe, *à peine me suis-je rendu ici.*

Gaiatateȣe, R. *amener quelqu'un.*

Kenθo ȣaχeȣe, *j'ai conduit jusqu'ici.*

Sateȣasennon ȣagaheȣe niontrendaientakȣa, *Elle a amené, elle est venue jusqu'à la moitie des prières.*

Est etiam rel. ȣahoñaheȣe, *on l'a amené.*

Gahasa, *passus, pas.*

Etiegahes v. Gahesonse, *on fait de grands pas.*

Tȣ aχaheson, *avoir de grands pas.*

Θo nieχahage, *combien de pas?*

Ohagenta, *suye de la cheminée.*

Gahagentóron, S. *estre sali de suye.*

Gahagentarigon, S. *être mangé de la suye;* riks, rig.

Gahagenten^c^ton, Ch. *abbattre la suye, ramonner la cheminée.*

Gahagentaȣagon, Ch. *la secouer.*

Gahatsi, S. *être enroué.* ȣaχatsi, *je suis enroué.*

Gahasen, Ch. sens, sen, senne; *tenir conseil, être assemblé.*

Gahasenton, Ch. *s'assembler souvent.*

Gahasentakon, Ch. *p.* & *f.* kȣa; *tenir conseil pour q. c.*

Gahensontion, Ch. *souffler dans la calumet.*

Kahenreton, S. θa, t, tanne; *faire un cry de nouvelle.*

Tajagohenretanne, *on vient en fesant le cry.*

Kahenra^c^ta^c^kon, S. *faire le cry pour q. chose.*

Gahenta, *prairie.*

Gahenton, Ch. tes, te, tonne; *aller le premier.*

Gahahenton, Ch. *faire le chemin.*

Gaihonhenton, Ch. *pescher à la façon des Onneiȣts qui chassent le poisson.*

Ohere, *canne de blé dinde, succets.*

Ganeriaχon, Ch. *en aller couper.*

Gaheragon, *en manger.* Aserag, *mange des succets.*

Aθeronni, Ch. *y en avoir beaucoup.*

Gahere, *estre couvert, vétue, avoir dessus.* S. *f.* rag; ȣakkere, sahere, rohere.

Ehorag, *qu'il soit couvert de sa robe.*

Roratie onnagentsa, *it y a sur luy une peau passée.*

Kaheren, *estre dessus;* rakȣe, re.

Θo gahere sontak, *ta chaudière est là dessus.*

In comp. Gaksahere, *un plat estre dessus.*

Gaharonnion, *quantité de choses être sur quelqu'un.*
Gaiatahere, *une beste ou autre chose vivante, &c.* Vide infra Gar.
Titkahere, *estre plein jusqu'à regorger.*
Titkannakȣahere onnenste, *caisse pleine de blé.*

Kaherhon, S. *faire cuire des citrouilles sur des pierres chaudes.*
Orakȣa, *une portion de telles citrouilles.*
Garakȣannegen, Ch. *en demander.*
Gaherakȣa, *plante de citrouille.*
Tsiatak niorentonte skaherokȣat, *une seule tige a sept plantes de citrouille.*

Gaheᵉta, *champ.* Johetθȣie, *terre en pointe.*
Joθetakton, *champ courbé.* Joθetagȣarison, *champ droit.*
Gahetonni, Ch. *faire des champs;* nisk, ni, nianne.
Gahetonnianni, R. *f.* nien.
Gahetajen, S. *avoir des champs.*
Jatonaronniaton ȣakketajentakȣe, *tout est gâté, perdu dans mon champ.*

Gahetkeñon, Ch. ens, en, ensere; *estre gâté.*
In comp. frequenter apud alias nationes.
Garihȣahetken, *méchante affaire.*
Gahetkense, neut. acq. *devenir mauvais à soimême.*
Gahetkenton, R. θa, t, tanne; *gaster, mal employer.*
Gahetkentsihon, Ch. *n'en pouvoir plus.*
Gahetkentanni, R. acq. *f.* ten.
Atatkenton, Ch. θa; *s'entregaster.*

Gahetkȣate, *estre courbé.*

Gahiȣentaon, Ch. θas, tanne, tasere; *douleur s'appaiser.*
Gahiȣentaon, neut. S.
Ostonha ȣagiȣentaon, *ma douleur est un peu appaisée.*
Gahiȣentaton, Ch. *ce qui fait appaiser la douleur.*

Gahiȣθion, Ch. θions, θie; *esguiser :* quando est passiv. est Parad. S.
Gahiȣθionse, R. *f.* ons.
Gahiȣθionkon, *eguiser avec q. c.* Onne johiȣθe, *cela est aigu.*
Intrat etiam in comp. Aserȣθion, Ch. *aiguiser une hache.*
Tagȣaserȣθionre, *éguise moi ma hache.*

Tiohiotsist, *chose salée.* Takkiosiston, *donne moy du sel.*
Gahiotsistarhon, *saler, être salé.* Ch. hos, he, hosere.

Kahogáton, Ch. tons, ton, tonsere; *éclairer.*
Te sogaton, *éclaire.* Tontaχogaton, *éclaire moi,* a Kahogatense, R.
Tiontogatonharakȣe, *chandelle.*

Gahontsi, Ch. *noir.* Inde Hatihontsi, *les négres.*
Gahontsista, in comp. Gahontsistio, *beau noir.*

Gahoñeja, *canot,* S.
Gahoñjonni, Ch. *faire un canot.*
Gahoñjonnianni, R. *faire un canot à quelq.; f.* nien.
Gahoñanniχon, Ch. *le coudre.*

Gahoñjonton, Ch. *estre à l'anchre; f.* te.
Gahoñjotáon, Ch. tas, tanne, tasere; *aborder.*
Gahoñjotaseron, *quantité de canots aborder.*
Gahoñjontagȣan, Ch. *desancher.*
Aθoñjontagȣan, pass. *idem.* Ch.
Gahoñaȣenron, S. *ne pouvoir pas contenir tout.*
Gahoñarion, S. *briser son canot.*
Gahoñaȣeronton v. rontaon, Ch. *canot tourner.*
Gahoñjo, *bon canot.* Gahoñaksen, *méchant canot.*
Gahoñagat, *canot que va viste.* Gahoñakste, *canot pesant.*
Gahoñjontion, S. *aller en canot, quitter le canot.*
Aθoñarégon, Ch. *mettre le canot à l'eau.*
Gahoñjogȣan, Ch. *le tirer de l'eau.*
Gahoñaratáton, Ch. *le lever en haut.*
Gahoñȣiseron, Ch. res, re; *traisner en chariot.* Est etiam R.
Takkonȣisere, *traine-moy.*

Gahȣae, *battre,* v. g. *le blé, les fezoles.*

Gahȣaeston, S. cum reit. *n'être plus en séve.*

Gahȣannhen, *lier,* R. Gahȣannhaston, gahȣannhaχon, atȣannhaχon, *être lié*

Gahȣaseron, R. rons, re, ronne; *depouiller quelqu'un.*
Gahȣaseron, neut. acq. *estre depouillé.*
Gahȣaserongȣan, R. Aθȣaseron, pass. Ch. *se depouiller.*

Gahȣatase, Ch. *tordre, tournoyer;* ses, se, ser. Aθȣatase, pass.
Hotkon tehatonhȣentsiatases, *Cacodæmon circuit terram.*
Gannatatase, Ch. *faire le tour du village.*
Tȣakȣatasehon, R. *tourner à costé de quelqu'un.*
Te-hok-ratases, *il va et tourne de costé et d'autre.* S.

Kahonre, S. *fusil;* raohonre, *son fusil.*
Kahonrio jate sȣateȣaθa, *bon fusil que ne manque point.*
Kahonraksen tiotsakton, *méchant fusil, tortu.*
Tȣaθonrannegaron, S. *fusil crever.*
Tȣaθonriagi, R. *fusil se rompre à quelqu'un.*
Tȣaθonrotagȣan, *se debander.*
Aθonraratie, S. *porter la culasse derrière l'épaule.*
Aθonrah-re, S. *le porter sur l'épaule.*
Atetatserȣtarhon kahonre, S. *sous le bras.*

Gahȣendo, *isle.* Gahȣendoge, *dans un île.*
Hahȣendagerha, *les Hurons.* Gahȣendȣt, *il y a une isle.*
Gahȣendȣtonnion, *quantité d'isles.*

Gahȣengare, Ch. *raquettes.*
Gahȣengariaχon, Ch. *en aller couper.*
Kahȣengaront, Ch. θa, ten, tanne; *aller en raquettes.*
Aθȣengaront, Ch. *les mettre.*
Kahȣengarȣtagȣan, *les oster.*

Gahȣengare significat etiam *buchette, soit pour festin soit pour autre entreprise.*

Gahȣengaron, R. *donner cette buchette, ce billet.*

Gahȣengarontion, S. *la jetter en quelque cabane.*

Gahȣengarontiense, R. Gahȣengaraȣi, R. *la donner.*

Onne ȣȣatkennison ȣakkengaraȣi, *Vous voila assemblé à qui j'ai donne la buchette, le bulletin.*

Gahȣennonni, Ch. nisk, ni, nianne; *arrondir, plier en ronde.*

Gahȣennonnianni, R. *f.* nien.

Aθȣennonni, S. *estre rond.* Jothȣennonni, *celà est rond.*

Gahȣennonni significat etiam *diverses cabanes sans palissades, sans ordre.*

Gahȣennonnige, g-nagre; *je demeure dans un village sans palissade.*

Gahȣennonniasion, Ch. *desvellopper.*

Aθȣennonniasion, S. *estre desvelloppé.*

Ohȣenria, *flegme.* Aθȣenriontion, S. *jetter un flegme.*

Ohȣensta, *escume, boue.* Gahȣenstoton, S. *bouer;* θa, t, tanne.

Gahȣesen, Ch. sas, sa, sanne; *polir, doler, gratter escorce.*

Gahȣesaton, Ch. θa, t, tanne; *doler avec q. c.*

Gahȣesase, R. *doler à quelq.*

Kannegȣesa, *petit fer dont on gratte les peaux.*

Gahȣisera, *force.* Akȣiseron, *s'efforcer;* atakȣiseron.

Gahȣiseñon, S. *estre accablé d'un fardeau, estre trop chargé;* ens, en, enne.

Onχȣisen, *je suis trop chargé.*

Gahȣisaton, S. *estre trop chargé par quelque chose.*

Gahȣinniaks, ȣakkȣinniaks, sahȣinniaks, rohȣinniaks, sagoȣinniaks.

Gahȣistoskon, Ch. *p.* et *f.* toske; *avoir froid.*

Gahȣistoon, S. *avoir eu froid.* Onne johȣisto, *cela est froid.*

Jotihȣistoon ongȣannoñonsera, *nos citrouilles ont eu froid.*

Gahȣistoton, R. *refroidir,* v. g. *la sagamité a quelq.;* θa, t, tanne.

Atahȣistoton, Ch. *se refroidir à soymeme.*

Ohȣistonsera, *graisse figée quasi refroidie.*

Gahȣistonserarhon, *engraisser.*

Gahȣistannaȣan, Ch. *le graisse qui etoit figée, se fondre.*

Gahȣistannaȣenton, Ch. *la faire fondre.*

Kakȣaton, Ch. θa, t; *tuer à la chasse oiseau ou beste.*

Θe nateskȣat oskennonton, *Combien as tu tué de chevreuils?*

Gakȣarinna, S. *dote d'une femme qui se marie.*

Gakȣarinnionton, Ch. *la porter dans la cabane où l'on se marie.*

Gaksa, *plat.* In comp. kerat; extra comp. gaksonni, *en faire.*

Gaksen, *laid, chétif,* in comp.

Hajataksen, *un chenitre, malfait.*

Garihȣaksen, *méchante affaire.*

Gaksaton, Ch. *gaster;* θa, t, tanne. Componitur cum infinitivo.

Gaksatanni, R. *gaster à quelq.*

Garihȣaksen, S. *estre méchant.*

Garihȣaksaton, pass. usitatius Atrihȣaksaton, Ch. θa, t, tanne.
Atriȣaksáon, R. *faire du méchant.*
Gaksenha, *idem* quod Gaksen, sed magis emphatice.
Gaiataksenha, *une méchante personne.*
Ataksen, S. *estre laid, vilain.*
Iotaksen v. Iotaksensa, *méchante chose.*
Ataksaton, Ch.; Atitaksaton, R. *gaster la fiente de quelqu'un.*

Akserie, *fil, filet.* Akserieta, in comp.
Gakserie, Ch. *faire du fil.*
Gakseriese, R. Gakserietonni, Ch. Gakserietonnianni, R. *f.* nien.

Gakste, S. *pesant;* te, teg. Intrat in comp.
Gaiatakste, *homme pesant.*

Gaksten, *vieillard,* S. Gakstensera, *vieillesse.*
Gakstenserio, *bonne belle vieillesse.*

Gaksia, *frère ou sœur aisné.* Caret singul.

Gaksot, *avoir pour grandpère ou grandmère.*
Raksôt, *mon g. père;* Aksôt, *ma g. mère.*

Gaiageñon, Ch. ens, enne, ensere; *sortir.*
Gaiagenseron, Ch. *sortir souvent.*
Gaiagense, R. acq. *sortir à ou sur quelq.*
Gaiagen[e]ton, Ch. θa, t, tanne; *sortir par quelq. endroit.*
Gaiagentakon, Ch. *idem.*
Gaiagenhon, Ch. hons, hȣe; *tirer, mettre dehors q. c.*
Gaiageñon, non componitur cum vocabulo significante rem vel personam egredientem; sicut componitur sæpe cum nomine signante locum unde exitur, quare non dices Gaiatageñon sed Gaiatinnigeñon, *quelque chose animée sortir de là,* a Gaiata et innigeñon, de quo infra in 4[a] conjug.

Gaiagon, Ch. aks, ag, aχe; *couper.*
Atiagon, pass. *être coupé.* Gaiakse, R. *f.* ks.
Tagiaks, *coupe moy cela.* Atiagi, R. *etre coupé à quelq.*
Kaiagon, Ch. *couper en deux.* Terhatijaks, *ils coupent en deux.*
De pluribus autem dic : Asen nihatijaks, *ils coupent en* 3.
Iagon, in comp. pro Gaiagon. Sic, Gannagariagon, *couper une perche.*
Iakse, R. Gannagariakse, *couper une perche à quelq.*
Iagon cum te affirm. et divisionis.
ȣaθoseriag, *il a passé l'hyver.* ȣaθagennhiag, *il a passé l'été.*
ȣatkannegaiag, *la pluye cesse.*
Kajahiagon, Ch. *passer la rivière;* ks, ag, aχe. Est etiam rel.
Kajahiakton, *l'endroit où l'on passe.*
Kajagon, Ch. *tirer de l'arc, du fusil.*
Tsiag, *tire.* Hetsiag, *tire sur luy.*
Kajakse, R. *tirer pour quelqu'un.*
Gaiaaχon, Ch. *aller tirer de l'arc, du fusil.*
Kaiagon, Ch. *gagner la partie.*

Gaiagonsera, *un morceau de peau à faire des souliers.*
Gaiaktanni, nisk, ten, nire, S. *etre arreté par le mauvais temps.*
Atiaktanni, pass. *idem.*

Gaianna, *piste.* Gaiannare, *il y a une piste.*
Gaiannaronnion, *il y en a beaucoup.*
Gaiannonni, *y avoir, en marquer.* Atiannonni, Ch.
Gaiannenhaȣi, *suivre les pistes de q. c. viv.*
Gaiannigen, Ch. *voir les pistes.*
Gaiannagennion, R. *vaincre quelqu'un à la course.*
Atiannison, Ch. *les pistes formés, savoir marcher.*

Gaianderesera, *noblesse,* S.
Gaiander, *homme ou femme considérable.*
Gaianderenston, R. *faire grand quelq. l'élever à la qualité de.*
Atiandereñon, S. *être bienheureux.*
Jojanderensta[c]kon nongȣatonnheston, *la grace.*

Gaiare, *sac.* Gaiaronni, *en faire;* nisk, ni, nianne.
Gaiaronnianni, R. *f.* nien. Gaiarison.
Atiaronni, Ch. *se faire un sac.*
Gaiareȣe v. Gaiarenha v. Gaiarenhaȣi, *porter le sac, faire des présents.* Ch.

Te gaiasere, *chose double.*
Kajaseron, Ch. *donner un captif; pr.* re.
Kajasaron, Kajasaronnion, *mettre le feu à un arbre coupé, pour le couper en diverses buches.*
ȣaθojasa[c]renhatie etiongȣaronni, si, ires; *il va fumant, il marche portant du feu.*

Gaiason, Ch. sk, s, sonne; *nommer, appeller.*
Θennon jejatsk, *quel est le nom de cela?*
Jesȣs ronaȣaθa, *il se nomme Jésus.*
Atiason, Ch. *estre nomme.*
Gaiason, neutro-pass. *impf.* atskȣa, *f.* hajatseg.
Θennon isaiatsk, *Comment t'appelles tu?*
Nota istud neutro passivum usurpari semper quando est sermo de actuali possessione nominis; sed quando sermo est de nomine suscipiendo usurpatur passivum, Atiason, v. g. Jesȣs ehatias, *il s'appellera Jésus.*
Gaiasonnion de multis, *nommer diverses choses.*

Gaiata, *chose vivante.* Tseiatat, *une seule personne.*
Te gaiatage, 2 *animaux.*
Gaiatagon, *dans le ventre,* Ch. Giatagon, *dans mon ventre.*
Gaiatagȣan, *prendre quelque chose vivante.*
Gaiatagȣanni, *f.* gȣas.
Gaiatagohon, hes, he, ha; *aller querir chose vivante.*
Gaiqtaiesáon, R. *ne trouver pas celuy qu'on cherche.*
Gaiatajesen, Ch.
Gaiatannogaron, S. res, re, rese; *faire une perte.*
Gaiatannogareton, R. *causer perte à quelqu'un.*

Gaiataro, Ch. *être présent, assister;* rakȣe, rag.

Gaiataragon, *assister pour quelque chose.*

Atiatarakon, *aimer quelque chose, ne vivre et ne subsister qu'en cela.*

Gaiatare, *Image*, R. significat *peindre, être peintre; f.* ren.

Gaiataronnion, *quantité d'images.*

Gaiatare, R. *f.* ren; *peindre, mettre quelq. en figure.*

Gaiati, cum notâ totalitatis, *par luymeme, par luy seul.*

Diȣ ate hajati roteȣejennonni garonhia jonhȣentsia onni, *Dieu a fait par luymême le ciel et la terre.*

Gaiatio, *bel homme ou femme.* Ch.

Gaiatioston, *rendre quelq. beau.*

Gaiatase, Ch. *jeune femme :* dicitur etiam de homine.

Gaiatagaion, *âgé de* 50 *à* 60 *ans.*

Gaiatasterist, *homme ou femme beau à voir.*

Gaiataterjon, S. ri; *faire une bonne rencontre.*

Ongiatateri, *j'ai fait une bonne rencontre.*

Gaiatison, R. *pr.* et *f.* sa; *faire créer.*

Diȣ sagoiatison ongȣe, *Dieu a fait l'homme.*

Atiatison, Ch. sas, sa, saanne; *estre vieux.*

Gaiationni, *estre étendu, couché par terre.*

Gaiatonni, *une poupée.*

Gaiatoton, *trahir quelq.* R.

Gaiatȣten, *estre ainsi fait, avoir cette coutume; pr.* t. tennen, tenhag. Neθo, nigiatȣten, *Je suis ainsi fait.* Vide ȣten.

Kajato°retou, Ch. θa, t, tanne; *examiner, penser, deliberer sur quelq. c.* Est etiam R. Te hoñajatoreθa, *on pense à luy.*

Kajatoretakon, *examiner quelque chose pour,* &c. Ch.

Gaiateñon, Ch. tens, tenne, tensere; *tomber.*

Gaiateñon, neut. acq. Ongȣajatens, *une chose vivante m'est tombée.*

Gaiatenton, R. *faire tomber à quelq.;* θa, t, tanne.

Atiatenton, Ch. *se faire tomber.*

Gaiaktanni, *f.* ten. Atiaktanni, neut. S. *etre arreté.*

Gaksaa, *petit enfant*, Ch. Gaksata, in comp.

Gakstesθa, *petite fille.* Gaksatio, *belle enfant.*

Gaksatajen, *avoir un enfant.*

Gaksôta, *estre grand père ou grande mère.*

Raksota, *mon grand père;* hiaksota, *ton g. père;* roksota, *son.*

Aχiksot ogon, *nos grandspères.* Gaksotsera, in comp.

Gakste, *pesant*, S.

Gaiehȣáon, S. hȣas, hȣa, hȣasere; *avoir besoin.*

Gaiehȣatanni, R. *rendre indigent.*

Gaien, *y avoir; impso.* takȣe, *imp.* tag, *f.* tasere, *f.* n. Componitur cum omnibus fere nominibus.

Gaien, S. *posséder.* Iȣagien, *j'en ai.* Jsaijen, ihoien, joïen.

Jaten te ȣagasaraien, *je n'a point de couteau.*

Gaien, Ch. *mettre en quelq. lieu.*

Isi snatsiaien, *mets la loin la chaudière.*

Gaiennon, Ch. *aller porter, mettre en quelq. lieu.*

Seksajenne, *va porter la plat.*

Gaienni, R. *f.* enhas; *mettre à quelq. mesdire de quelq.*

ȣagonriȣajenhas, *je te mets l'affaire entre les mains.*

Hesnontarajenhas, *garde, mets luy de la sagamité.*

Gaienton, multipl. *y en avoir en quantité,* S.

Jagoienton, *on en a en quantité.*

Gaientaon, S. tas, tanne, taȣere; *posséder, avoir.*

Niahoθennon taongi tanne tsinni rannregagaoθa, *je ne puis rien avoir tant il est yvrogne.*

Gaientatie, Ch. *aller en ayant quelque chose.*

Jaten hoθennon te ȣagientatie, *je n'apporte rien.*

Gaientaon, *tomber,* Ch. ȣahajentanne, *il est tombé.*

Kajen, Ch. *jouer, parier; imp.* Enhakȣe, *f.* en, *f. n.* enne.

Taetnien, *jouons nous deux.* Te gienne, *je vas jouer.*

Kajentakon, *prs.* et *f.* kȣa, kȣanne, Ch. *jouer quelque chose.*

Ostarakȣa te gientakȣanne, *je vas jouer de la rassade.*

Kajenni, R. *jouer pour quelq.* N. te hoñajennire, *on va jouer pour N.*

Gaien v. **Gaieña,** *avoir pour enfant.*

χeiña, *c'est ma fille, ce sont mes enfants.*

Hieña, *c'est mon fils;* Sagoieña, *sa fille;* Roieña, *son fils.*

Gaien onton, *devenir enfant de q.*

Onne roieña jotañon, *il est devenu son fils.*

Onnontio songȣajeña, *Onnontio nous a adopté pour ses enfans.*

Gaieon, *estre éveillé; pns.* habitum significans, Ihaies, *il s'éveille; pns.* actum significans, Ihojeon, *il est éveillé; f.* Ehaja. Tsnie, *éveillez vous.*

Gaiete, R. θa, t, tanne; *éveiller quelqu'un.*

Gaiehȣat, Ch. *estre éveillé.*

Raiehȣat, rajehȣatakȣe, *il est, il étoit éveillé.*

Atiehȣat, Ch. *se tenir éveillé.*

Hontiehȣaθa, *solent vigilare.*

Hondatiehȣat, *actu vigilant; f.* ehontiehȣaton, ehondatiehȣatag.

Atiehȣat, R. *veiller quelq.*

Hoñatiehȣaθakȣe rannaskȣa, *on veillait le captif.*

Gaiehȣaton, *se tenir éveillé pour quelque chose.*

Naie jongȣajehȣaθa si ontajon χirorianne, *ce qui nous tient éveillés, c'est qu'on nous a donné nouvelle.*

Gaienna, Ch. nas, na, nasere; *prendre,* est R.

N. ȣasagorienna, *N. l'a pris.*

Te sagoiatannegen, *il en a pris 2.* Itienna, *prends.*

Gaiennaȣagon, S. *embrasser, tenir ferme.*

Te ȣagiennaȣagon Jesȣs raorihȣa, *j'ai embrasse l'aff. de Jésus.*

Gaiennaȣase, R. *aider quelq.; f.* ȣas, ȣasere. Tagiennaȣas, *aide moy.*

Gaienna, *huile*, in comp. Genje, extra comp.
Gaiennarhon, Ch. hos, ho, hosere; *frotter d'huile.*
Jaten te ȣȣagiennajen, *je n'ay plus d'huile.*
Gaiennat, *il y a de l'huyle la dedans.*
Gaiennare, *il y a là de l'huyle.*
Gaiennógȣan, Ch. *lever l'huyle ou graisse liquide.*

Oiengen, *abbrevoir des bestes fauves.* Oiengensera, in comp.
Atiengenserannonna, *estre à l'affût.*
Atiengensori; gaiengenseraraon, *venir à l'abbrevoir, y arriver,* dicitur tam de homine qui insidias ponit quam de belluis.

Ojengȣa, S. *petun.* Gaiengȣio, *bon petun.* Ojengȣatet, *petun fort.*
Atiengȣison, *le petun est meur.*
ȣagatiengȣisaanni, *le petun est meur pour moi.*
Gaiengȣata, *en mettre dans le calumet.* Ch.
Tagien gȣatas, *mets moi du petun.*
Gaiengȣagasta, *consommer du petun.*
ȣaskiengȣasas, *tu consommes mon petun.*
Te gatiengȣakariask, *je suis malheureux n'ayant point du petun.*
Gaiengȣannion, S. *etre chiche à donner du petun.*
ȣagatiengȣanninnonre, *je viens acheter du petun pour moi.*

Gaiengȣire, *flèche.*
Gaiengȣiron, Ch. res, re, rese; *chasser, aller à la chasse du cerf.*
Gaiengȣironse, *chasser pour quelq.* R.

Garihȣaiengȣironse, R. *quereller, accuser.*

Gaiennenon, in comp. ens, enn, ensere; *tomber.*
Garihjennenon, *l'affaire tomber.* Ch.
Garontiennenon, Ch. *arbre tomber.*
Gaiennenon, S. *tomber sur quelqu'un.*
ȣahorontiennens, *un arbre est tombé sur luy.*
Gaiennenton, *faire tomber.* Similiter in comp. θa, t, tanne; est etiam R.
Gaskontariennenton, *faire tomber escorce.*

Gaienrha, extra comp.; Ojengȣara, in comp., *fumée.*
Gaienrhare si etiongȣannonsȣte, *il y a de la fumée dans notre cabane.*
Gaienrharáon, si, ras, ranne; *avoir de la fumée.*
Etiengȣaronni, *il y a de la fumée.*
Atiengȣaronni, Ch. *estre à la fumée, en avoir.*
Atiengȣaronniation, Ch. *en causer par q. c.;* θa, t, tanne.
Est etiam R. ȣaskȣatiengȣaronniat, *tu me fais de la fumée.*
Gaiengȣarȣtanni, R. *f.* θas; *donner signal par la fumée d'un feu fait exprès.*
Atiengose, S. *ébloüy de la fumée.* Kaiengȣarose, *idem.*

Gaienratonni, R. *mesdire de quelq., l'offenser par rapport.*

Gajenseron, Ch. rons, re, ronne; *escorcher.*
Gaienseronse, R. *f.* rons. Atienseron, pass. *etre ecorché.*

Gaienreñon, R. *se blesser, se mettre une épine au pied.*

Ojente, S. *du bois*, extra comp. Gaienta, in comp. *bois.*

Gaientonni, Ch. *faire du bois.* Gaientonnanni, R. *f.* nien.

Atientonni, pass. S. *y avoir du bois.*

Iotientonni si etiongȣannataien, *il y a bien du bois là où est notre bourg.*

Gaientagohon, Ch. *aller querir du bois.*

Gaientagȣan, Ch. gȣas, go, gohe; *faire, lever du bois.*

Gaientagȣanni, R. *f.* gȣas; *en faire pour quelqu'un.*

ȣahoientagaten, *il y a bien du bois.*

Gaientȣt, *il y a un bucher.* Gaientȣton, *il y a plusieurs buchers.*

Gaientȣtagȣan, Ch. *enlever, defaire un bucher.*

Gaientȣtagȣanni, R. *f.* gȣas.

Gaienton, R. θa, t, tanne; *frapper.*

Skajenton, *rendre la pareille, refrapper.*

Gaientatonton, R. *satisfaire pour quelqu'un blessé ou tué.*

Gaienton, Ch. *faire tendre les lacets au chevreuil.*

Gaientonnon, *en aller tendre.*

Gaienθon, Ch. *avoir des champs;* θos, θo, θosere.

Ka etisaienθon? *Où as tu ton champ?*

Gaienθoton, Ch. *faire son champs de quelque chose.*

Gaienteron vel **Gaienteréon**, *connoitre, s'accoutumer*, Ch. tes v. ten, terenne, terese.

Quando signatur actualis notitia dic Gienteri, *je le sais bien* : a quo formantur Gienterinnen, *sciebam;* Agienterenne, *sciam.*

Quando autem signatur notitia habitualis dicendum : Iaten te skienteres? *non me nosti?*

Gatihȣajenteron, Ch. *savoir l'affaire.*

Gaienteton, *faire connoitre.*

Naie hoñajenteton, *on le connoit par cela.*

Gaieren, *faire*, Ch. rha, re, sanne; *dire.* Garihȣajeren, Ch.

Sahojerat, *c'est sa coutume, son ordinaire.*

Saojerat v. Saot v. Saejatȣten, *c'est la coutume.*

Atieren, depon. *faire.* Hot nisatierha? *Que fais tu?*

Atieren, pass. Hot njotieren jonhȣentsiagon? *Quid fit in inferis.*

Gaieraton, *faire ainsi, de cette façon.*

Atieraton, S. *etre fait ainsi.*

Gaierase, R. *f.* ras; *faire à quelqu'un.*

Gaieren, cum reit. *ressembler*, quasi dicerent : *refaire.*

Sojeren ronniha, *il ressemble son père.*

Atieren, cum reit. *estre semblable.*

Te skiatieren, *elles se ressemblent.*

Gaieri, *quatre.*

Gaierion, cum te affirm. *estre juste accompl.;* ris, ri, risere.

Iate gaieri v. Gaieri tsihon, *it y en a autant qu'il en faut.*

Gaierise, R. *f.* ris : Eȣagieris, *j'en aurai assez.*

Garihȣajerion, Ch. *l'affaire estre juste.*

Kajeriton, act. Ch. ris, rit, riθe; *parfournir, donner le reste.*
Tatierit, *tu fais juste.*
Tasrihȣagerit, *tu dis vray la chose comme elle est.*
Karihȣajeriton, act. Kajense, R.
Jate songȣajens, *il nous a donné à tous ce qu'il nous fallait.*
Gaȣendajeriton, R. *accomplir la voix de quelqu'un.*

Gaieron, R. rons, ron, ronne; *faire tort.*
ȣaskieron, *tu m'as fait tort.*
Atieron, Ch. *fair un mauvais coup, faire méchant.* Atieronnion.

Gaieronge, Ch. *corps.*
Gieronge jotoñon, *il est devenu un autre moimême.*

Gaiesáon, Chi sas, sa, sasere; *etre pauvre, misérable.*
Gaiatajesaon, *ne pas trouver ce qu'on cherche.*
Gannenrajesaon, S. *une armée s'en retourner sans avoir rien fait.*
Gaiesaton, R. θa, t, tanne; *rendre misérable.*
Garihȣajesaton, Ch. *se railler de quelque chose.*
Ganniehajesáton, R. *ne pas venir manger ce qu'on avait preparé.*

Atiesaton, Ch. *abuser, prodiguer, ne tenir compte.*
Atiesatanni, R. *f.* ten.
Atiatajesaton, Ch. *se rendre impitoyable.* Depon.
Atiatajesatanni, R. acq. *se rendre impitoyable à quelq.*

Gaiesen, non est in usu, nisi in comp.
Gannenraiesen, *grande armée.*
Gannonserajesen, *citrouilles romaines grosses.*

Atiesen, *cela est facile;* ȣatiesen, ȣatiesennen, aontiesenhag.

Atiesen, *estre liberal,* S.

Gaieson, S. sons, son, sonne; *rire.*
Gaiesonnion, *plusieurs rire.* Gaiontienni, S. *éclater en riant.*

Kajeston, Ch. θa, t, tanne; *adjouter, mesler.*
Gannatarok kahik te gaieston, *pain assaissoné de fruit.*
Kaihestanni, R. *f.* ten, tongatiesten, *adjoute m'en encore.*

Gaihonha, *rivière, ruisseau.*
Te jonnihahógen, *rivière fourchue.*
Te gaihonharoñȣa, *rivière qui vient de travers et se jette dans un autré.*
Si johoñasereñon, v. Tsi etiondatraon, *confluant de 2 rivières.*
Jonnihonhagȣaton, *rivière qui serpente.*

Gaionni, S. *collier de porcelaine.* Gaionjonni, *en faire.*
Te johahasen, *a 20 rangs.*

Gaioteñon v. **Garihonteñon,** S. te, ten, tensere; *être empèché.*
ȣagiotekȣe, *j'étais occupé.*
Gaiotennion, S. *plusieurs être empèches.*
Gaiotati, R. ts, ts, tire; *empècher, retarder quelqu'un, l'amuser.*
Atatiotati, Ch. *s'amuser soy-meme.*

Gaion, *entrer,* Ch. Gaionton, *faire entrer.*

Gaionȣe, *une claye d'osier pour faire sécher quelque chose.*

Gaon, *un van d'écorce.*

Gaonȣajen, *sorte de chant quand on fait festin de chien.*

Gaȣann-ka, Ch. *folatrer, jouer.*

Gaȣejenda, *addresse.* Gaȣejendaksen, Ch. *estre maladroit.*
Gaȣejennajanton, *adroit à tout.*
Gaȣejennagateñon, Ch. *faire quantité de choses avec addresse.*
Gaȣejennentáon, Ch. *se reposer, cesser de travailler;* tas, tanne, tasere.
Gaȣejennharaon, *avoir beaucoup d'occupations.*
Ateȣejennonni, Ch. *faire avec addresse.*
Gaȣejenteton, Ch. θa, t, tanne; *sçavoir* est R.
Gaȣejentetaᶜkon, *la main droite.*
Gaȣejentetáon, *idem;* tas, tanne, tasere. Est etiam R.

Gaȣejenθon, in comp. *etre calme.*
Gandigonraȣejenθon, R. *appaiser quelqu'un.*
Gandigonᶜraȣejenθoton, *appaiser avec quelque chose.*
Gandiataraȣejenθon, *le lac calmer.*

Gaȣejonta, *bec d'oiseau.*

Gaȣen, S. *appartenir à quelqu'un.* ȣageȣan, *mon bien.*
Gaiataȣen, *avoir pour sujet.* R.
Songȣajataȣen Raȣendio, *Dieu nous a pour créatures.*
Gaiataȣenston, R. *s'assujetir quelqu'un.*

Gaȣenda, Ch. *voir, présent.*
Tioton niaȣendage ennoȣarane, *la famille de la tortue a 9 voix.*
Gaȣendio, *parler bien.* Gaȣendaksen, *mal parler.* Ch.
Aθȣendaksaton, Ch. *parler mal, mauvaise langue;* θa, t, tanne.
Gaȣendaroten, *voix affable.*
Gaȣendasȣaten, Gaȣennannegaron, *voix rude.*
Gaȣendasnore, Ch. *parler viste.* Gaȣendasaien.
Gaȣennarakon, *obéir à quelqu'un; pns.* et *f.* kȣa, kȣanne.
Gaȣennajesaton, R. *mépriser la voix de quelqu'un.*
Gaȣendasteriston, R. *estimer la voix de quelqu'un.*
Gaȣendaᶜteᶜton, S. *voix forte aigue.*
Gaȣendarision, Ch. *se dédire, defaire ce qu'on, &c.*
Atȣendarision, Ch. Gaȣennannoton.
Gaȣendatogen, Ch. *parole qui ne change point.*
Gaȣendasatáon, *etre convaincu, mis au sac.*
Gaȣennaráon, S. *regarder en songe.*
Gaȣennoretakon, R. *se moquer de quelqu'un.*
Gaȣennentáon, Ch. tas, tanne, tasere; *conclure quelq. chose, porter sentence, arrest, definir.*
Atȣendajenton, Ch. *parler haut en colère;* tons, ton.
Gaȣennaragȣan, R. *donner le désir d'un autre;* gȣas, go.
Gaȣennáton, S. *nier;* θa, t, tanne.
Gaȣennont, R. θa, ten, tanne; *mettre la voix de quelqu'un.*

Atȣennont, pass. akte ȣasatȣennonten, *tu expliques autrement sa voix.*

Gaȣendȣteñon, Ch. tens, ten, tensere, tenhag; *parler d'une manière.*

Atȣendȣteñon, Ch. satȣendȣten, *parle haut, fais le cry autour du village.*

Gaȣendȣtatie, Ch. *aller parlant comme quand ils vont en ambassade.*

Atȣendȣtakȣaton, R. *demander à quelqu'un quelque chose.*

Gaȣendanniont, Ch. *attacher, pendre la voix de quelqu'un;* θa, ten.

Atȣendanniont, Ch.

Gaȣendio, Ch. *estre le maistre.*

Gaȣendioston, R. *reconnoître quelqu'un pour maître.*

Atȣendioston, Ch. *se rendre le maistre;* θa, t, tanne.

Gaȣendiostakon, R. *obéir à quelqu'un pour quelque chose.*

Gaȣenton, *couper en large,* Ch. Gaȣentagȣanni, R. *f.* gȣas.

Gaȣera, *le vent.* Vide Oȣeron. Gaȣerio, *bon vent.*

Atkaȣera^c^kȣan, *venter avec véhémence; pns.* kȣe, kȣa.

Atkáȣerátase, *venter en tourbillon en rond.*

Kanongati tagoȣerenhaȣit, *de quel costé vient le vent?*

Atkaȣerentáon, Ch. *le vent s'appaiser.*

Kaȣerogaton, S. *avoir vent devant.*

Ateȣeronton, Ch. θa, t; *avoir vent arrière.*

Keȣerarohon, S. *vent de costé.*

Gaȣeton, Ch. tonsk, ton, tonre; *enfanter.* Ateȣeton, pass. *idem.*

Gaȣie, *éventail.* Ateȣiaȣat, Ch. *esventer.*

Gaȣiahontsa, *aisle.* Kaȣiahontsont, Ch. *avoir des aisles.*

Gaȣinnon, *monialis, jeune fille pas encore mariée.*

Gahoñȣinnon, *trainer canot;* v. nes, ne, nesre.

Gaȣiongoton, R. θa, t, tanne; *une armée faire coup dans les champs.*

Gaȣionsera, *une navette.*

Gaȣira, S. *partus.*

Gaȣiron, R. *donner un enfant à quelqu'un, le lui attribuer.*

Gaȣirata, *la mettre dedans, engrosser.*

Gaȣiraksen, *méchant enfant.* Gaȣirio.

Gaȣirarharaon, Ch. ras, ranne, rasere; *avorter.*

Atatȣirarioon, Ch. *tuer sa production.*

Atȣironni, Atatȣironnianni, *se faire des enfants.*

Onne hotatȣironnianni ȣasagoteȣeton hotinnonsionni.

Atȣirajen, S. *animal avoir des petits.*

Atȣirajenni, R. acq. *f.* enhas. Atȣirannonste, S. *aimer ses petits.*

Gaȣisa, extra comp. S. *glace.* Joȣise, *il y a de la glace.*

Gaȣisera, in comp. Egaȣiserat, Egatenti, *je partirai quand il aura de la glace.*

Gaȣisanniraton, *le glace estre forte.*

Gaȣisogȣan, Ch. *la glace se déprendre.*

Atȣitsiagi, *la glace se rompre sous quelqu'un.*

Gaȣisoserhon, Ch. *l'eau surnager sur la glace.*

Kaȣitskȣan, Ch. *glisser.* ȣatioȣiskȣat, *il fait glisser.*
ȣatioȣiskȣentare, *il y a du verglas.*
Oȣisk-ra, *gresle.*
Gaȣiskerontion, Gaȣisontion, *tomber de la gresle.*
Gannaarhon, Ch. hosk, ho, hosere; *escrire.*
Gannaarhose, R. *f.* os; *escrire à ou pour quelqu'un.*
Gannaarhontsera, *escriture.*
Onnaa^cta, *un plat costé.* Gnaatakske, *au costé.*
Gannaatihen, Ch. *avoir mal au costé.*
Onnagara, *corne.* Kannagaront, S. *avoir des cornes.*
Te jotinnagaronton, *des moutons.*
Gannagaronni, S. *etre considérable.*
Kannagarȣt, S. *etre assis sur son derrière, accrouppi.*
Gannágare, *perche, grand baston.*
Gannagariagon, Ch. *couper une perche.*
Tsonnagariagon, *castor.*
Gannagararohon, Ch. *perche de travers.*
Onnagensa, *peau passée.*
Gannagȣaton, Ch. ts, t, θa; *semer.*
Gannagȣati, R. *f.* ts; *semer pour quelqu'un.*
Gannagȣatsera, *semence.*
Gannagȣatserison, Ch. *avoir achevé de semer.*
Onnagȣara, *peau d'homme ou de —.*
Gannagre, Ch. gre, greg; *demeurer, y avoir, etre.*
Jaten te skannegorhannagre, *il n'y a plus de porcelaine.*
Jaten te tsiennagre, *il m'y a plus personne.*
Katke tsi snagre, *Combien? quel âge as tu?*
Gannagratsera, *lieu où l'on demeure, la terre, son pays.*
Taonχen sȣannagratserio, *O le beau, bon pais que le vôtre.*
Gannagraton, S. θa, t, θa; *s'habituer en quelque lieu.*
Gannagreñon, S. *avoir abondance de q. ch.;* ens, ens, ensere.
Ronnagrenseron, *il a beaucoup de.*
Gannagrenton, S. θa, t, tanne; *faire avoir abondance,* est R.
Gannageranni, R. *f.* ren; *imiter quelqu'un.*
Gannageraton, Ch. *se servir de règle, juger par q.*
Atennogeraton, depon. Ch. θa, t, tanne.
Naie jagȣatennageraθa onne ajehejonsere, *Nous connaissons, jugeons par cela qu'on va mourir.*
Onnahost, *citron.*
Gannaie, Ch. *glorieux, superbe, arrogant.*
Gannaie, *sac de toile.*
Gannajetakon, R. *se moquer de quelqu'un, railler, leur attribuant ce qu'ils n'ont pas; p.* & *f.* kȣa.
Ganna^ckon, S. Raonnakon, *sa quaisse, tambour.*
Ganna^ckonni, Ch. *en faire une.* Gannakonnianni, R.
Ganna^ckȣi, *la quaisse est pleine.*

Ganna^{c}kȣihen, *elle est à demi pleine.*
Ganna^{c}kȣagareraston, Ch. *battre la quaisse.*

Ganna^{c}kȣa, *mariage, coitus,* Ch.
Ja^{c}ten ranna^{c}kȣio, *il n'est pas bon mary.*
Ganna^{c}kȣare, Ch. *p.* rha, *f.* ren; *faire mal.*
Ranna^{c}kȣarhannionsk, *il est à toutes les femmes.*
Ganna^{c}kȣagarien, Ch. componitur cum infinitis prope.
Ganna^{c}kȣaχȣan, R. *enlever la femme d'autruy.*
Ganna^{c}kȣenhaȣi, Ch. *mener sa femme avec soy.*
Gannakȣagenteiase, R. *perdre sa femme.*

Gannakȣáton, *estre faché par quelque chose;* *θ*a, t, tanne.
Ronnakȣat, Rotannakȣat, *il prend plaisir à faire fascher le monde.*
Gannakȣatanni, R. *f.* ten; *fascher quelqu'un.*
ȣahagnakȣaten, *il m'a fâché.* Ronnonȣenserannakȣat.
Gannakȣeñon, S. *de dépiter, être en colère;* χȣens, kȣen, ensere.
Ganna^{c}kȣase, R. *mettre quelqu'un en colère.*
Gannaχȣentáon, S. *la colère s'appaiser.*
Gannaχȣensera, *colère.*

Gannakiȣan, R. *ne pouvoir attraper à ce qu'on pursuit.*
ȣagȣannakiȣe okȣari, *nous n'avons pu joindre l'ours.*

Gannakte, S. *natte, lieu où l'on couche.*
Gannaktohare, Ch. *laver la natte,* dit on quand on jette de la porcelaine sur un corps mort.
Gannaktaseronni, Ch. *faire accommoder sa natte.*

Gannakti, S. *un fuseau au bout duquel est enté un petit baston que les enfans font courir sur la glace.*

Gannaon, in comp. nas, nanne, nasere; *regretter.*
ȣagonhȣentsiannanne, *je regrette ta terre.*
Hontennasere rotiksten ogoña, *les anciens vont.*

Gannannon, act. *remplir;* nas, ne, nanne.
ȣahannanne skajarat, *il a rempli un sac.*
Gannannon, pass. *être rempli.*
Onne ratinnannons v. ratinnatsihon, *tout est plein, ils remplissent la cabane.*

Gannannaȣan, extra comp. S. *être humide, mouillé.*
Jonnannaȣan, *cela est humide.*
Gannannaȣenton, S. *humecter.*
Gannaȣan, in comp. Ganniannaȣan, *des mitaines,* S.
Onnenhannaȣan, *du blé trempé dans l'eau.*
Gannaȣenton, in comp. Gasirannaȣenton, *humecter, mouiller une couverte.*
Ja^{c}ten sorihȣannaȣan, *il ne prend plus en jeu.*
Ja^{c}ten te tsiorihȣannaȣan, *ce n'est plus un jeu.*

Gannanni, R. *injurier quelq.* ȣasknanni, *tu m'injuries.*
Gannanniserongȣast, R. gȣas, go, gohe; *injurier beaucoup.*
Gannanniharon, *idem.*

Gannaȣa, *rivière.* Gannaȣate^{c}ton, S. *rivière rapide.*
Gannaȣandóron, pass. S. Ongnaȣannorons, *mihi est difficilis fluvius.*
Gannaȣen^{c}ton, Ch. θa, t, tanne; *descendre la rivière.*
Gánnaȣaráon, Ch. ras, ranne, rasere.
Gannaȣatéron, Ch. ros, ro, ronne.
Jonnaȣerȣt, *source, fontaine.*
Gannaȣakeha, *loup cervier.*
Onnaȣatsista, *sorte de mouche.*
Onnaȣe tsonnito, *testicules du castor.*
Onnaȣenskeri, *balieures.* Gannaȣenskerinnigeñon, *jetter dehors les ordures.*
Onnaȣatsta, *boue, terre grasse, &c.* Onnaȣatstage, iges, *je, &c.*
Gannaȣatstarhon, *bouziller*, Ch.
Gannaȣatstannetska, *terre, boue glissante, mouvante.*
Onnáȣak, *crible.* Gannaȣagon, S. *cribler.*
Onnaȣenha, *moustache*, S. signat etiam *ce q'on met en travers comme une tringle. pr.*
Gannaȣi, S. ȣis, si, ȣisere; *prendre quelque chose soit à la chasse avec des trappes, soit à la pesche.*
ȣahotsiannaȣi, *il a abondance de poisson.*
Onnaȣi, *dent*, S. extra comp. ȣagnaȣige, *à ma dent.*
Gannaȣira, in comp. gannaȣires, *dent grande.*
Gannaȣirio, *bonne belle dent.* Gannaȣiragetȣt, S. *dent se montrer.*
Gannaȣirannoñagon, *y avoir mal.*
Gannaȣirȣθie, S. *dénts aigues.*
Kannannet, *être double*, Ch. θa, t; sumitur etiam active.
Kannannetarion, *avoir beaucoup de do^{s};* active sumitur in comp.
Te horihȣannetarion, *il a joint diverses choses.*
Kannia, *pierre à fusil.*
Kanniohare gaiengȣire, *fleche ayant une pierre au bout.*
Gannas, Ch. *être couché*, anomal. Gannaskogon, *dans le sein.*
Gannaskȣagon ȣahorori, *étant couchés ensemble, il luy a dit.*
Onnas, S. *plume.* Gannasoñt, *avoir des plumes.*
Gannasôtagȣan, Ch. *oster les plumes, les arracher.*
Gannasôtagȣanni, R. *f.* gȣas.
Gannaskȣa, Ch. *esclave, estre esclave.*
Gannaskonni, R. *faire un esclave.*
Atnaskonni, Ch. *se faire prisonnier.*
Gannaskȣeȣe v. Gannaskȣenhaȣi, *amener des prisonniers.*
Gannasta, *perches à faire cabane, celle de dedans que l'on courbe pour servir de moule à la cabane.*
Gannastȣt, Ch. *les dites perches être mises.*
Gannastonni, *les mettre*, Ch.
Gannáta, *village.* Gannatȣannen, Gannataȣiriens, *grand village.*
Nigannataa v. Nigannatasa, *petit village.*
Kannátakȣan, Ch. *pns.* et *f.* kȣa, kȣe; *n.* kȣanne.
Gannatonni, Ch. *faire un fort.*
Gannationni, *là où est le fort, l'armée est campée.*

Gan^{c}nata, S. *sac à petun ou autre petit sac, pochette.*
Gan^{c}natatsera, in comp.
Gannatatserȣrarhon, R. *mettre le sac à petun à quelq.*
Gan^{c}natatserage^{c}te, S. *porter un sac comme les vieillards.*

Onnátak, *crapaud.*

Gannátarok, *pain*, S. Gannataronni, *faire du pain*, Ch.
Gannataronnianni, R. *faire du pain à quelqu'un.*
Gannataronniaton, Ch. *le faire de quelque chose.*

Gannaton, *nommer*, Ch. tons, ton, tonne; est etiam R.
Hesnaton, *nomme-le.*
Gannatonkon, Ch. *nommer comme cela, de ce nom;* kȣa, kȣe.
Gannatonni, R. *f.* tonhas; *montrer à quelqu'un quelque chose.*
Tagnatonhas, *nomme, montre moy cela.*

Gannatsa, *clunes.* Gnatsaske, *àmes.*
Gannatsarégon v. Gannatsaiagon, R. *fouetter;* ks, g, χe.

Gannaθaron, Ch. res, pro habitu; re, pro actu; *f.* re, *fn.* resere, *visiter.*
Gannatareskon, *elle visite souvent.*
Jesannaθarennaȣire, *on te vient visiter.*
Gannaθaron, R. Gnaθahre, *je viens visiter.*

Kanne, *graine de semence, blé ou autre chose.*

On^{c}nega, S. *eau;* Gan^{c}negio, *bonne eau;* Gan^{c}negaksen, *méchante eau.*
Gannagaksaton, *gaster l'eau*, Ch.
Gannegonni, *faire de l'eau*, Ch.
Atnegonnion, Ch. *se fondre, se dissoudre.*
Atnegontion, Ch. *eau bouillir.* Ongȣan^{c}negos.
Gan^{c}nego, *il y a de l'eau.* Gannegonnion, *il y en a beaucoup.*
ȣaongion^{c}nonne, *l'eau entre dans notre cabane.*
Onnegage ratentieskȣe Jesȣs : *Jésus marchait sur les eaux.*
Etgannegatironθa, *il y a marée.*
Onsagannegatire, *elle monte.*
Gannegañhonθon, *donner médecine.*
Gannegoon, *eau déborder*, S. Gannegogȣan, *oster l'eau de.*
Atnegogȣan, *l'eau sortir, se repandre.*

Ganneganni, R. *f.* gen, *demander.* Gannegen, *demander.*
ȣagonnegen, *je te demande.*
Gasaranneganne, *je viens demander un couteau.*

Gan^{c}negaron, S. *méchant.* Atennegaron, Ch. *devenir méchant.*

Gannégen, in comp. *joindre.* Te ȣasarannegen, *il y a 2 couteaux.*
Gannegenseron, *joindre beacoup de choses.*
Aχinnatannegenseron garennajenhaga aχinnatagarien, *nous défimes plusieurs villages Hurons.*
Garannégen, extra comp. Ch. Te srannegen, *joins ces 2 choses.*
Tȣatrannégen, Ch. *être joint l'un contre l'autre.*
Te tsiatrannegenhag, *soyes l'un contre l'autre.*
Gannegen, eum nota localit., *empirer.*
Ontagannegensere, *il va empirant.*

Onnegri, *herbe, foin, paille.*

Gannegriagon, Ch. *couper de l'herbe.* Asare jennegriakta, *une faux.*

Ganneg-ro, *de la paille ou autre ordure être dans l'eau.*

Eskennegrose, *tu feras tomber l'ordure dans* v. g. *ma sagamité.*

Gannegroskaron, Ch. *faucher, couper l'herbe.*

Gannegrenhe, *manche*, extra comp. Gannegrenhetsera, in comp.

Gannegrenthetseronni, Ch. *en faire un.*

Gan^cnegaron, S. *estre méchant.* Rojatannegaron, *méchant homme.*

Kan^cnegaron, in comp. *se crever, s'entrouvrir.* Karan^cnegaron, extra comp.

Tȣatran^cnegaron, Ch. *s'entrouvrir, crever.*

Tȣajataran^cnegaron, S. *aller dur à la selle.*

Etȣatonhȣentsian^cnegáre, *la terre s'ouvrira.*

Onnegorha, S. *porcelaine.* Raondegorha, *sa.*

Gannatsia, in comp. Ontak, extra comp. *chaudière.*

Ontakonȣe, *chaudière de terre.* Ontak otsogri, *chaud. ronde.*

Gannatsionni, *en faire.*

Gannatsianneron v. Gannatsianni^ekon, *la raccommoder, recoudre.*

Gannatsionnikonse, R.

Gannatsiarȣton, Ch. *chaudière de guerre où les guerriers chantant.*

Gannehon, *une peau non passée*, extra comp. Gannehȣa, in comp.

Skannehȣat, *une seule peau.* Gannehȣio, *bonne peau.*

Gannehȣakste, *peau qui peze.* Onnehȣa, *peau mediocre, demy castor.*

Gannenhȣa, Ch. Gannenhȣasen, *avoir pour beau père ou belle mère. Imp.* takȣe, *f.* tak, Ch.

ȣagnenhȣage, *chez mon beau père ou belle mère.*

Snenhȣage. Gannenhȣasenton, de multis.

Gan^cnekȣáón, Ch. *couler.* Eso ontagannekȣa ȣaθonannentsargarog, *il a bien coulé quand on l'a saigné.*

Onnenhare, *raison.* Ganneharon, R. *surmonter quelq.*

Ganneharon, neut. S. *estre vaincu.*

Ongennehare, *je suis vaincu,* v. g. *dans un festin où l'on ne peut pas tout manger.*

Gannéon, R. *vaincre; pns.* ȣas, quasi a Gannеȣaon.

Sagonneȣas, *il les a vaincus.*

Sagotinnéon agotsagannha, *il a defait les Loups.*

Gannehȣaton, *vaincre avec q. c.*

Naie jonχinneȣaθa jaten te jongȣahonraien, *on nous surmonte parceque nous n'avons pas de fusil.*

Ganneies, *grand*, Ch.

Ganneȣaron, R. rons, re, ronne; *surprendre.*

Gaiatanneȣaron, R. *donner une fausse alarme.*

ȣagonjatanneȣare ne gonnhongon, *je t'ay surpris, t'ayant oppelé.*

Ganneȣaraton, S. *sentir avoir mal au cœur, estre provoqué comme à vomir, à ouyr ou voir quelque chose desplaisante;* d'où vient ce mot si usité parmy les Agniers: Jonneȣarat, Jonneȣarata, *chose fesante mal au cœur.*

Ganneȣaratanni, R. *f.* ten.

Kannegota, *échelle.* Kannegotatiron, *la dresser*, Ch.
Kannegotiennenton, *la retirer, l'abbaisser.*

Gannenhison, Ch. sons, son, sonne; *faire sagamité.*
Gannenhisaonni, R. *f.* sen; *la faire pour quelq.*
Gannenhisaton, Ch. θa, t, tanne; *la faire de q. c.*
Gennenhisatsera, Ch. *assaisonnement.*

Onnentia, *blé.* Gannenhagaion, S. *vieux blé.*
Gannenhannaȣenton, *en faire tremper.*
Gannenhenson, *blé grouler dans les cendres pour faire de la farine épaisse.*
Gannenhenson[c]kȣa, *blé ainsi groulé.*
Gannenhensonkȣagon, Ch. *en manger;* ks, g, χe.

Gannenkaton, R. *peccare, rem habere.*

Onne'ja, *pierre*, S. Gannejonni, Ch. *faires des petites bales.*
Atnenjonnian, Ch. *pierre se former.*
Ganneñjat, *il y a du plomb dans le fusil.*
Onnenjogon, *dessous la pierre.*
Onnenyara, *il y a des pierres.*

On[c]nennata, S. *pommes de terre.*
Gan[c]nennatágon, Ch. *en manger.*
Gannennatagȣan, Ch. *en cueillir.*

Gannennianni, R. *surprendre quelque bande ou armée, la defaire entièrement.*

Gannenton, Ch. tons, ton, tonne; *admirer*, est R.
Hoñannenton, *on l'admire.*
Gannennonton, *admirer à cause de q. c.*
Atatnenton, Ch. *s'admirer soymême.*

Kannennage, *l'automne.* Kannennagenne, *pendant l'automne.*
Kannennageka, *chose d'automne*, v. g. *canot, castor, &c.*

Gannenna, *hardes*, S. in comp.
Gannennio, *beaux habits, bonnes hardes.*
Atnennokte, Ch. θa, ten; *estre à bout de ses hardes.*
Gannennaton, in comp. Gannonsa gannennáton, *avoir envie sur la cabane, vouloir sa destruction.*
Songȣannonsagannennaθa Onnontio.

Gannenskȣan, Ch. kȣas, ko; *dérober.*
Gannenskȣaton, Ch. *lieu où l'on dérobe, ou chose pourquoy on dérobe.*

Onneñon, *s'affaiser*, in comp. est R.
Gaȣiseronneñon, *la glace s'affaiser*, S.

Gannen[c]ra, *armée, bande, troupe de guerriers, compagnie.*
Gannen[c]ronni, Gannenrorogon, *assembler l'armée ou compagnie.*
Gannen[c]raregon, Ch. *pousser l'armée, la faire marche.*
Gannen[c]rinnon, Ch. *aller en armée;* nes, na, nesere.
Gannen[c]rarion, R. *rompre, défaire l'armée;* ris, ri, risere.
Gannenragarien, R.
Gannenrȣt, *l'armée se poser.*
Gannenrȣtágȣan, Ch. *la faire lever.*

Gannenrentanni, R. *f.* ten; *dresser ambuscade.*
Gannenrajesaon, S. *armée s'en retourner sans rien faire.*
Atnen^c^raton, S. *armée estre perdue.*

Gannentsa, Ch. *bras.* Atnensaget, *le plier.*
Atnentsagȣarision, *le dresser.*
Kannentsaȣeston, *le percer, saigner.*
Gannentsa, R. *prendre le bras.*

Gannentágon, in comp. Garannentagon, extra comp. *estre attaché, collé, appliqué.*
Gannentakton, *attacher.*
Gaiatannentagon, Ch. *être attaché chose vivante.*
Gaiatannentakton, *attacher*; θa, t, tanne.
Hoñajatannentakton osȣengarege, te gaientannhare, *on l'attacha sur la croix.*
Garannentakton, Ch. *joindre, attacher q. c.*

Onnenste, *blé*, S. Gannenstontion, S. *semer.*
Gannenstarongȣan, Ch. *l'égrainer.*
Gannensto, S. *le mettre tout entier bouillir.*
Kannensto^c^kon, S. *l'assaissonner ainsi bouïllie de.*
Kannenstiagon, Ch. *l'écraser entre 2 pierres.*
Gannenstase, *blé nouveau.* Gannenstatken, *id. pourri.*

Gannera, *virga*, S. raonn.
Eθo si etȣagneristonte ȣagnonhȣaktannik, *doles in virga.* Signat etiam *peste.*
Ganneratarinnon, Ch. *la peste courir.* Neutraliter sumptum, *avoir la peste ou autre maladie contagieuse.*
Jongȣann-ratarinnes, *nous avons une maladie contagieuse.*
Fit etiam substantivum. Aseronnige etiotention onneratarinnes, *la peste est venue des Europeans.*

Ganneragoon, S. *admirer;* gȣas, go, gohe. Est etiam R.
Ganneragȣaton, S. *admirer pour q. c.*
Jonneragȣat, *cela est admirable.*
Rojatanneragȣaton, *c'est un homme admirable en beauté.*
Gannero^c^kȣannoñagon, Ch. *cupere, &c.*
Gannero^c^kȣenton, S. *s'être accouplés.*

Gannéron v. **Ganneragon**, Ch. in comp. *se méprendre.*
Garihȣanderagon, Ch. ks, g, χe; *pécher.*
Garihȣanderagi, R. *f.* ks; *faire pécher quelq'un.*
Garihȣanderakton, Ch. *pécher par quelque chose.*
Garihȣanderaχon, *pécher souvent.*
Rorihȣanderaskon, *grand pécheur.*
Gannonsannerágon, Ch. *prendre une cabane pour une autre.*
Gaiatannerágon, *prendre une personne pour une autre.*
Atȣennannerágon, *dire une parole pour une autre.*

Onnerasa, *tondre champignons.*

Onnerate, *feuille.* Ganneratont, *y avoir des feuilles;* θa, ten, tanne.
Gannera^c^tentaon, Ch. *feuilles tomber;* tas, tanne, tasere.

Onneregȣare, *bouclier.* Gannerekenθore, *fonds de caisse.*

Onnerenha, *vers.* Gannerenhat, S. *avoir des vers.*

Gannerenhata, Ch. *mettre des vers dedans.*

Gannerenhatatakȣan, Ch. est etiam R., *tirer les vers du corps.*

Atennrenhorioon, S. *estre malade des vers.*

Atennerenhorianni, S. *vers se remuer dans le ventre.*

Tagnonkȣatseranhonθo gontiagentakȣa onnerenha, *donne moy médecine pour faire sortir les vers.*

Ganneraθen, S. *être vieux, décrépit, blanc de vieillesse.*

Gannéron, Ch. *être enceinte.*

Ganneron, Ch. *lever des écorces;* rons, re, ronne.

Ganneᵉrase, R. Ganneronhon, Ch. he, ha.

Gannesahre, *la neige porte,* Ch. Gannesaᵉronk.

Gannesen, Gannesenton, S. Si etionnesenton, *là où il y a du sable.*

Onnestagȣara, *crasse.* Gannestagȣaroron, *estre crasseux.*

Onneᵉta, *gomme, bray, pin.* Ganneᵉtarhon, Ch. *gommer.*

Ganneᵉtaarongȣan, Ch. *estre de gomme.*

Eθo si jotnetonni, *là où est un pin.*

Ganneχereñon, S. ens, en, ensere; *ignorer,* est R.

Garihȣanneχereñon, S. *ignorer l'affaire, ne pas connoître.*

Ganneχerenston, S. *faire ignorer,* est etiam R.

Ongnontaranneχeron, *je ne sais ce que c'est que sagamité.*

Gannaháon, R. nhas, nhanne, nhasere; *commander.*

Atennháon, act. *commander,* Ch.

Rotennhaskon, *le grand commandeur.*

Gannhaton, R. θa, t, tanne; *récompenser* seu *commander par q. c.*

Θennon eskennhat, *que me donneras tu pour récompense.*

Gannhateñon, Ch. ens, en, ensere; *regretter q c.* est R.

Hoñannhátens, *on le regrette.*

Gannhatenston, Ch. *regretter pour quelque chose.*

Onnhate, *bûche fourchu, gros bois.* Tejonnhatogen, *fourchu.*

Gannhe, R. nhas, nhe, nhesere: *aider, défendre quelqu'un.*

Gatagonnhe, *aide moy.*

Gannhe, Ch. *défendre quelque chose, prohibere.*

Rannhesk Diȣ ajennesko, *Dieu défend le larcin.*

Est etiam R. Hagennhes, *il me défende, m'empeche de.*

Jotennhaskon, *une querelleuse à l'occasion,* v. g. *de ses enfants qu'elle protége.*

Kannheks, extra comp.; Gannhesa, in comp. *ceinture, babiche.*

Gannhesonni, *faire une courroye,* Ch.

Gannhesagȣetaron, Ch. *couper une babiche.*

Kannhen, in comp. *ceindre.*

Kannatannhen, *ceindre, assiéger une ville,* Ch. *f.* enhag.

Gaiatannhen, R. *ceinturer quelq.*

Atiatannhen, S. *etre ceint.*

Gannhaston, Ch. *se servir de q. c. pour ceinture.*

Gaiatannhaston, Atiatannhastion, Ch.
Gannhasion, in comp. *oster ceinture.*
Gaiatannhasion, R. sions, si, sionhe; *deceindre quelq.*
Jontiatannhasθa, *ceinture.*
Atiatanhasion, *ôter sa ceinture.*

Onnhenha, *urine.*

Onnheta, *porcépi.*

Gannhetien, S. Gannhetiensera, in comp. *femme.*
Gannhetienserio, *bonne femme.*
Gannhetienseraksen, *coureuse.*
Gannhetienserannonhȣéon, Gannhetienseragasθa, *aimer les femmes.*
Gannhetienserare, *il y a une femme.*

Gannhigon, S. his, hig; *ignorer, bégayer.*
Ganhȣannhigon, S. *ne savoir pas les affaires.*
Gannhiton, impers. S. θa, t, tanne; *faire ignorer.*
Jonnhit jagotrens, *on bégaye, on a de la peine à chanter.*
Gannhitannî, R. *f.* ten; *faire ignorer quelq.*
Atonnhitannî, pass. N. S. *f.* ten; *estre caché à soymeme.*
Kannhi, *grand baston dont on abbat les nids des tourtes.*

Gannhoha, *porte.*
Gannhohandoron, S. *avoir de la peine à ouvrir ou à entrer.*
Gannhohahȣiseñon, S. *parte difficile à ouvrir.* Neut. acq.
Gannhohajengȣiron, Ch. *frapper à la porte.*
Gannhohajagon, R. *provoquer au jeu quelq.*
ȣaonχinnhohajag, *on a frappé à notre porte, on nous a provoqué.*
Gannhohontion, S. *partir, abandonner sa porte.*
Te snihohatógen, *dresses la porte.*
Te gonninnhoharonnion, *plusieurs portes.*
Kannhote, *à la porte.* Skannhohati, *à l'autre bout de la cabane.*

Onnhonsa, S. *œuf.* Annhonsen, Ch. *pondre.* 1ae conj.
Onnhonsatarion, *elle a quantité d'œufs.*
Jonninnhonsajentackȣa, *le nid où elle pond.*
Gannhonsaiesaton, Ch. *perdre ses œufs.*
Te jonninnhonsiagon, *elle a éclos.*

Gannhontren, terhaon in comp. *mettre bout à bout;* terha, tranne.
Te sasȣengarannhontren, *mets les planches bout à bout.*

Gannhonθon, R. *mettre dans la bouche;* D. θosk, θo, θosere.
Gannonckȣatserannhonθon, R. *donner médecine.*
Gannhonθoseron, R. *donner beaucoup.*
Gannhonθoton, Ch. *ce qu'on donne ou pourquoi on donne.*
Enninnhoskȣannhonθon, R. *prendre dans sa bouche pour le jetter dans la bouche d'un autre.*
Te senninnhoskȣarontat, *souffle ce que tu as dans la bouche.*
Atennhont, Ch. *avoir ou mettre dans sa bouche;* θa, ten.
Atennhontagȣan, Ch. *s'oster de la bouche.*

Gannhoton, Ch. tons, ton, tonne; *fermer la porte.*
Gannhotonse, R. Atennhoton, S. *se fermer.*
Atennhonse, neut. acq. *trouver la porte fermée.*
Gannhotongȣan, Ch. gȣas, go, gohe; *ouvrir la porte.*
Gannhotongȣanni, R. *f.* tongȣas.

Gannia, *doigt*, in comp. Ganniagatste, Ch. *estre cruel.*

Ganniagenon, *s'eschapper, guérir;* ens, en, ensere. Assumit notam reiteratio : Onsahanniagenne, *il s'est enfuy, il est guéri.*
Ganniagense, R. acq. *s'enfuir à quelq.*
Onsahoñatinniagens, *ils leur ont échappé.*
Ganniagenton, *faire échapper.*

Ganniagon, *se marier*, S. ks, g, χe.

Ganniagȣari, *Une ourse :* C'est le nom de l'Agnier.

Ganniaha, *manger repas.*
Areko ongenniahonsori, *je n'ai pas encore.*
Sȣanniahentaon, *vous avez mangé, dîné.*

Onniara, *tête coupée.* θo ganniarah-re, *il y a la dessus une tête.*
Ganniareñon, *baisser la tête;* ens, enn, ensere.
Ganniarenton, R. *couper la tête, tuer des ambassadeurs ou autres venus;* askennen.
Ganniariagon, R. *couper le col.*
ȣagenniarenni ȣagnonhȣaktannik, *j'ai mal au col.*

Onniare, *serpent.*

Onniata, *gosier*, S. Ronniatonne, *à son gozier.*
Ganniataθenon, S. *avoir le gozier sec.*
Ganniatannaȣenton, R. *l'humecter, donner à boire.*
Ganniataraon, S. *estre pris au gozier pour avoir pris un trop gros morceau.*
Ganniatannoñagon, S. *avoir mal au gozier.*

Onniasa, *col.* ȣagenniasatske, *à mon col.*
Ganniasotarhon, S. hos, ho, hosere; *mettre au col.*

Ganniaskaron, *avoir le hoquet*, S.

Onniatsara, *porcelaine que les femmes attachent aux cheveux que leur pendent derrière la teste.*

Ganniat, S. *avoir des nasses.* Ganniatoon, *les mettre dans l'eau.*

Onniataraa, *toile.*

Ganniaskari, S. ris, rig, riχe; *agraffer*, est R.

Ganniatare, *lac.* Ganniatarigon, *traverser le lac.*
Ganniatariakton, Ch. *le passer pour q. c.*

Ganniatren, R. trens, tren, trenχe; *étrangler.*

Ganniahonkon, Ch. *enfoncer dans la neige molle.*

Ganniegóton, *oiseau rouge.*

Ganniejeñon, *avoir eu de la neige.* Impers. Onniente, in comp.
Ganniejenna, *il y aura de la neige.*
Gannientannaȣan, *neige molle.*
Gannientannira°ton, neut. impers. *la neige s'endurcir.*

Gannien, Ch. niha, nie, nianne; *japper,* est R. *japper à quelq.*
Ganniannion, *japper souvent,* Ch.
Jonniaskon satsennen, *ton chien est grand jappeur.*

Gannien, Substant S. *blé.*
Agȣa igen ongȣannien, *comme si vous aviez du blé.*
Ganniense, R. *dérober du blé.* Il se dit aussi de toute autre chose semée, comme fezoles, citrouilles, etc.
Ganniehon, Ch. *aller ceuillir des chataignes.*

Kannien, extra comp. } *batte feu.*
Ganniensera, in comp. }
Jatente ȣagennienserajen, *je n'ai point de batte feu.*
Ganniegarannie, *frotter entre ses mains 2 bois pour faire du feu.*

Gannienton, Ch. *venir demander q. chose; avoir quelque raison d'entrer chez quelqu'un.*
Θennon senniente? *Qui t'amene ici?*

Onnienta, *jambe.* Agennientarig erhas, *un chien m'a mordu à la jambe.*

Gannienθarhon, *bander fusil,* Ch. Gannienθaragȣan, *le débander.*

Onnienskȣire, *branche d'arbre.*

Onniera, *le dedans de la noix.*
Gannieratakȣan, Ch. *le tirer de dedans.*
Onnierágon, *O que le dedans de la noix est bon!*

Ganniero, Ch. ros, ro, ronne; *pécher au petit poisson avec un panier.*

Gannieton, in comp. *donner commission.*
Garihȣannie^c ton, R. θas, t, tanne.
Atinnie^c ton, Ch. *donner charge.*
Atrihȣannieton, Ch. *idem.*
Etkatrihȣanniet neȣagnagren, *je donnerai commission au cas que j'en aie beaucoup.*

Kannigat, extra comp. } *une pile,* S. Ronnigataien, *il a une pile.*
Kannigata, in comp. }
Gannigatonni, Ch. *en faire une.*
Gannigatiagon, Ch. *la couper.*
Tagennigatiaχe, *Viens me couper une pile.*

Onnigensa, *cheveux des femmes pendants derrière.*
Tagenniastren, *lie moi ma queue.*

Gannigenteron, Ch. takȣe, tag; *homme de 35 à 40 ans.*
Rannigenteronseraksen, *chétif homme.*

Onnigȣensa v. Gannegȣe, *sang.*
Jaten te gannigȣensentas te hoñannentsaȣeston, *le sang ne s'arrête pas où l'on la saigné.*
Gannigȣensinnigeñon, Ch. *le sang sortir.*
Gannigȣentsoron, neut. S. *estre sali de sang.*
Gannigȣensohare, Gannigȣensageȣennion, Ch. *laver de sang.*

Onnigȣenta, *la panse, le ventre.*

Onnigȣentara, *rouge.*

Kannigȣati, Ch. *gauche.* Sannigȣati, *il est gauche.*

Kannigonron, *pointe d'une enclume.* Ils nomment ainsi un cochet, parcequ'il a le museau ainsi fait.

Kannigonron, S. *couvrir le temps, ne dire mot de dépit; f.* re.

Kannigotstiagon, Ch. *baisser la tête de honte.*

Ganniharon, inusit, sed ejus loco Atonniharon.

Gannikon, Ch. kons, kon, konne; *coudre.*

Gannikonse, R. Atennikon, pass. Ch.

Gannikonsiongȣan, Ch. gȣas, go; *découdre.* Atennikonsiongȣan.

Gannikonkon, Ch. *coudre avec quelque chose.*

Tagroñaron jontennikonkȣa, *donne moi une aiguille.*

Ganni v. **Ganniha,** *être père, avoir pour père.*

Raganniha, *mon père.* Hianniha, *ton;* ronniha, *son.*

Dicunt Ragenni in vocat. v. subjungunt genha. Raȣenheion sagȣanni genha, *notre père est mort.*

Gannisen, *avoir un père;* takȣe, tak.

Jate ronnisen, *il n'a point de père; il est incertain, on le desavoue.*

Ganninnon, R. *traiter, acheter de quelqu'un;* nons, non, nonre.

Ganninnon, Ch. act. componitur cum omnibus fere substantivis.

Ganneganninnon, *traiter de l'eau de vie.*

Gasiranninnon, *traiter de l'étoffe.*

Atahianninnon, Ch. *traitter des fruits.*

Gahianninnon, R. ȣagonjasaranninnonre, *je viens te traiter un couteau.*

Atenninnon, pass. Ch. *traitter.*

Atenninnonseragon, Ch. *aimer à traitter.*

Atenninnonsera, *traitte, vente.*

Ganninnonse, R. acq. *traiter pour quelqu'un.*

Tagȣanneganninnonsere (nniha), *Va traiter de l'eau de vie pour moi.*

Ganninnonton, Atenninnonton, Ch. *acheter avec quelque chose.*

Gandigon^{e}ra, *esprit, pensée,* S.

Gandigonrio, *avoir l'esprit bien fait,* Ch. R. S.

Gandigonrȣannen, S. *avoir grand esprit.*

Gandigonraȣihon, S. *savoir bien quelqe chose.*

Gandigonrat v. Gandigonret, S. *avoir de l'esprit;* takȣe.

Gandigonraton, S. *avoir perdu l'esprit.*

Gandigon^{e}rata, R. *donner de l'esprit.*

Gandigonroge, S. *être beste.*

Gandigonrhatannion, R. *tromper quelqu'un.*

Gandigonrare, S. *penser à quelque chose;* rarakȣe, rag.

Gandigonriagon, S. neut. *perdre espérance.*

Gandigonriaktanni, R. *f.* ten; *faire perdre espérance.*

Gandigonragennion, R. *surpasser quelqu'un en esprit.*

Gandigon^{e}raχahon, S. *joindre ses pensées, ses opinions.*

Gandigon^{e}raksaton, R. *gaster l'esprit à quelqu'un, le fâcher.*

Gandigonraȣenrion, S. *esprit se brouiller, varier.*

Gandigont, *avoir de l'esprit*; takȣe, tag (rarum usit. nisi in comp).
Gandigontarion, R. *appaiser quelqu'un.*
Gandigonkennion, R. *tromper quelqu'un.*
Gandigonkenheion, Ch.

Gandigonrheñon, S. ens, en, ensere; *s'oublier.*
Garihȣandigonrheñon, S. *oublier une affaire.*

Gannigonhare, S. *bretelles.*
Gandigonharagete, Atendigonharagete, *porter bretelles*, S.

Gannihare, *jusque là.*
Ganniharhon, Ch. hos, ho, hosere; *aller jusqu'à un terme.*
Tsonnontȣann nahanniharho, *il a compris Tsonnontȣan.*

Gannihen, R. *prester.* ȣagonni, *je te preste;* tagni, tagȣanni.
Gannihase, R. *emprunter de quelqu'un;* ȣgonjenniase.

Gannio, *germer*, S. impers. Tontajonnio, *elle a repoussé.*

Gannio, R. *passer la rivière dans un canot.*
Tagȣannio, *passe moi la rivière.*
Gannioho, *aller passer quelqu'un.*

Gannion, S. *avare, chiche.* Rostarokȣannion, *il est avare de rassade.*

Kanniogȣa, *cramaillere.*

Ganniong, Onnionsa in comp. *nez, muffle.* ȣagennionge, *à mon nez.*
Kannionsaȣeston, S. *avoir le nez bûché par un rhume.*
Skannionsa, Skannionsȣann, *orignal.*
Tȣatkonniokon, Ch. *faire la nazade.*
Kannionkon, S. *pns.* et *f.* ka; *saigner du nez.*
Ti agotkonniaeston, *Nez Percés.* 1[ae] conj.

Kannionra, *trou de la cheminée.*
Kannionragarenton, *la où est le trou de la cheminée.*
Kannionraȣerhon, Ch. *boucher le trou de la cheminée.*
Tagennionraȣerhos, *bouche moy le trou de.* R.
Kannionraȣeragȣan, Ch. *le déboucher;* gȣas, go, gohe.

Onniongȣar, *épine, ronce.*

Gannioron, Ch. *pns.* et *f.* re, *n.* resere; *aller en canot.*
Gnioresere, *je dois aller en canot.*

Gannioron, impers. pass. *f.* rog; *la neige se pressera, s'abbaisera.*

Ganniont, θa, tan, tanne; act. plerumq. comp. *attacher, suspendre.*
Garihȣanniont, Ch. *joindre une affaire.*
Sasarannionton, *attache, pends ton couteau.*
Snatsionnionton, *pends la chaudière.*
Ganniontagȣan, Ch. *détacher, dépendre.*
Ganniontase, R.

Ganniot, Ch. θa, t, tanne; *être planté droit, dresser, mettre debout.*
Sniôten, *dresse*, v. g. *ce pieux.*

Onniòsk, *cayeux.* Gannionseronni, Ch. *faire un cayeux.*

Ganniron, *être fort, dur.*
Gannonsan[c]niron, *cabane dure forte.*
Gannironse, neut. acq. S. Ongnironse, *je le trouve dur.*

Ganniraton, Ch. *affermir;* θa, t, θe.

Gannirhaon, S. *pns.* et *f.* rha; *s'affermir, s'endurcir.*

Gannisegȣan v. **Ganniskȣan,** Ch. kȣas, ko, kohe; *différer, délayer.*

Rannisegȣas tiotkont kanniga ires, *Il est toujours lent quelque part qu'il aille.*

Gannisegȣaton, Ch. *différer pour ou par q. c.*

Gannisten, *avoir pour mère.*

Gannistensen, *avoir une mère,* R. Gannistensera, subst.

Gannistigarȣt, Ch. θa, ten; *faire un boucle.*

Gannistiagéon, S. ges, ge; *pisser.* Est R.

ȣahiannistiage, *il a pissé sur toi.*

Gannistiageston, S. *lieu où l'on pisse.*

Gannisterohon, Ch. *Danse des Agoianders où l'on donne de la porcelaine aux spectateurs.*

Onniste, *la queue, le pecoul d'un fruit.*

Garoñare te jonnistonte, *un clou.*

Ganniténton, *Battre sur les écorces le soir qu'on a brûlé ou tué quelque prisonnier, pour chasser l'âme du défunt.*

Onnitskera, *crachat,* extra comp. Oskera, in comp.

Ennitskerontion, S. *cracher.*

Ennitskerontiense, R. *cracher sur quelqu'un.*

Gaskeroserhon, *mouiller de crachats,* R.

Onnitsehȣa, *la pance, le ventre.*

Gannitseho, *avoir gros ventre,* S.

Kennihonnitsehȣagarate, *il a le ventre gros comme celà.*

Kannitsehoren, S. *la pance se fendre, crever.*

Gannitsokȣaron, S. *avoir de la grosse gale.*

Ganno, *froid.* Onneganno, *eau froide.*

Gaiatanno, *corps froid.*

Gaiatannoston, S. *s'affraichir, prendre le froid.*

Kannogariagon, S. *avoir mal aux dents.*

Onnogȣa, *blé mangé par les souris.*

Onnogȣario, *farine épaisse détrempée dans l'eau froide, ou blé à demi cuit qu'on écrase ou pile, et que l'on mange sans autre assaisonnement.*

Gannogȣari, S. ris, risere; *se faire un manger de cette sorte.*

Ohare, in comp.; Gannohare, extra comp. *laver.*

Gannatsiohare, Ch. *laver la chaudière.*

Gannohareton, Ch. θa, t, θe; *laver avec quelque chose.*

Gannôha, R. *être oncle :* Ragnoha, *mon oncle;* Hiannoha, *ton oncle;* Ronnoha, *son oncle;* Aχinnoha, *nos oncles.*

Gannohon, impers. *blé raffiné dans la boue qui sent un peu.*

Gannokȣa, *une grenouillere, eau de pluye qui a fait comme un marais.*

Eθo ȣage si tgannokȣajen, *je vais à la gren.*

Gannokȣanneron, *lier un sac, un bourse.* Ch.

Gannokȣason, Ch. *ramasser par ci par là;* kȣas, kȣa.

Gannontarannokȣason, *manger de la sagamité par cy par là dans les cabanes.*

Onnokȣisen, extra comp. } *farine épaisse.*
Onnȣkȣisera, in comp. }

Gannokȣiseragon, Ch. *en manger.*
Gannokȣiserôon, Ch. *faire de la farine épaisse, sagamité.*
Gannokȣiseroken, Ch. *en faire de quelque chose.*
Gannokȣiseroserhon, *la détremper dans l'eau froide.*
Tagnokȣiseroseras, *détrempe moi de la farine.*
Ongnokȣiserasti, S. *je suis pris au gozier de la farine.*

Gannoña, *fonds de l'eau.* Gannoñagon, *au fond.*

Gannoñagon, Ch. ks, g, χe; *avoir envie de manger*, Ch.
Garihȣannoñagon, Ch. *avoir envie d'une affaire*, seu *chercher querelle, attaquer le premier.*

Gannongȣentaon, R. *brûler les cabanes*; tas, tahȣe.
Θorie rotonni saonχinnoñgȣentaȣe onseronni, *il naquit lorsque les Français bruslerent nos maisons.*

Onnongȣira, S. *corde de porcelaine.*
Θo nigannongȣirage, *combien de cordes de pourcelaine.*
Gannongȣirontion, S. *jetter une corde de porcelaine.*

Gannonhȣaktannion, S. nisk, ten, nire; *avoir mal.*
Jonnonhȣakte, *cela est douloureux.*
Gannonhȣaktâton, S. *causer la douleur.*
Atatnonhȣaktâton, Ch. *se causer de la douleur.*
ȣagnonhȣaktannik, si, sonnhe; *je t'aime, ta vie m'est précieuse.*

Gannonhȣéon, Ch. hȣes, hȣe, hȣenne; *aimer quelqu'un ou quelque chose.* Est R.
Gandigon^c^rannonhȣéon, R. *aimer le naturel de quelq.*

Onnonhȣara, *la cervelle*, S.
Gannonhȣara^c^ton, S. *être ivre, avoir perdu le cerveau.*
Gannonhȣara^c^tonton, S. *ce qui enivre.*
Gannonhȣariaχon, Ch. *casser le cervelle à quelqu'un.* Est R.
Gannonhȣariagon, S. *avoir mal à la teste.*
Gannonhȣariakton, R. *causer mal à la teste à quelqu'un.*

Onnonhȣârore, Onnonhȣarorotseron in comp. S. *bonnet.*
Gannonhȣaroron, S. *avoir un bonnet* seu *la tête couverte:* a Garoron, *couvrir*, et Onnonhȣara.
Atiataȣit gannonhȣarorotseront, *capot qui a un bonnet, capuchon.*
Gannonhȣarata^c^kȣan, Ch. *tirer la cervelle.*

Kannonhiannion, S. nisk, ni; *avoir peur, être effrayé, apprehendre.*
ȣaθonninhianni ȣasagaonnhet te hoñagonhen, *Il a eu peur, il a donné la vie a son esclave.*
Kannonhianniton, S. *causer cette frayeur.*

Kannonhȣeron, R. *saluer quelqu'un;* ronsk, ron, ronne.
Kannonhȣeronton, R. *saluer, remercier par q. c. ou pour.*

Onnonhȣeri, *poil qui croist sur le corps.*
Atnonhȣeronnion, S. pass. *avoir du poil, estre velu.*
Kennihonnonhȣéres, *il y a du poil de cette longueur.*

Gannonhȣarori, S. *Chanter chanson de mort ou autre, pourvu qu'on chante seul sans qu'aucun réponde.*

Gannonhȣaroriáton, S. *chanter telle chanson.*

Gannonhȣarorige, *dans la tabagie où l'on s'entredemande ses desirs.*

Jonnonhȣarorigȣanni, dit on d'une coureuse.

Gannonhȣaroriase, *le faire pour quelq.; aller courir et demander le desir d'un autre.*

Gannon^{c}karon, R. *p.* rons, *f.* re; *faire les cheveux.*

Gannon^{c}karáton, Ch. *avec quoy on coupe les cheveux.*

Gannonkȣe, R. *avoir pour parent.*

Songȣannon^{c}kȣe Jesȣs saonχiseraȣe, *Jésus nous adopte pour ses parents quand on nous baptise.*

Gannonkȣarita, *cheveux brouillés*, S.

Gannon^{c}kȣaritagenrat, *chevelure blanche.*

Jonnon^{c}kȣaritaksen, *injure.*

Onnonkȣeñonte, *épi de blé.* Gannonkȣeñagon, Ch. *manger des épis.*

Onnon^{c}kȣat, S. *médecine.* Onnonkȣatsera, in comp.

Gannonkȣatserannhonθon, R. *donner médecine.*

Onnon^{c}kȣis, *cheveux.* Onnon^{c}kȣisere, in comp.

Gannonkȣiseras, *longs cheveux.*

Gannonkȣiserare, R. *arracher les cheveux.*

Gannonna (est etiam R.), Ch. *impf.* nakȣe, *f.* ne, *n.* nanne; *garder.*

Gannatannonna, Ch. *garder le village.*

Garihȣannonna, Ch. *garder, attendre le succes d'un affaire.*

Gannonnannion, *avoir envie d'aller au quelque lieu; avoir pour but de son voyage.*

Gannonnatanni, *faire venir l'envie de q. c. en la montrant.*

Onnoñsera, S. *citrouille.* Gannonserajesen, *grosse citrouille.*

Gannoñonsero, Ch. *en faire bouillir.*

Gannoñonseront, Ch. *en faire cuire sous les cendres.*

Gannoñonserontanni, R. *f.* θas.

Atnonoñseront, pass. Atnononserontanni, pass. acq.

Gannonnaȣan, S. *calumet.* Gannonnaȣenta, in comp.

Jaten te sȣagnonnaȣentajen, *je n'ai plus de calumet.*

Gannonnatanni, *faire venir l'envie de q. c. à quelqu'un;* R. *f.* ten.

Gannonȣajenton, Ch. θa, t, tanne; *tenir la foire.*

Gannonȣireton, S. *se perdre, s'abîmer, disparaitre.*

Garihȣannonȣireton, S. *quitter le soin des affaires.*

Gannoȣen, S. *menteur, estre menteur.*

Gannoȣenton, S. *mentir;* θa, t, tanne.

Atennoȣenton, R. *dementir quelqu'un.*

Gannoȣentanni, *faire mentir quelqu'un; lui attribuer ce qu'il n'a pas dit.* R.

Gannoñȣensera, *gueuserie.* Gannonȣenseraksenha.

Gasatennonȣenserinnet, *que ta gueuserie s'en aille.*

Gannonsa, *cabane.* Gannonsȣt, *il y a une cabane;* takȣe, tak.
Gannonsȣton, *il y a des cabanes.*
Onneneja gannonsȣtakon, *maison de pierre.*
Gannonsogeronte, *maison, cabane dont le toit est en talus.*
Gannesonni, *cabane, ronde par le bout.*
Gannonsonni, Ch. *faire une cabane.*
Gannonsonnianni, R. *f.* nien.
Gannonsison, Ch. *achever ou avoir achevé la cabane.*
Gannonsisaanni, R. *f.* sas.
Gannonsanneron, Gannonsannikon, Ch. *accommoder, recoudre la cabane.*
Gannonsarïsion, Ch. *la défaire.*

Onnonra, S. *chevelure.* Kannonra^c^kȣan, R. *enlever la chevelure.*

Gannonrare, Ch. *avoir chance au jeu tout blanc ou tout noir.*

Gannonre, S. *avoir gisté, couché en chemin.*
Ka nisannonre^c^kȣe? *Où as tu couché?*

Gannonsen, R. *marquer sur le corps avec la pointe d'une aiguille.*
Atnonsen, S. *être marqué.*

Gannonsen, R. *f.* enhas; *faire cuire de la viande pour quelqu'un.*

Gannonste, R. *impf.* tekȣe, *f.* teg; *aimer.*
Gannonstaton, in comp. *garder, protéger.*
Gaiatannonstaton, R. ts, t, θe; *garder quelqu'un.*
Gannonstati, R. *f.* ts, tatseg; *refuser à quelqu'un.*
Jonχinnonstati ajagȣatenti, *on nous a empêché de partir.*

Onnonta, *lait*, S.
Gannontat, *il y a du lait.*
Gannontatata, *se faire venir du lait.*
Gannontatakȣan, Ch. *tirer la lait,* v. g. *à la vache.*
Gannontat^c^kaon, C. kaȣas, kaȣa, kaȣasere; *quitter la mammelle.*
Gannontakȣion, S. *estre saoul de teter.*
Gannontonte, *elle a des mammelles formées.*

Onnontara, *sagamité.*
Gannontario, Gannontaragon, *bonne sagamité.*
Gannontaragasθa, Ch. *qui mange beaucoup de sagamité.*

Onnonte, *montagne.*
Onnontes, *longue ou haute montagne.*
Onnontagenhiat, *au dessus.* Onnontoharage.
Gannontaráon, Ch. ras, ranne; *la monter.*

Gannontégon, Ch. ks, g, kse; *boucher, fermer quelq. vaisseau ou quaisse.*
Gannontekton, Ch. *le boucher avec quelque chose.*
Gannonteksion, Ch. *le déboucher.* Gannonteksions^e^.
Atnonteksion, pass. Ch. *se déboucher.*

Gannonten, R. tens, ten, tenre; *donner.*

Gannonton, inusit. In comp. *fouiller, interroger.*
Garihȣannonton, Ch. *demander de nouvelles;* tons, ton, tonre. Est etiam R.

Garihȣannontonre, *je te viens interroger.*

Rarihȣannontonskon, *curieux, grand demander de nouvelles.*

Gannonton, Ch. *s'ennuyer, s'impatienter d'attendre quelqu'un ou q. c.*

Θosa tesennontong nastennhâon, *Ne t'impatientes pas en attendant ce que tu m'as commandé de faire.*

Gannonton, Ch. tes, te, tesére; *jetter de la porcelaine pour les morts.*

Gannonteton, Ch.

Gannontráon, R. *attraper quelq. après qui l'on court, l'atteindre.*

Onne ȣagonnontranne, *je t'ai atteint;* tras, tranne, trasere.

Gannontraseron, *de multitud.*

Onnontsi, Onnontsista in comp. S. *tête.*

Gannontistagarien v. Gannonkarien, *manger la tête.*

Onnora, S. *tresse de blé.*

Gannoronni, Ch. *tresser le blé.* Gannoronnianni, R. *f.* nien.

Gannonrarhon, *les mettre sur les perches.*

Asen nagonnoron, *je te donne 3 traisses.*

Neθo nigannorage tsinni jeȣendage ahetȣannorarorog hatitsihenst, *Donnons autant de tresses de blé, qu'il y a de voix aux robes noires.*

Gannóron, Imps. *être difficile, prétieux,* S. rong.

Gannoron^{c}kon, Ch. *pns.* & *f.* kȣa, kȣag; *n.* kȣanne, *estimer q. chose, la faire précieuse.* Est R.

Jatan te sknoron^{c}kȣa, *tu ne fais pas cas de moy.*

Garihȣannóron, *chose d'importance.*

Gannonsandóron, *cabane où l'on a peine à entrer.* S.

Gandoronnaon^{c}tenti, *il y a de la peine à marcher.*

Atennoron^{c}kon, S. *être rendu difficile, de prix par q. c.*

Gannonron^{c}kȣanni, R. *f.* kȣen; *faire q. c. prétieuse, chère.*

Gannoron^{c}kȣaton, Ch. *le faire chèr pour celà.*

Gannoronse, neût. acq. S. *trouver difficile;* rons, rons, ronsere.

Ongrihȣannorons nagrihȣiost, *Je trouve difficile d'être Chrétien.*

Gannȣsen, R. sas, sa, sasere; *porter envie.*

Gannȣsen, Gannȣsenha, *beaupère.* Sagonnȣsenha, *son beaupère.*

Onnȣsera, *galle.* Gannȣseraon, S. sas, sa. Gannȣserarhon, R. *la donner.*

Onnȣta, *coton, duvet.*

Nondȣtage^{c}te, *la guerre.* Hotinnondȣtagatete, *les soldats.*

Onne tetsiongiatógen nondȣtagete, *J'ai fait divorce avec la guerre.*

Kannotoñagon, Ch. *avoir les dents agacées.*

Onnotsia, *dent.*

Areko ronnotsiȣt, *il n'a pas encore de dents.*

Kannotsiongo^{c}ton, S. *avoir mal aux dents; θa,* t, tanne.

Kannotsiotagȣan, Ch. *arracher la dent.*

Kannotsiotagȣanni, R. *f.* gȣas.

Gannotsiotarhon, *avoir quelque chose entre les dents.*

Tȣannoserigon v. Tȣannogaranniehon, *grincer des dents.*

Gan^{c}dȣton, Imperson. S. *être profond.*

Θo nijon^{c}dȣtes, *Combien est-il profond?*

Ken ni ondȣtesons, *Il est de cette profondeur.*

Ken ni on[c]dȣtesa, *un peu profond.*

Gan[c]dȣton, Neutr. acq. S. *être profond à quelq.;* tons, ton, tonne.

Ongȣennȣton si etiagȣenniat, *Nous avons trop d'eau là où sont nos nasses.* Intrat in comp.

Kenniȣenheiontandȣtes gagerontatie, *Il y a des corps morts de cette hauteur.*

Ken ok tsion[c]dȣtes, *Il n'y a plus que cette hauteur*, v. g. *dans le baril.*

Gar et gare, *être, mettre dessus, peindre, paraitre.*

Composita ex gar, *être, mettre dessus.*

Jaten te garihȣare niotaksen nongȣarihȣiosta[c]kon, *Il n'y a rien de mauvais dans notre créance.* Vel Jaten te gare garihȣaksen.

Garaton, act. *mettre auprès non pas immédiate.*

Okniorea te srat, *Mets ces deux choses près l'un de l'autre.*

Garon, pass. *mettre près, après.*

Joskenhen sron, *mets près après,* v. g. *ces graines.*

Atron v. atren, *être à quelque distance;* trons, trons, tronne, tre.

Joskenhen ate tȣatre, *Sumus proximi.*

Kene nate giatréa, *Ces deux choses sont l'une contre l'autre.*

Ok niore ken niorea, *tout près.*

Garagȣegan, Ch. *effacer;* geȣas, geȣe, geȣasere : fere semper cum nota reitere, Garageȣenni, R. *f.* geȣas, *effacer à quelq.*

Onsahagrageȣas nagrihȣanderen, *Il m'a effacé mes péchés.*

Atrageȣen, pass. *s'effacer, se décolorer.* Atrageȣenni, pass. recip.

Atrageȣaton, θa, *ce quoi avec on efface.*

Sȣatrageȣaθa niagȣarihȣanderask Jesȣs raonnigȣensta, *Ce qui fait effacer nos péchés, c'est le sang de J. Christ.*

Garonnion, ons, on, onne; *Y avoir par ci par là.*

Garihȣaronnio njojandere, *Il y a par ci par là q. c. de bon.*

Gar, cum partic. motus atie signat *aller avec q. c., l'accompagner, se faire avec ou en même temps.*

ȣaseraratie sinni ȣenniseres, *La hache frappait tant que le jour dura.*

Garihȣaraties, *l'affaire va, suit en même tems.*

Jaten te jondegorharation onne jagoiateñon jonhȣentsiagon, *La porcelaine n'est pas allée en enfer avec ceux qui y sont.*

Gara[c]kon, Ch. kȣa, *f.* kȣe, kȣanne; *mettre dans q. c.*

Naie ensrakȣe, *tu mettras la dedans.*

Ontakne tsnirakȣe, *mettes dans la chaudière.*

Hoñajatarakon garontotserage garistatsi, *On le mit dans un cercueil de métail.*

Gara[c]kon, *estimer, priser.* R.

Jaten te θariakȣa, *Il ne t'estime pas.*

Jaten χetarakȣa onseronni, *Je ne crains, ne fais point de cas des Français.*

Gaȣennara[c]kon, R. *obéir;* kȣa, kȣe, kȣag, kȣanne.

Atȣennarakon, pass. *être obéissant.*

Atiatarakon, Ch. *se plaire à q. c.;* *être tout la dedans.*

ȣagatiatarakon nondȣatagete, *Je me plais à la guerre.*

Hennegen hetsegonsarakȣat, *Fais luy mettre la face en haut,* ut solent facere aliquid sorbentes.

Garakȣanni, R. *f.* kȣen, *mettre à quelq.*

Ontakne tagrakȣen, *Mets moy à manger dans la chaudière.*

Garanni v. Gatsientanni, R. *f.* rhas, *mettre à manger pour quelq.;* nik, nire.

Tontagerhas, *redonne m'en encore.*

Garagȣan, Ch. gȣas, go, gohe; *ôter de dedans, trier, choiser;* srago, *choisis.*

Garihȣarágȣan, Ch. *avoir égard à q. c.,* dite par mégarde.

θosa tesrihȣarágo hoθennon ȣairon jagonnegiren, *N'aye pas égard à ce qu'on dit dans l'ivrognerie.*

Atiataragȣan, Ch. *s'ôter, se retirer de q. c.*

Gaiataragȣan, R. Hetsiarago rokskoña, *descends cet enfant de dessus.* Signat etiam *choisir quelq.*

Atrihȣaragȣan, *une chose se retirer, n'y penser plus* : a Garagȣan, *descender q. c., l'ôter de dessus.* Vide infra Gahre.

Aθaragȣari, Ch. *s'ôter du chemin, se détourner.*

Aθaragȣanni, R. *f.* gȣas, *se détourner pour laisser passer un autre.*

Garáon, R. ras, ranne, rasere; *trouver quelq.*

Aχerasere jagoiengȣiron, *Je vas trouver ceux qui sont à la chasse.*

Gannontaráon, Ch. *monter une montagne.*

Tȣatráon, Ch. tras, t-ranne, t-rasere; *se rencontrer.*

ȣaθontranne, *ils se rencontrèrent.*

Tȣat-raseron, Ch. *de multis.*

Tȣat-raton, Ch. *faire rencontrer;* θa, t, tanne.

Ateráton, Ch. *passer.* Ateráton, *mesurer.* Ch.

Asen naháterat honajengȣanninnons, *Il donne* 3 *longueurs de tabac.*

Garaon v. **Garaȣi,** R. *habiller, couvrir quelq., calumnier, accuser.*

Jotsannit naongras! *C'est étrange qu'on m'impute celà!*

ȣagonras, *je te couvre.*

Garagaraȣi, Garagarhon, R. *accuser, quereller quelqu'un.*

ȣaχeragarhosera v. ȣaχeragaraȣire, *je m'en vas quereller.*

J. ejongȣarihȣaranne, *l'affaire tombera sur nous.*

Garáon, act. *vouloir, consentir.*

Jaten horas, *Il ne veut pas consentir.*

Onne ȣahatiranne rotiksten, *Les anciens consentent, il font le cry d'approbation, le* Niohen.

Garase, R. *f.* ras, *consentir à quelqu'un.*

Onne gonrase, *J'approuve ce que tu.*

Gaȣennaráon, Ch. *avoir vu en songe.*

Gaȣennaragȣan, R. *parler en faveur de quelqu'un qui demande ses desirs dans L'*onnonhȣarori.

Gar, *paraitre, reluire.* Imp. garakȣe, *f.* garag.

Onne igar, *le soleil luit.* Ason tegar, *la lune n'est.*

Onne iskar, *nous avons nouvelle lune.*

Entiek négárák, *à midy.*

Atra, pass. Esȣatrat, *quando erit nova luna.*

Onne tsiot ragarhon, *en nova luna.*

Onne sȣa-traθe, *la lune va renouveller.*

Atraton, neut. sumpt.

Areko tetsiongȣat-ráton, *Nous n'avons pas encore nouv.*

Gar, cum part. kon.

Ken nongati garakennen, *le soleil étant au dela de midi.*

Garakȣa, *le soleil.*

Garakȣannontakton, Ch. θa, t, tanne; *attacher le soleil.* Ab Ora^c^kȣannentágon, quod sæpius pro sole simplicitur usurpatur.

At-takȣaton, *Impson.* Onne ontrakȣaton, *nous avons éclipse.*

Garakȣt, *Imp.* takȣe, ten, tanne; *faire bien chaud.*

Taonχen jorakȣt, *O qu'il fait chaud!*

Garakȣataton, S. *le soleil être piquant, ardent.*

Garakȣatiron, Ch. *le rayon du soleil passer en quelque lieu.*

Garakȣinnion, cum part. loc. *le soleil passer au travers,* v. g. *une vitre.*

Garakȣinnegeñon, ens, enne, enhȣe; *le soleil se lever, sortir de la nue.*

Garakȣaȣiaχon, Ch. *aller à la chasse des tourtes la nuit.*

Karakȣaȣerhon, Ch. *être, se mettre à l'ombre.*

Garakȣaȣerhoston, *faire de l'ombrage.*

Atrakȣaȣerhoton, Ch. *se mettre à l'ombre.*

Jagotrakȣaȣerhosθa, *un parasol.*

Tȣatronrose, S. *être ébloui du soleil.*

Gar et **Gare,** *peindre.* Gaiatare, *peindre quelq.* R. re, ren, ranne.

Tagiataren, *peinds moi.* Gaiatare, act. *peindre.*

Gaiatare, pass. Eθo rajatare Jesȣs, *Voilà l'image de J. C.*

Hatiataronnion hotiatatogeton, *les images des saints.*

Onka ken gaiatare, *De qui est cette image.*

Gar, *être, mettre du nombre;* re, rag, ranne.

Ja nennaie se gar, *Cela n'est pas compris.*

Naie onni igar, *Cela y est aussi compris.*

Gaiatare, Ch. *estre du nombre, être présent.*

Esiatarag n'egatennioten, *Tu assisteras à mon festin.*

Gaientare, *comprendre, faire cas.*

Jaten te gaientareha ȣaontatsiararágo, *Cela n'est rien, qu'on arrache les ongles.*

Jaten te χeintarha areko jagorihȣioston, *Je ne comprends pas les infideles.*

Gaiataratie, *aller en la compagnie de quelqu'un.*

Ehojataratie, *il est allé en la bande,* v. g. *des guerriers.*

Gaiatarágȣan, R. gȣas, go, gohe; *ôter du nombre, excommunier.*

Satiatarágo, *retire toy de cette compagnie.*

ȣahoñajatarágo notiokȣatogetonge niagorihȣioston, *On la ôté du nombre des Chrétiens.*

Gahre, rakȣe, rag; *être, mettre dessus.*
Θo gaksahre, *le plat est la dessus.* Vide sup. Gahre.
Ennisne gahra°kȣe, *Cela était sur l'andichon.*
Gaiatahre, *une chose vivante être dessus.*
Atiatahre, Ch. *se mettre dessus quelque chose.*
Ga°ráon, *tomber dessus;* ras, ranne.
Onksiraranne, *du feu est tombé sur moy.*
Enniserage agaiataranne tsinnoȣen, *La souris est tombée sur l'andichon.*
Gara°gȣan, Ch. *ôter de dessus;* gȣas, go, gohe.
Snatsiahrágo, *ôte la chaudière de dessus le feu.*
Garagȣanni, R. *f.* gȣas, *ôter de dessus à quelqu'un.*

Garagohon, Ch. *aller quérir de nids de tourtes.*

Ga°re, re, ranne, rasere; *monter en haut.*
Agannonsaranne, *la cabane va montant en haut.*
EΘa tagan°negaranne si etiontiatannhasΘa, *L'eau monte jusqu'à la ceinture.*

Gahre, re, ren, ranne; *mettre, lever en haut.*
Θosren, *mets là dessus.* ȣakren, *j'ai mis.*

Gahráon, *f.* has, R. *mettre dessus pour quelqu'un.*
Tageksagerhas, *mets moy le plat la dessus.*
Tagientaherhas, *mets moy ce bois sur ma charge.*

Gaharatáton, Ch. *lever en haut;* ts, t, θe.
Sagenharatat, *trousse ta robe.*

Gahren, *le coup tomber sur quelqu'un;* ras, ra, ranne.
Jaȣetȣan ȣaonkranne, *J'ai reçu quantité de coups.*

Garagarere v. **Garagarhe,** *imps.* S. *faire du bruit.*
Gannakȣagareraston, Ch. *jouer du tambour.*
Garistagareraston, Ch. *sonner la cloche.*
ȣahotakȣarere, *ses souliers font du bruit.*

Garahiatakȣan, R. kȣa, kȣe; *agacer, irriter.*
Atrahiatakȣan, Ch. kȣa, kȣe, kȣanne; *refuser de faire q. c.*
Atrahiatakȣanni, R. *f.* kȣen, *refuser à quelqu'un.*

Garannie, es, e, ese; *frotter.*

Garagenrje, R. jes, e, jehe; *rouler, volutare.*
Otsirege hoñaragenrie, *On l'a roulé dans le feu.*
Atragenrie, pass. Otonkȣagon jonr-ragenriehon te jagotonnhakarien jonhȣentsiagon, *Les damnés se roulent dans les flammes.*

Ga°rarágon, Ch. raks, rag, raχe; *percer, trouer.*
Ga°rarági, R. *f.* ks. Gararakton, Ch. *trouer avec quelque chose.*
Jerontararakta, *une tarière.* JerontararakΘa.

Garannaȣan v. **Gannaȣan,** *être humeoté, un arbre être en séve.*

Garanniston, Ch. θa, *ne pas écouter.*

Garáta, *talon.* Tagratonnien, *Couds moi le talon de mes souliers.*

Garáte, Ch. tes, ten, tensere; *aller le long de q. c.*
Θo garates tsinnoȣen, *La souris monte le long, &c.*

Tȣaratatou, *courir*, Ch. ts, t, θe. Est R. ȣaθoñara^c^tat, *on sauta, courit sur luy.*

Garaθen, Ch. θens, θen, θensere; *monter.*
Jeraθensθa, *une échelle.*

Gararhon, Ch. hosk, ho, hosere; *aborder en canot.*
Jeraroθa, *débarquement, lieu où on aborde.*

Gara^c^ȣen, Ch. imperf. takȣe, sen; *faire cuire dans l'eau.*

Garaskȣa, *portion de sagamité.*
Garaskȣatarihaton, Ch. *la faire rechauffer.*
Garaskȣaȣeron, Ch. *renverser un plat de sagamité.*

Garégon, Ch. rks, reg, rekse; *pousser.*
Setsitareg, *attise le feu.* Jahakrekȣe, *il m'a poussé.*
Garaseron, frequent. Setsistareseron, *attise ces tisons.*

Tȣ–Atatreseron, Ch. *s'entrepousser.*

Kȣatre, *mon petit fils ou p. fille.* In voc. vid. sup. Atrea. χeiatrea, *ma petite fille.* Hiatréa, *mon;* Sagotre ogoña, *ses petits fils.*

Gare, cum redupl. *un nombre au dessus de dix.* Oieri, skat, skare, *onze.*
Ojeri nihati tegni satire, 12 *homines;* tegni skontire, 12 *fœmenœ.*
Componitur cum Gaiata, et dicunt : Asen satiatare, *ils sont douze.*
Ojeri ȣaθagennhongo gaieri skagennhare, *il a passé* 14 *ans.*
Skat tsioserare oieri sané, *onze hyvers.*

Garenda, S. *prière, chanson, festin, sort.*
Rarendio, *sa chanson est belle.*
Garennentáon, Ch. *achever sa prière, sa chanson.*
Atrendagent, Ch. ensk, en, enne; *prier.*
ȣagatrendajentakȣe, *j'avois prié.*
Jontrendajentakȣa, *une chapelle, lieu où l'on prie.*
ȣagatrendajennonnen, *j'étais allé à la prière.*
Atrendajentagȣan, Ch. *avoir prié.*
Atrendajenni, R. *f.* enhas, *prier pour quelqu'un.*
Tagȣatrendajenhas, *prie pour moi.*
Atrendȣt, Ch. θa, ten, tanne; *chanter.* Garendȣt, act. idem.
Atrennonnianni, R. *jetter des sorts; f.* nien.
Garendahetken ȣahorio, *C'est un sort qui le tire.*

Garennhaon, Ch. nhas, nhanne, nhasere; *s'accoutumer.*
Are^c^ko rorennhaon, *Il n'est pas encore accoutumé.*
Iotrennhat, *on s'accoutume.* Est R. Hoñarennháon, *on est accoutumé à luy.*

Atrenranni, R. *aimer quelqu'un, aller à quelq. sitôt qu'on le voit.*

Garenha, *cime d'arbre.*
Garenhoskaron, Ch. *ébrancher une arbre;* rons, ron, re.
Garenhoskaronse, R.

Gareñja, *bûche.* Karenjoren, *fendre une bûche.*

Garennhon, R. *scarifier, faire incision;* nhens, nhon vel nenn.
ȣahatatrenn, *il s'est coupé.*
Atattrennhon, Ch. *se scarifier.*

Garensa, *corde de rassade, chappelet, jambe.*
Tagrenson, *donne moy un chapelet.*
Garensannoñagou, S. *avoir mal aux jambes.*
ȣahotrenso, *il a la jambe enflée.*
Garensotari, Ch. risk, ri, riχe; *bander un arc.*
Garensotarision, Ch. *le débander.*
Garentagáron, Ch. rons, re, ronhe; *rechausser le blé.*
Ga^{c}renton (dic Orenton, extra comp.), *pendre en bas.*
Jo^{c}rentonkȣe, *cela pendait en bas.*
Ejorentonhag, *que cela pende en bas.*
Ab Enton, in comp. S. *chose qui pend.*
Joristenton, *du fer qui pend.*
Entonkon, act. *pns.* et *f.* kȣa, kȣanne; *faire pendre, suspendre q.c., descendre q. c.*
Entonkȣanni, R. *f.* kȣen, *faire descendre à q. chose, la dévaler.*
Hennegen ȣaθonasitanneren ok ȣahoñagonsajentonkȣat, *On luy lia les pieds an haut et suspendit la tête en bas.*
Gareȣaton, R. θa, t, tanne; *punir, tancer.*
Atreȣa^{c}ton, Ch. *s'opposer à q. chose, la blâmer.*
Ratreȣaθa n'ontredajen, *Il blâme la prière.*
Ionχireȣaθa n'ongȣarihȣioston, *On nous blâme, nous autres;* χens.
Garha, *forest.* Garhio, *belle forest.* Garhasen, *il y a une forêt.*
Garhate, *il y a.* Garhatajenton, *il y a des forests.*
Garhison, Ch. sas, sa, saanne; *faire une forest.*
Garhatageha, *des bluets.* Garhatagentiag.
Garhagonha, *oiseau de proye, vautour.*
Garhit, *arbre de bout.* Potius dicit. Gerhit, gerhitakȣa.
Garhare, Ch. vel S. rekȣe, re, reg; *attendre, espérer.*
Est R. Jesarhare, *on ta attendu.*
Garharaston, Ch. *attendre pour q. chose.*
Garharastanni, R. *f.* ten; *faire attendre, promettre à quelqu'un.*
Jesȣs songȣarharastanni garonhiage, *Jésus nous a promis le ciel.*
Garhate, S. *coureur qui n'arrête en nulle place.* Male sonat, quando dicitur de muliere.
Garhegaton, Ch. θa, t, tanne; *desirer en quelque lieu.*
Gerhegaθa garonhiage, *Je souhaitte le ciel.*
Garhegatanni, R. *f.* ten; *desirer de voir ou d'être avec quelqu'un.*
Ogarhenta, *massue d'armes.*
Garheñon, S. ens, enne, ensere; *être jour.*
Ejorhenne egatenti, *Je partirai demain,* seu *quand il sera jour;*
Oia etsiorhenne, *après demain;*
Orhonge, *le matin;* Orhongetsi, *de très grand matin.*
Garheñon, neut. *arriver au jour.* S.
Oskeronge onsahorhenne, *à peine a-t-il revu le jour.*
Niaȣen Jesȣs oskennen onsajon gȣarhenne, *Grâces O Jésus de ce que nous avons revu le jour.*

Karhenton, Ch. *faire arriver au jour, surpasser tout la nuit;* θa, t, tanne.
ȣaθarhent ȣahotonkȣarho, *Il a eu la fièvre toute la nuit.*
Garhenton, Ch. *citrouilles qui passent la nuit à cuire sous les cendres.*
Ontaterhentannik jontataȣiatanni, *On fait cuire des citrouilles pour ses hôtes.*
Garhentagȣan, Ch. gȣás, go, gohe; *dérober les dites citrouilles, les tirer des cendres.*

Orhesk, *espine.*

Garhon. *berceau.* Garhonsera, in comp.
Garhonne, *être au berceau.* Garhonseronni, *en faire un.*
Garhonseronnianni, *f.* nien
Garhonseronniaton, *le faire de quelque chose.*
Serhonserȣten, *dresse le berceau.*
Eserhonseriennent, *tu feras tomber le berceau.*

Garhon, Ch. *frotter, induire de q. chose;* hosk, ho, hosere.
Gajennarhon, Ch. *frotter d'huyle.*

Karhon, *mettre au jeu.*
Hoθennon te serho, *Que mettras tu au jeu.*

Garhóron, *couvrir, envelopper;* roks, rog, roχe. Est etiam R.
Aterhoron, pass. Ch. *se couvrir, s'affubler.*
Gasa satiataȣit agaterhorog, *Donne moi ta robe que je me couvre.*
Garhoroᶜkon, neut. *être couvert de quelque chose.*
Garhorokton, Ch. θa, t, tanne; *envellopper avec quelque chose.*
Garhoroksion, Ch. *dévellopper, découvrir.*
Aterhoroksion, Ch. *se découvrir;* sions, si, sionhe.
Garhoroksionse v. Garhoroksiongȣanni, R. *déplier à quelqu'un.*

Orhotsera, *la gousse des fezoles.*

Garhotonni, N. nisk, ni, nianne; *addoucir quelq.*

Gari, inusit., *être cuit.* Onne jori, *cela est cuit.*
Ejorihag, *qu'il soit cuit.* Niare egarig, *attends qu'il soit cuit.*
Jaten te garisere, *Non coquetur.*
Gariton, Ch. *faire cuire;* θa, t, tanne.
Garitanni, R. *f.* ten, *faire cuire à quelqu'un.*
Garise, R. acq. *coqui alicui.*
Jaten te gerhe eȣagrisennire, *Je crois que cela ne se cuira pas à moi.*
Jonnorári, *le blé est meur.*
Jesȣs songȣannoraritanni, *Jésus a fait meurir nos bleds.*

Garigon, Ch. ris, rig, riχe; *mordre.*
Jaten tagarig, iaten te skannotsiôt: *Il ne mordra pas, il n'a plus de dent.*

Karigon, *joindre ensemble.*
Te giatontarigon, *Kébec, deux rivières qui se reunissent.*
Ati sȣendarig sȣaksten ogoña, *Convenite simul et deliberate.*

Kari, *être chaussé.* Garisk, *chausse.*
Garisk oñȣe, *des mitasses.* S. Raorisk, *ses mitasses.*
Garisk te jositonte, *Des bas qui ont le pied.*
Te satri, *mets tes bas.* Garisera, in comp.
Tagriseragȣetare ne sósa, *Coupe moy des bas à ta couverte.*
Garisi onton, *On est reduit à la besace, il ne reste plus rien.*
Garis ȣagatkannonni, *Je ne suis plus rien.*
Tȣatrision, S. *se déchausser.*
Karision, R. *déchausser quelqu'un.*
Kariskaȣe, *aller déchaussé*; kaȣas, kaȣe.
Te horiskaȣe iras, *Il va jambes nues.*

Garienna, *charge de bois.*
Gariennagete, S. *porter une charge de bois.*
Gariennontion, *jeter par terre.* S.

Garihenon, In comp. *être chaud.*
Atariheñon, pass. S. ens, en, ensere.
Jotarihen, *cela est chaud.*
Joroñaratarihen, *le fer est chaud.*
Atariheñon, neut. S. *avoir chaud.*
Origȣatarihen, *j'ai chaud.*
Garihâton, Ch. θa, t, tanne; *faire chauffer, bouillir*
Snotaratarihat, *faire chauffer la sagamité.*
Garihatanni, R. *f.* ten.

Garihȣa, *chose, affaire, discours, nouvelle,* S. Raorihȣa.
Garihȣio, *bonne affaire, estre bon.* S.
Horihȣio, *il a l'esprit bien fait.*
Garihȣastanni, R. *f.* sen, *tancer quelqu'un.*
Atatrihȣastanni, *se repentir, blâmer.*
Garihȣioston, Ch. θa, t, tanne; *croire, être Chrétien.* Quasi diceres *faire une bonne fortune.*
Garihȣiosta^c^kon, Ch. *pns.* & *f.* kȣa, kȣanne; *croire par q. c.*
Garihȣison, Ch. sas, sa, saanne; *achever une affaire, conclure.*
Garihȣisaanni, R. *f.* sas.
Jesȣs songȣarihȣisaanni ȣȣat-rageȣaθa niagȣarihȣanderask, *Jésus nous a fait une bonne affaire pour effacer nos péchés.*
Garihokte, Ch. θa, ten, tanne; *conclure son discours.*
Atrihokte, Ch. pass. *une affaire être à son bout.*
Onne ontrihokten ongȣarihȣa genha, *Notre affaire est à bout, est perdue.*
Garihoktanni, R. *f.* θas; *achever une affaire, discours, nouvelle.*
Garihont, *y avoir quelque liaison, rapport entre q. c.*
Jaten te tsiorihont, *Il n'y a plus sujet de, plus de rapport.*
Garihont, θa, ten, tanne; *donner quelque charge à quelqu'un.*
Atrihont, S. in *pnt.* et Ch. in *fut.; être officier, capitaine.*
Θone eθotrihontakȣe Konskȣirat ronajatskȣe, *Ponce Pilate étoit alors gouverneur.*
Garihontagȣan, R. *dégrader quelqu'un.*

Garihontakon, *pns.* & *f.* kȣa, kȣanne; *faire q. c. à dessein.*

Garihȣtaon, Ch. tas, tanne, tasere; *arriver nouvelle.*

Garihȣtase, R. acq. θas, in *f.*

Atrihontagȣan, Ch. *se démettre de sa charge.*

Ejorhenne ejongȣarihȣθas, *Demain la nouvelle nous viendra.*

Garihȣenhaȣi, Ch. *porter l'affaire, apporter la nouvelle.*

Rarihȣenhaȣis Diȣ raorihȣa, *Il porte la voix de Dieu.*

Garihȣeȣe, neut. Ch. *nouvelle être affirmée.*

Atrihȣinneton, Ch. θa, t; *la nouvelle venir de quelque lieu.*

Ganniege tontrihȣinnet, *la nouvelle vient d'Agnier.*

Garihȣasθoton, Ch. *diminuer, amoindrer la chose.*

Garihiagon, *couper la discours*, Ch. ks, g, χe.

Garihiagi, R. *f.* hias.

Asongȣarihias, *Il a coupé son discours pour l'amour de nous.*

Atrihiagon, *rem cessare, n'en parler plus.* Melius dicunt : Önne jorihȣagaion, *c'est une vieille affaire.*

Jorihȣagon, *c'est une bagatelle, nouvelle sans fondement.*

Garihȣanniont, Ch. θa, ten, tanne; *attacher l'affaire, un present.*

Garihȣannageraton, Ch. *faire des affaires.*

Garihȣannhatanni, R. *aggrandir le mal, faire l'aff. plus mauvaise.*

Garihȣa[c]raon, Ch. *avoir attrapé l'affaire;* ras, rȧnne, rasere.

Garihoteñon, S. *être empêché.*

Gario, *beste fauve.* Gariota, in comp.

Gariotannagre, *il y a bien des bestes.*

Gariotannagȣr, Ch. *être bon chasseur.*

Garotatsannit, *bête monstrueuse.*

Gario, R. os, o, osere; *tuer, battre :* ȣagonrio, *je te tue;* ȣahorio, *il l'a tué;* ȣaχetario, *je tue leur fiante.*

Atrio, Ch. *se battre;* trios, trio, triosere.

Atatrio, Ch. *se tuer soymême.*

Gariose, R. *f.* rios; *tuer à quelqu'un.*

ȣasongkȣannaskȣarios, *Il nous a tué notre animal domestique.*

Atriose, *se battre pour quelqu'un.*

Gario, *valoir, être le prix de quelque chose.*

Θennon jorios sonnonaȣan? *Que te donnera-t-on pour ton calumet?*

Garioton, *tuer, frapper, acheter avec q. c.;* θa, t, tanne.

Garioon, cum reitr. *quelque semence mourir*, v. g. *blé, fezoles, &c.*

Onsajorio ȣagnagȣaton[c]nen, *Le blé que j'avais semé est mort.*

Tsioriosere, *il mourra.*

Gariose, neut. acq. S. Onne tsiongȣariose, *nos bleds sont morts.*

Tsiorioθa, *du blé qui n'est pas venu à maturité.*

Ka[c]rion, Ch. ris, rinne, risere; *s'user, être usé, brisé.*

Te jo[c]rion, *cela est usé; farine bien pilée, brisée, menue comme sable.*

Gajanna[c]rion, S. *être brisé, las, fatigué.*

Karise, R. *f.* ris; *s'user à quelq.*

Te ȣagatakȣarise, *mes souliers sont usés.*

Garira, *corde* (Onnejȣt).
Ga^e^riron, Ch. ris, rire, risere; *répandre quelque liqueur.*
ȣasnegarire, *tu répands l'eau.*
Ga^e^rise, R. *f.* ris. Asongȣannatsiaris, *il a répandu notre chaudière.*
Onχrisehatie, *cela va se répandant sur moy.*

Gari^c^ton, *gland, chesne.*

Ka^e^rison, Ch. θa, t, tanne; *briser, rompre.*
ȣatetkrit, *je brise;* ȣatesrit, ȣaθarit.
Oȣaron te gariton, *chair brisée en petits morceaux.*
Karitanni, R. *f.* ten; *briser à quelqu'un.*
ȣatesknatsiariten, *tu m'as rompu ma chaudière.*

Orite, *tourte.* Garitetsera, in comp. ȣasriteserag, *mange des tourtes.*

Garistatsi, *fer, métail;* Garistatsisera, in comp. Garistonni, *en faire.*
Raristonnisk, *armurier, qui travaille sur le fer.*
Garistȣt, *il y a du fer.*
Garistȣton raota, *il a des cloux à ses souliers.*
Garistandóron, *or, argent, métail prétieux.*

Karistiagon, Ch. *battre du blé entre 2 pierres;* ks, g, χe.
Karistiagi, R. *f.* ks; *en écraser pour quelq.*
Oriste, *blé ainsi écrasé après avoir été trempé dans l'eau.*
Garistagon, Ch. *en manger.*

Garo, *en deçà;* regit aoristum.
Garo nagaihoriati, *en deçà du ruisseau.*
Skaihoriati, *au delà du ruisseau.*
Garo nagannatati, *en deçà du bourg.*
Garo gaset, *viens en deçà.*

Garógon, Ch. *bûcher, faire du bois;* roks, rog, roχe.
Kannentsarógon, Ch. *saigner, frapper le bras avec du fer.*
Garógi, R. *f.* roks; *faire du bois à quelqu'un.*
Atat-rogon, Ch. *se frapper avec sa hache.*
Garokton, Ch. *bûcher avec q. chose.*
Garokte, *viste, promptement.*

Garoñare, *fer pointu par un bout.*
Garoñare jontennikonkȣa v. teratakonniaθa, *alêne.*
Garoñare te ȣatroñarongoθa v. garoñaragarent, *aiguille.*
Garoñare te jonnistonte, *un clou.*
Garoñarȣton raota, *il a des cloux à ses souliers.*
Garoñarȣt, Ch. *ficher un clou.*

Garongȣan, *ramasser q. c. répandue par terre.*

Garokȣa, *une pipe, touche de petun.*
Garokȣentaon, Ch. *achever de fumer.* Atrokȣajenton, Ch.
Atrokȣaχahon, Ch. *être assis les uns près des autres, comme en conseil, à cause qu'ils y petunent.*
Tȣatrokȣannegen, Ch. Tegni tetgarokȣentanne jenseȣe, *Tu y arriveras après avoir fumé deux fois.*

Ga^c^ronhon, Ch. hos, hȣe; *mettre* v. *être de travers.*
Gannagara^c^ronhon, *barre de travers.*
Ga^c^roñȣase, R. *f.* ȣas; *attendre quelq. en chemin.*

O^c^roñȣe, Oroñȣe, *il y a un vallon.*
O^c^ronȣagon, son, *le long du vallon.*
Etioroñȣennion, *il y a quantité de vallons.*
Ga^c^roñȣennion, *se promener.* Ch.

Garonhia, *le ciel.* Garonhioron, *le ciel nébuleux.*
Garonhiaksat — Joronhiogeȣen, *beau ciel.*
Garonhiaksaton, Ch. *le ciel se brouiller.*
Ongȣaronhiaksat, *Nous avons mauvais temps;* a Garonhiaksaton, S. neut.
Garonhiaenton, R. *caresser.* Raro dicitur ab Iroquaeis Agnier.
Garonhiatiron, *ciel droit.*

Garonhiageñon, Ch. ens, en, enne; *souffrir.*
ȣasronhiagen, *tu as bien de la peine.*
Garonhiagense, R. acq. *endurer pour quelq.*
Garonhiagen^c^ton, R. *faire souffrir quelq.*

Garonkȣannion, S. *démanger.*
Ongronkȣens, *il me démange.* ȣagronkȣannion.

Oron^c^kȣenna, *leschine, l'épine du dos.*

Garon^c^kȣenstare, S. *parler haut, confusion de voix.*
Garon^c^kȣenstȣannen, *grande confusion et multitude de voix qui parlent ensemble.*
Atron^c^kȣenstȣannen, Pass. S.
Atronskȣenθoton, Ch. *Diminuer ce bruit et cette confusion.*
Ateronkȣanni, R. *chasser, expeller; f.* kȣen. Steronkȣen, erhar.

Garonta, *arbre.* Garontiagon, *couper un arbre.* Ch.
Karontorenseron, Ch. *le fendre.*
Garontiennenon, Ch. *un arbre tomber.*
Garontaga^c^te, *un arbre coupé.* Garontagannha, *un piquebois.*
Garontotsera, *un coffre.* Te garontȣte, *une souricière.* S.

Garóri, R. *raconter*; risk, ri, rianne. Hesrori, *raconte luy.*
Atrori, Ch. pass. *raconter.* Satrorianne, *Va raconter.*
Garoriaton, R. *raconter avec q. chose.*
Atroriase, *raconter de quelq.;* R. *f.* ras.

Garorogon, Ch. roks, rog, roχe; *assembler.* Garorogi, R. *f.* roks.
Gannestarorógon, Ch. *assembler, amasser du blé dans un tas.*
Atrorógon, Ch. *s'assembler.*
Atroroχon, Ch. χes, χe; *s'aller assembler, aller voir.*

Garȣston, Ch. θa, t, tanne; *invoquer l'Otkon sur q. c. songée qu'on donne.*
Garȣstanni, R. *f.* ten.

Garȣt, Ch. θa, ten, tanne; *petuner.*
Garȣtagȣanni, R. *f.* tagȣas; *Prendre le calumet de quelqu'un qui petuner pour fumer.*
ȣagonrȣtágȣas, *que je fume dans ton calumet.*

Garȣt, R. *manger la portion d'un autre.*
Ehiarȣt, *il mangera ta part.*

Garȣten, S. *être affable.*
Gaȣendarȣten, S. *avoir la voix douce, affable.*
Gan^c negatȣten, *eau douce.*
ȣagon^c neganhonθo onnegarȣten askennen asinnontonnionheg, *Je te donne un doux breuvage pour que – – –.*

Otsihȣa^c rôten, *peau passée d'orignac ou vache sauvage.*
Gasihȣarótonni, Ch. *en passer une.*

Gas v. **Gasa**, *donne apporte.*

Gasaa, Ch. *enfant : on nomme aussi ainsi un puisné ou puisnée.*

Gasa, *bouche.*
Gasaga^c renton, Ch. *avoir la bouche ouverte.*
Gaskȣegon pro Gasagȣegon, R. ks, g, χe; *fermer la bouche.*
Ataskȣegon, *fermer sa bouche.*

Gasagaionton, Ch. cum nota local, tes, te, tesere; *faire le cry de victorieux*
Tajesagaiont, *on fait le Kohe.*

Gasaien, S. *être lent.*
Gasajatanni, R. *f.* ten; *retarder quelq. par sa lenteur.*
Gasajáton, *rendre lent; θa*, t, tanne.

Osaheta, *fezolles.* Gasahetageñjon, Ch. *escosser des fezolles.*

Gasatáon, Ch. tas, tanne; *tomber à la renverse.*

Gasaten, R. *porter sur le dos;* tensk, ten, tensere. Inde Agosatensk, *un cheval.*

Gasenda, Ch. *nom, avoir réputation, être considérable.*
Hatisenda son, *ils sont tous considérable.*
Gasendȣannen, Ch. nen, nennen; *être considérable, grand guerrier*
Gasendȣannhaton, R. *rendre, faire quelqu'un considérable.*
Atsendȣannhaton, Ch. *devenir brave.*
Gasendȣtagȣan, R. gȣas, go, gohe; *faire mourir un considérable.*
Atsendȣtagȣan, Pass. Ch. *un capitaine considérable mourir.*
Gasennajen, R. *honorer quelq. huro.*
Atsennajen, Ch. *être beau, bien fait.*
Atsennajenton, Ch. tons, ton, tonsere; *idem.*
Gasendare, Ch. *avoir son nom écrit.*
Gasennaronnion gannearhonge, *leurs noms sont dans le livre.*
Gasennon, R. *donner un nom à quelqu'un.*
Satesnisenda, *Vous avez le même nom.*

Gasennon, *au milieu.*
Sateȣasennon itȣes, *Nous sommes à moitié chemin.*

Gasennion, R. nies, ni, niese; *vaincre quelq.*
Gasennion, Neut. S. *être vaincu.*
Ongesenni, dit on v. g. *dans un festin où l'on ne peut pas tout manger; je suis vaincu.*

Gasense, *haïr*, S. *être fâché.*
ȣaksense nagrihȣanderen, *Je suis fâché d'avoir péché.*

Gascnnonni, minus usitat apud Agnier, *caresser quelq.* Sed
Atsennonni v. Atsennonnion, utriusq. parad. *être heureux, bien*
Taonχen rotsennonni! *O qu'il est aise!*
Atsennonniaton, Ch. *être heureux pour ou par q. c.*

Gasendio, *bon tireur,* Ch.
Gasendaksen, *mauvais tireur, maladroit.*
Atesendioston, *prendre bien sa visée.* Ch.

Gaseráton, Ch. tonsk, ton, tonne; *tendre une peau.*
Gaseratonni v. Gaseratonse, R. *f.* tons; *tendre à quelq.*
Gaseratongȣan, Ch. *destendre une peau.*
Gaseratongȣanni, R. *f.* gȣas.

Gaserohen, Ch. *être méchant homme.*
Atserohâton, Ch. θa, tanne; *faire une méchante action.*
Gaserȣannen, *grande faute.*
Ojerȣannen okti asȣegon aχeion, *Il faudrait bien en avoir pou j'en donnasse à tous.*

Oserenta, *sommeil.*
Gaserentagon, S. *aimer le sommeil, grand dormeur.*
Gaserentonianni, R. *f.* nien; *troubler le sommeil à quelq.*
Gasentaráon, S. taras, ranne, rasere; *avoir sommeil.*
Gaserentio, S. os, o, osere. Gaserentioston, Ch. *avoir beau s*
Gaserentaksenon, S. sens, sen, sensere; *avoir mauvais songe*
Gaserentaȣenrion, *avoir eu un mauvais songe suivi de quelq heur;* ries, rie.
Gaserentontarhon, R. *immitere soporem.*

Gaserhon, Ch. serask, seraȣe; *arroser, jeter l'eau.* Est R. *baptiser.*
Katke eskeseraȣe? *Quand me baptiseras-tu?*
Gaserhoton, Ch. *mouiller avec.*
Gaiatoserhon, S. *être mouillé de la pluye ou autrement.*
Gandigon^c^raserhon,

Oserha, *quelque chose liquide qui s'est épaissi,* v. g. *de la sagamité.*
Oserha ȣasatkaston, *Tu as fait de la bouillie bien épaisse.*
Gaserhonni, Ch. *en faire.*
Ateserhonni, Ch. *de la bouillie s'épaissir.*

Gaseron, Ch. res, re, resere; *suivre, poursuivre.* Est R.
Sagonieres, *il les poursuivent.*
Atatseron, Ch. *idem.*
Tȣataseron, Ch. *aller à 4 pattes.*
Tȣategiseron, *aller sur son derrière,* v. g. *de cane.* Ch.
Gaseriθa, *une traîne, une chariot.*
Gontiseras agosatensk, *les chevaux traînent.*

Oseks, *gomme, bray.* Oseskta, in comp.
Gasestarhon, Ch. *gommer, mattachier* v. g. *une peau.*

Gaseronni, Ch. *accommoder q. c. faire une hache.*
Inde vocant Europæi, sed est 1ae conj. Aseronni, Ch.
Onseronni, adv. *ensemble, au même lieu.*

Onseronni ȣahontien, *Ils sont dans la même cabane.*
Skaseronni, Ch. *satisfaire.*
Jesȣs soseronni nyongȣarihȣanderen, *Jéus a satisfait pour nos péchés.*
Gaseronniaton, Ch. *accommoder avec q. chose.*
Gaseronnianni, R. *f.* nien; *accommoder à quelqu'un.*
Gaseronni, *habiller quelq.* R.
Atseronni, Ch. *s'habiller, s'accommoder.*
Atseronniaton, Ch. *s'accommoder avec q. c.*
Gaiataseronni, R. Atiatseronni, Ch.
Gaseronniasion, R. *déshabiller quelq.*
Atseronniasion, Ch. sions, si, sionhe.

Gasie, R. *porter sur son dos comme à cheval.*
Gasiharon, Ch. *boucher.*
Atsiharon, Ch. *être bouché, fermé.*
Gasiharongȣan, Ch. *desboucher.* Atsiharongȣan, Ch. *se desboucher.*
Gasiharon^c^kon, Ch. *boucher avec q. chose; p.* & *f.* kȣa.
Kasiharáon, Ch. ras, ranne; *être trop pressé.*
Kasiharase, neut. acq. S. *être trop à l'étroit.*
ȣatȣagesiharas, *cela ne peut pas entrer où je le voulais mettre.*

Osinnigota, *cheville du pied.*

Gasire, *une couverte à grand poil,* v. *étoffe Iroquoise.*

Gasisat, *un pilon.*

Kaskaráon, S. raȣas, raȣe; *ouvrir la bouche.*
Kaskaraȣaton, S. *boâiller.*
Gaskaraton, S. θa, t, θe; *être amer, désagréable au goût.*
Kaskaratonȣe, neut. acq. S. tons, ton v. tonhas.
Gaskáren, Ch. *mordre;* rha, ren, ranne. Est R.
Roskoraskon, *le grand mordeur.*

Oskaro, *du chanvre.* Gaskorohon, Ch. *aller chercher du chanvre.*

Gaskenn, *corpus a quo discessit anima.*
Hatisken agon, *manes.*
Eskennannigé, *au pais des âmes.*
Ti saskennennont, *tu as un visage de mort.*
Gaskennonton, Ch. tes, nont, tese; *aller au pays des âmes.*
Inde forte Oskennonton, *Cerf* quia timidum est animal quod se semper putet esse mortuum.
Gaskennonteton, *locus quo itur post mortem.*
Garonhiage jeskennonseθa niagorihȣioston, *Les Chrétiens vont au ciel après la mort.*
Naie jeskennonteθa^c^kȣa nonhȣentsiagon nierihȣanderaχon, *C'est le péché qui fait aller aux enfers.*
Gaskennonteton, R. *faire mourir quelqu'un de peur.*
Gaskendendis, R. *porter malheur à quelqu'un.*
ȣahotiskennendis, *Il y a eu un mauvais presage contre eux.*

Gaskennatiagon, S. *avoir la jaunisse.*

Oskennen, *en paix, doucement.*
Tosken, toskenha, *loin.*
Toskenha etȣagatention, *a longe profectus sum.*

Gaskenra, *la guerre.* Inde
Hoskenragetete, S. 2ae conj. *soldat; impf.* takȣe, *f.* tak.
Oskenrha, *la rouille.*
Gaskenrhare, *il y a de la rouille.*

Oskokȣa, S. *portion des Agoianders.* Raoskokȣa.
Gaskokonni, Ch. *faire de ces portions, mettre en réserve pour les anciens et considérables.*

Gasko, *être dans la chaudière,* dicitur de re quæ habet vel habuit vitam: *quelque animal estre dans l'eau.* Desinit in O in omnibus temporibus.
Erhar ȣahasko, *Il a fait festin d'un chien mis dans la chaudière.*
Atatesko, *mettre pour soi dans la chaudière quelq. animal.*

Gaskoon, Ch. kos, konne, kosere; *s'enfoncer dans l'eau, se noyer.*
Gaskoton, R. *faire noyer, enfoncer dans l'eau.*
Gaskohon, Ch. *mettre quelq. animal dans l'eau non pas pour l'y cuire.*
Annoȣara hoskohon, *Il a mis une tortue dans l'eau;* os v. ohose.
Gaskose, R. *mettre dans l'eau pour quelq.*
Hotkon hoñaskose, *On lui a mis du venin dans sa tasse.*
Hotkon hoteskohose, *Le démon s'est mis dans son plat.*
Gaskogȣan, R. gȣas, go, gohe; *retirer de l'eau.*
Onsahoñaskógo, *on la tiré hors de l'eau.*
Ateskogȣan, Ch. *se retirer soymême hors de l'eau.*
Gaskonsage, *au saut ainsi appellé par les Iroquois,* a Gaskonsa, *dent. Saut à pic.*
Etioskonsenton, *Idem quod* Gannaȣenton, *chute d'eau, cascade.*

Gaskȣa-egon, Ch. *battre le blé ou autre légume;* ks, g, χe.

Gaskont, act. θa, tan, tanne; *rostir quelq. animal.*
Seskonten, *rostis* v. g. *ce poisson.*
Ateskont, Ch. *rostir pour soy.* Gaskont, pans. *être rosti.*
Gaskont jongȣannenhisacton, *Nous avons assaissonné de poisson rosti.*
Gaskontaon, Ch. tas, tanne, tasere; *animal tomber dans le feu, se brûler.*
ȣahaskontanne, *il est tombé dans le feu.*
Gaskonθanni, *f.* θas, R. *rostir à quelqu'un.*
Tageȣaronθas, *fais moi rôtir de la chair.*
Gaskonθon, R. *faire tomber dans le feu.*
ȣahoñaskonθo, *on l'a brûlé, mis dans le feu.*
Gaskontagȣan, R. *retirer du feu,* cum part. reit. Jesȣs sesongȣaskontagȣan jonhȣentsiagon.

Oskȣira, *branche d'arbre.*
Hoskȣiriaχon, *il est allé couper une branche.*
Kaskȣiriagon, Ch. *quitter son pays pour demeurer chez l'ennemi.*
Onne ȣatieskȣiriag, *Voila qu'on se réfugie chez son ennemi.*

Askonte, S. *écorce.* Gaskontara, in comp.
Raoskonte, *son écorce.*
Gaskontario, *belle écorce.* Okario, *idem.*
Gaskontaraton, Ch. tons, ton, tonne; *mettre des écorces sur l'échafaud.*
Gaskontaragohon, Ch. *en aller querir.*

Gasniennon, R. nons, non, nonre; *travailler pour quelq.*
Atasniennon, Pass. Ch.
Gasniennonron, *aller travailler pour quelq.*
Atasniennonron, *idem.*

Gasnonge, *doigt*, Ch. Gasnonsa, in comp.
ȣaθoñasnonsiag, *on luy a coupé le doigt.*

Gasnoron, Ch. re, reskȣe, reg; *aller faire viste q. chose.*
Josnore, *impson.* Agosnoreg, *cela seroit bien viste.*
Ejosnoreg, *ce sera bien viste.*
Raȣendasnore, *il parle viste.*
Gasnoraton, Ch. *dépêcher q. chose, haster.*
Gasrihȣasnorat, *expédie viste l'affaire.*
Atisnore, *croître promptement en âge.*
Hondatisnore, *ils vieillissent bientôt.*

Osogȣa, *noix*, S. Raosogȣa, *sa noix.*
Gasnora°kon, R. kȣa v. kȣe; } *reprocher à quelqu'un qu'il a dit ou*
Gasnorakȣanni, *f.* kȣen, } *fait q. chose.*

Gason, *faire.* In comp. frequens; *pns.* & *f.* sa, n, saanne.
Diȣ raonhȣentsison, *Dieu a fait la terre.*
Sagoiatison ongȣe, *Il a fait l'homme.*

Gason, *achever, consommer*, Ch.
Onne ȣaksa v. ȣakson, *j'ai tout achevé.*
Atson, Ch. *être consommé, brûlé.*
Onna ontsa gannatarok, *Le pain est brûlé, réduit à rien.*
Atiatatson, Ch. *brûler.*
Gasaanni, R. *f.* sas; *consommer à quelqu'un q. chose.*
ȣaskȣannenstasas, *Vous nous consommes notre bled.*
Atsaanni, R. recip. *être consommé à quelqu'un.*
Ongȣatnenstasas, *Mon blé s'est consommé à moi.*
Garihȣision, Ch. *conclure l'affaire.*
Areko jongȣatrihȣisaanni, *Notre affaire n'est pas encore faitte.*

Gason, *tuer*, (*de multitudine.*)
ȣaonχisa, *on nous a tué.*
Ontagasaaton, Ch. θa, t, tanne; *épuiser tout.*
Ontagasat, *elle a tout épuisé.*
Tȣatsaaton, Ch. *être épuisé totalement.*
Onne ȣaθontsat ȣahontenti, *Ils sont tous partis.*
Onne etiogatsaaton, *tout est épuisé.*
Onne eθondatsaaton ehotiageñon, *Ils sont sortis tous.*

Gasogeñon, Ch. ens, en, ensere; *broncher d'un cheval.*
Gasogenskon, freq. S.
Jaten gaiannatogen agosatensk josogenskon, *Mon cheval bronche sæpe.*
Gasogenton, *faire broncher.*
Atesogenton, *se mettre à broncher.*

Gasonne, *le dos*, Ch.
Gasonnionkon, *deffendre, vêtare.* V. Sup. 1ª conj.

Osonȣe, *fosse, creux, trou profond.*
Ken niosonȣa, *Il y a un trou de cette grandeur.*
Gasonjonni, Ch. *faire un trou, creux, fosse.*

Gasonraton, Ch. θa, tanne. Gasonratanni, *f.* ten.
Josonrataskon, *fainéante qui a de la peine à tout.*

Gasonrion, Ch. *gouster;* ries, ri, riese.
Jaten te jonnatasonrion ok eθo ȣagȣajatȣten, *Elle n'entra pas dans le fort, elle fût brûlée là même.*
ȣage ȣarasonri, *J'ai goûté de la chair.*
Gasonrieᶜton, *faire goûter.* R.

Gasȣan, S. sȣas, so, sohe; *flairer, sentir.*
Ongeso, *j'ai flairé.* Ongeȣaraso, *j'ai senti la viande.*
Gasȣaton, R. *faire flairer.*
Atesȣaton, Ch. *faire flairer à soimême.* Satesȣat.

Kasȣannet, Ch. *doubler;* θa, t, tanne.
Atasȣannet, S. *être double.*
Gasȣannetarion, Ch. *doubler de plusieurs doubles.*
Atasȣannetarion, S.
Gasȣannetase, R. *doubler, augmenter à quelq.*
Te horihȣannetarion, *Il a joint plusieurs affaires*, a Kannannet. (Onnejout.)

Gasȣaton, S. *être méchant;* ȣa, t, tanne.
Josȣat, *Que cela est fâcheux.*
Rosȣat, *le méchant, l'importun.*
Gasȣaton, S. *haïr pour q. chose.*
Gasȣatanni, R. *f.* ten; *haïr quelqu'un ou quelque chose par l'importunité et incommodité qu'on en reçoit.*
Gasȣenon, Ch. ens, en, ense; *haïr.* Est R.
ȣagonsȣen, *je te hais.* Gasȣenseron, freq.
Atatsȣeñon, Ch. *se haïr, détester sa vie.*
GasȣaθeÑon, Ch. θens, θen, θensere; *avoir envie de manger q. chose de bon.*
Gasȣaθenston, *être la cause de cette envie; causer le manquement d'assaisonnement ou de q. c. de bon.*
Gasȣaθeton, S. θa, t, tanne; *éclairer*, cum nota local.
Te taksȣatet, *éclaire moy.*
ȣatiosȣaθe gȣann, *Il se fit un grand jour.*
Te josȣaθeθa, *la lumière.*

Osȣen v. **Osȣenta,** *charbon éteint, du noir.*
Osȣentȣskon, *de pur noir.*
Gasȣentarhon, Ch. *marquer avec du noir.*

Osȣengare, S. *une planche.* Gasȣengaronni, Ch. *en faire.*
Jesȣengaronniaθa, *un moulin à planche.*

Ostarokȣa, S. *de la rassade. Ils appellent aussi ainsi du menu plomb.*

Gastaθeñon, S. extra comp. Aθeñon, in comp. *être sec;* θens, θen, θensere.
Jostaθens, *cela est sec.*
Ganniataθeñon, S. *avoir soif, avoir le gozier sec.*
Ganniataθenston, *ce qui fait sécher.*
Gastaθaton, act. θa, t, tanne; *faire sécher.*
Sestaθat, *fais sécher.*
Gastaθase, R. *f.* θas; *faire sécher à quelqu'un.*

Gastahron, Ch. rons, re, ronne; *ne trouver pas ce qu'on cherche.*
Gaiatastahron, R. *ne pas trouver quelqu'un.*
Garihȣastahron, Ch. *ne pas trouver l'affaire, la nouvelle.*

Gastaront, Ch. θa, ten, tanne; *sucer, tirer avec les lèvres.* Est R.
Hetsestaronten, *Donne lui à tetter.*
Gastarontanni, R. *f.* θas; *sucer quelqu'un, nourrir quelq. à q. chose vivante.*
Takstaronθas v. Tagestaronθas neȣateȣeton erhar, *Nourris moi un petit chien quand ta chienne portera.*
Gastarontagȣan, Ch. *se déprendre de ce qu'on suce.*

Kastegenhejon, Ch. hejons, heje, hejonsere; *désespérer, perdre patience.*
Kastegenhejaton, idem, *perdre l'espérance.*
Kastegenheiase, R. *faire perdre l'espérance à quelqu'un.*

Kasteriheñon, S. ens, en, ensere; *être pressé, avoir hâte.*
Kasterihaton, S. *se hâter pour q. chose.*
Kasterihaton, R. *hâter quelq.;* θa, t, tanne.
Tetkonsterihatanne, *Je retourneray te hâter.*
Tetkasteriheñon, *à la haste.*

Gasteronhon, *refuser de faire q. c. qu'on commande;* hons; hȣe.
Jontasterhoñhȣe, dit on d'un enfant qui n'obéit pas aux commands de ses parents.

Ostiesera, *les poûmons.*

Gastonton, S. tons, tonte, tonne; *prétexter q. chose.*
Θennon ȣagostonte, *Quel prétexte a-t-on eu?*

Gastonrion, R. *toucher au mal de quelq. et luy causer de la douleur.*
ȣaskistonri si etȣagnonhȣaktannik, *Tu m'as fait mal là où je suis incommodé.*

Gastontere, S. *jointure des os.*
Atestonteragȣan, *un os être demis.* S.

Gastoron, re, reg, Ch. Sastóron, *dépêche, fais viste.* Hæc 2ª persona sola ferme est in usu. Tsiastoron, *vos 2.*

Ostosera, *plumes d'oiseau qu'on a plumé.* S.
Gastosaron, Ch. ronsk, ron, ronhe; *plumer.*

Gastotsiron, *baiser.*

Gasθon v. **Gasθonha,** in comp. *être petit.*
Gannatsiasθonha, *petite chaudière.*
Gasθoton, Ch. θa, t, tanne; *faire petit.*
ȣasrihȣasθot, *tu amoindris l'affaire.*
Gasθotanni, R. *f.* ten; *faire petit à quelqu'un.*
Gasθose, neut. acq. S. *f.* θos; *trouver petit.*
Ongȣasθos, *cela me semble peu.* Oȿtonha, *un peu.*

Gat, in fine vocabuli cui præponitur par la redup. signat *unitatem.* S. *vel* Ch.
Skat, *un.* Skarihȣat, *une chose.*
Tsionhȣentsiat, *un seul pays.*
Tsagiatat, *Nous ne sommes qu'un, nous sommes frères.*
Sajatat, *un seul;* Skajatat, *une seule.*
Sic Sagat *vel* Sagarihȣat, *idem est.*
Sajonhȣentsiat, Sa-agiatat, Sa-agȣajatat, Sahatiatat, *eædem sunt;* Sagontiatat, *eædem sunt.*

Gata, in comp. Gatara, *fange.*
Okti jotara, *parole de mépris, homme de néant.*
Gataragetskȣan, S. *se lever,* dit on d'un malade qui a peine à se relever.

Gataχon, Ch. *p.* & *f.* χ, n, χese, *courir;* χes, pro habitu.
Θo gataχi erhar, *le chien court.*
Ontahataχe, *il vient en deçà en haste.*
Gataχeton, quando locus exprimitur ad quem pergimus; θa, t, tanne.
Ken nongȣati esotaχeton, *Il s'en est couru de ce côté là.*

Gatagȣentaron, *être gisant.*

Kataon, *se lever debout.* Vide Conj. anomalium.
Tektas, ȣatektanne, tektasere, dicitur tertas de habitu.
Onne gen te hatas nhetsieña, *Ton enfant est il asses fort pour se tenir debout? Se tient-il debout?*
Te gete, de actu; te sete, te hate.
Katastou, R. sθa, st, stanne; *faire tenir debout.*

Gatase, in comp. stum, *tourner autour;* stes, se, sese.
Eθotinnonsatases, *ils tournent autour de la cabane.*
Ganniengȣatases, *la neige pirouette.*

Garatase, in comp. cum voce pass. *entortiller, tordre.*
Joteratase, *cela est entortillé, enlacé.*
Joteroñaratase, *un fer tordu,* seu *une vrille percerette.*
Joterontatase, *arbre, colomne fait en vis* seu *canalée.*

Gaθare, *parler;* tarha, taren, taranne. Assumit in dual part. dualit.
Te jagniθarha, *Luy et moi parlons ensemble.*
Gaθaron, *de multit.*
Gaθaranni, R. *f.* θarhas, *tancer quelqu'un.*

Gate, *être;* takȣe, teg.
Toskenhe etkáte, *cela est bien loin, différend.*
Gate, in comp. *être présent.*
Jaten sondigon^crate, *Il n'a pas d'esprit.*
Ken ongȣentiokȣate, *Nous autres qui sommes ici en bande.*
Ti gate, *être différent.* Ti hatite, *ils sont différents.*
Ti ejatate v. Ti jejatennon, *C'est une autre sorte d'homme.*
Te hatiatate onseronni te hatiatennon hotinnonsionni, *Les Français sont différents des Iroquois.*

Katen, anom. tens, ten, tensere; *se lever en haut.*
ȣatiagȣaten, ȣatitȣat, ȣatisȣat, ȣaθatit, ȣatkontiten.
Katenston, *faire lever en haut.*
Te gȣatenston okȣesen, *On a fait lever la perdrix.*
At de homine qui evehitur in altum dic : Te hoñajatakȣan v. Te hoñajaratato n, *On a levé en haut.*
Katense, R. *se lever pour ou contre quelqu'un.*
Ti hetsetens, *assurge illi.* ȣaθonatitens, *on se leva sur eux.*

Gatennion, in comp. nions, nion, nionhe; *changer.*
Garihȣatennion, Ch. *changer l'affaire.* Est R.
ȣahoñarihȣatenni Onnontio, *On a change l'affaire d' Onnontio.*
Gaiatatennion, Atiatatennion, S. *se déguiser.*
Atrihȣatennion, Ch. *l'affaire se changer.*
Atrihȣatennionse, R. *l'affaire se changer à quelqu'un.*

Gatenson, *impf.* tensonnen, *f.* tensa; *épais, gros.*
Ken nigatens, *épais de cela.* Nigatensa, *un peu épais.*
Nigagenhatensk, *de la toile.*
Gagenston, *faire épais.*

Gatentaron, Ch. *estendre au sec;* tarons *vel* tara, taron, taronhe.
Snenhatentaron si etiorakȣt, *étends le blé au soleil.*
Gatentaron^ckon, Ch. *ce sur quoi l'on estend.*
Gatentaronse, R. *f.* rons; *estendre au sec pour quelq.*

Ga^cte^cra, *racine à coudre canot.*
Gaterogeñion, Ch. *netoyer, racler des racines.*
Ga^cterogeniase, R. *accommoder des racines à quelqu'un.*

Gateronkȣanni, R. nisk, kȣen, nire; *chasser, éloigner.*

Gateronni, S. *être poltron.*
Gateroñon, S. ons, onn, onsere.
Gat-ronton, S. *craindre pour q. chose.*
Gat-rontanni, R. *f.* ten; *faire craindre quelqu'un.*

Gaθeñon, In comp. tantum.
Jostaθen, *sec.* Gaȣaraθen, *chair sèche.* Vide supra Gastaθeñon.
Gaθase, R. ȣageȣaratase; *Je trouve la viande sèche.*
Gaθeñon, S. *ne vouloir pas;* θens, θen, θensere.

Oθesera, S. *farine.* Raoθesera, *sa farine.*
Gaθeseronni, Ch. nisk, ni, nianne; *faire de la farine.*
Gaθeseronnianni, R. *f.* nien.

Gaθeseronniaton, Ch. *en faire avec q. chose.*
Jeθeseronniaθa, *un moulin à moudre du blé.*
Gaθeton, Ch. θa, t, tanne; *piler farine ou autre chose.*
Gaθetanni, R. *f.* ten; *piler à quelqu'un.*
Gaθeta[c]kon, Ch. *ce avec quoi ou le lieu où l'on pile.*

Gatie, *voler* (tie pro actu, ties pro habitu), tie, tiese.
Gontities, *les oiseaux.*

Kato, S. *nasse.* Raota, *ses.*
Gatoseronni, *faire des nasses.*
Gatoserohon, Ch. *les mettre dans l'eau.*
Gatoseroñonnon, *aller pêcher avec des nasses.*
Gatoserogȣan, *les tirer de l'eau.*

Gatogen, Ch. toχa, tog, toganne; *s'appercevoir, savoir.*
Areχo te getoχa, *Je n'en sçais encore rien.*
ȣagrihatoganne, *Je va m'informer de l'affaire.*
Songȣandigon[c]ratoχa Diȣ, *Dieu voit cœurs.*
Gatogen togenske, *il est vrai, être vrai.*
Hajatógen garonhia rotaȣejennonni, *Il y a une personne déterminée qui a fait le ciel.*
Egatogenne egarihȣatogenn, *Cela se vérifiera.*
Areko jorihȣatógen, *la nouvelle n'est pas encore assuré.*

Gatógen, regit futurum quando signat *à fin que.*
Agȣast asrihȣiost gatogen esatsennonni garonhiage, *Sois bon chrestien à fin que tu sois heureux au ciel.*

Gatogase, S. *s'appercevoir de quelq. action d'un autre; f.* togas.
Gatogáton, *s'appercevoir par q. chose.* Ch.
Θennon ȣastógat, *Quel indice as tu de?*
Jaten skat te ȣagtogaton, *je n'ay aucune preuve.*

Gatogeñon, S. in comp. Gandigonratógen, ens, en, ensere; *sçavoir.*
Jaten te ȣagennigonratogen, *je ne suis pas assuré.*
Gatogenston, *s'assurer par q. chose.*
Gatogenstanni, *f.* ten, *assurer quelqu'un par q. chose.*
Tagrihȣatogensten, *Eclaircis moy de la nouvelle.*

Gatogenton, *être liberal, avoir grand cœur.* S. θa, t.

Gatoge[c]ton, *choisir, marquer, déterminer.*
Senniseratóge[c]t, *marque le jour.*
Gatoge[c]tanni, R. *f.* ten; *marquer, déterminer à quelqu'un.*

Gatoge[c]ton, etiam pass. signat *estre saint.*
Gaiatatoge[c]ton v. Gaiatatogeston, S.
Enniseratogeton, *jour saint, le dimanche.*
Ejorhenne ejongȣentatogestanne, *Nous aurons dimanche.*

Te gatorarágon, Ch. raks, rag, raχe; *presser, serrer.*
ȣateskȣasitorarag, *tu me presse, foule le pié.*
Te gatorarakton, Ch. *presser avec q. chose,* a Garagon, in comp. tantum usitatum.
ȣahagonsorarag, *il s'est frissé le visage.*

Te gatoraraksion, Ch. *séparer se qui étoit joint ensemble.*
Te sȣatoraraksion, *se séparer.*
Tonsontoraraksi, *Cela s'est séparé.*

Gatsannion, Ch. nis, nig, nisere; *craindre.*
Garihȣatsannion, *apprèhendre une affaire.* Est R.
Jaten te getsannise, *Je ne les crains pas.*
Gatsanniton, *être formidable.* S.
Rongȣetatsannit, *homme redoutable.*
Jotsannit v. Jotsaniθa, *chose étrange.*
Atetsanniton v. Atetsannitanni, R. θa, t; *épouvanter quelqu'un.*

Gatsaste, Ch. *être fort;* tekȣe, teg.
Gaȣendatsaste, *voix forte, efficace.*
Atȣendatsaste, *rendre sa voix efficace.*
Atesatste, Ch. *s'efforcer, faire un dernier effort.*

Gatse, S. extra comp. Gatsita, in comp. *gourde, bouteille.*
Gatsetonte, *il y a des bastions.*
Gatsetogon, *gourde vuide.*

Gatsennen, S. *animal domestique, serviteur*, *esclave.*

Otsera, *chaussée.* Te gatseraronhon, *y avoir un chaussée à travers.*
Jaten te ontnegongot agȣat ȣatkannegata si etiotseraronȣe: *L'eau ne passe point, mais s'arrête à la chaussée.*

Gatsiaraȣi, R. *donner du petun; f.* rhas.

Katsiahon, R. hons, hon, honsere; *parler à l'oreille de quelqu'un.*
Tetsiáron, *id. tous les deux.*

Gatsien, S. *plat,* extra comp. N. Raotsien, *C'est le plat d'un tel.*
Gatsiaȣesen, Ch. *polir un plat.*
Gatsienton, Ch. θa, t, tanne; *puiser de.*
Gannegotsienton, *puiser de l'eau.*
Satogȣatserotsient, *prens en une cuillerée.*
Gatsientakon, Ch. *puiser avec q. chose;* kȣa, kȣanne.
Gannaᶜkon jetsientakȣa, *un sceau.*
Gatsienhon, Ch. hes v. he, ha, hese; *aller puiser de l'eau.*
Gatesientanniseron, R. *aller puiser de l'eau pour quelqu'un.*
Gatsientanni, R. *f.* ten; *donner à manger à quelqu'un.*
Tagetsienten, *Donne moi à manger.*

Gatsienton, R. θa, t, θe; *médeciner, guérir quelq.*
Sagotsientannion jegaiontas, *Il guérit tous les malades.*
Hatetsiens, *médecin.*
ȣatetsiens v. ȣatetsienha, *chose médicinale.*
Atetsientakon, Ch. *se servir de q. c. pour médecine.*

Gatsienha, *foyer.*
Katsienhiagon, Ch. *diviser le foyer.*
Skatsienhat, *un seul feu.*
Te jagȣatetsienhannegen, *Nos foyers sont les uns près des autres.*
Te jotignitsienhat, *Nous sommes au même feu.*

Neθo nonȢe te jagȢatetsienhatre, *Nos foyers sont à cette distance l'un de l'autre.*

Gatsiaregon, Ch. *pousser le feu, l'atiser.*

Gatsiareseron, Ch. *éparpiller le feu à fin qu'il s'allume.*

Gatsihajen, Ch. *tenir conseil;* takȢe, èn, enne.

OtsigȢara, *charbon allumé.*

KenniotsigȢarandȢtes, *brazier àrdent.*

GatsigȢaront, Ch. *faire un nœud.*

JotsigȢaronton, *il y a des nœuds.*

Otsihensta, *noir.* Gatsihenstatsi, *être noir, vêtu de noir.*

Gatsinn, Ch. *masle;* tam de hominibus quam belluis, extra comp.

Gatsinnata, in comp. v. Gatsitsera.

Ratsitserio, *bon chasseur.*

Gatsinnogáton, Ch. *boetter.*

OtsinnigȢar, *couleur verte, bile.*

RotsinnigȢaraksen, *bilieux, colère.*

GatsinnigȢaraȢenrion, S. *La bile se remuer et causer vomissemens.*

Otsinneta, *lente vermine.* Tsinnon, *des poux.*

Otsinnetare, *il y a des lentes.*

Gatsinnionkera, *morue.*

HotsinnionkȢarȢt, *il y a de la morue.*

HotetsinnionkȢarȢtatie, *il va avec la morue.*

GatsinnionkerageȢen, Ch. *se moucher.*

GatsinnionkerageȢenni, R. *moucher quelq.*

Onniatarajenti gatsinnionkerageȢaθa, *un mouchoir.*

Otsinnoñа, *vers.* Gatsinnoñagon, *être plein de vers.*

Otsinnonhiaᵘta, *veine, nerf.*

Katsinnonhiatiagi, R. *seigner quelq.*

Katsinnonhiatannerágon, Ch. *prendre une veine pour l'autre.*

Otsire, *feu.* **Gentsirat,** *il y a du feu.*

Agentsiraranne, *le feu est tombé.*

Gentsiraieri, S. *tenir conseil.*

Gentsiranno, *le feu être éteint,* seu *le conseil fini.*

Gatsiregon, S. *succer.*

GatsirontagȢan, Ch. *prendre du feu.*

Gatsirontaton, Ch. *branler un brandon de feu.*

Gatsirentaon, Ch. *douleur s'appaiser;* tas, tanne, tasere.

Gatsirentaton, Ch. *faire appaiser la douleur.*

Gatsio, os, S. *être infirme, maladif habituellement.*]

Gatsioston, *rendre infirme.*

Gatsiohontorianni, S. *ressentir des atteintes de quelque indisposition habituelle.*

Gatsiostanni, R. *causer quelq. infirm habituelle.*

Gatsista, *feu.* Gatsistaien, S. *tenir conseil, allumer le feu du conseil.*

GatsistontagȢan, Ch. *oster du feu.*

Gatsistontagohon, *aller querir du feu.* Ch.

Otsistok, *étoile*, S. Otsistokȣa, in comp.
Gatsistokȣarannentágon, *étoile attaché.*
Gatsistokȣarannentaᶜkton, Ch. *attacher des étoiles.*
Gatsistogatannion erhar, *chien moucheté blànc et noir.*
Gatsistȣt, *avoir une taye.* S.
Otsiokȣa, S. *portion, morceau de chair.*
Asen niȣatsiokȣage, 3 *portions.*
Gatsiokonni, Ch. *faire les portions d'un festin.*
Otsitsia, *fleur, houblon.*
Gatsitsiararágon, *fleur épanouye.*
Gatstitsionni, Ch. *faire de la bière.*
Jotsitsiont raonnonhȣarore, *Il a une fleur à son bonnet.*
Kakȣan, Ch. kȣa, kȣe, kȣanne; *lever de terre.*
ȣatkekȣe, *je prends, je leve de terre;* ȣatisekȣe, ȣaθakȣe.
Te sekȣa, *lève cela de terre.*
Kajatakȣan, R. *enlever q. c. vivante.*
Gakȣan, R. *enlever à q. l., luy oster q. c.; p. & f.* kȣa, kȣasere.
ȣahoñaχȣa, *on luy a osté.*
ȣaontatekȣa, *on s'entrepille.*
Gaχare, S. *brayer.* Raoχare, *son brayer.*
Ateχare, *avoir un brayer;* re, ren.
Ateχarotsion, Ch. *oster son brayer.* Est etiam R.
Gaχen, cum part. te, *joindre.*
Te hieχen, 2 *jumeaux.*
Te gannehȣaχen, 2 *peaux cousues ensemble.*
Tontageχas, *joins moy cela.*
Gaχahon, *plusieurs choses jointes.*
Te tȣaȣendaχahon, *joignons nos voix.*
Te jongȣandegonraχahon, *nos pensées, esprits sont unis.*
Kaχasion, *desjoindre*, Ch. v. Kaχasiongȣan, est R. *partager, séparer.*
Tȣateχasion, *se séparer*, Ch.
Gaχȣa, *morceau.* Gaχȣio, *bon morceau.*
Gaχȣentaon, Ch. *avoir achevé sa portion.*
Gaχȣannen, Ch. *grand mangeur, gourmand.*
Katson, R. *gaigner au jeu quelq ; p. & f.* sa, *n.* tanne.
Katsannon, freq. Atentson, pass. Ch. *gagner au jeu.*

VERBA 3ae CONJUGATIONIS.

Ehiaᶜraon, Ch. re, ranne, v. rag, rasere; *se souvenir.*
Ehiaᶜrakon, Ch. *se souvenir par q. c.*
Ehiaᶜrakȣanni, R. *f.* kȣen; *faire souvenir quelqu'un.*
Ehiarase, R. *se souvenir de quelqu'un.*
Ekiaron, R. rons, ron, ronne; *nourrir, élever quelqu'un.*
Atchiaron, Ch. *croître en âge, devenir grand.*

Ejen, R. ensk, en, ensere; *encourager.*
Hetsijen Jesȣs, *exhortes, pries Jésus.*

En, In præt. ttum est in usu, *dire.*
Jȣagen, *j'ai dit.*
Isen, Ihaȣen, Raȣen, Jaȣen, &c. *præs.* et *imp.* supplentur per Igatonk, *je dis*; Gatonhakȣe, *je disois. Fut.* et *aorist* supplentur per Egiron, v. simpliciter engi esiron v. ensi.
F. N. Jaten hoθennon tagironne v. te gatonne.

Igen, Igennen, aliquando supplet. verbum subst. sum, es, est.
Raȣendio igen, *il est le maître.*
Aliquando signat. diminutionem rei, v. g. Hinnonha igen, *un peu loin.* Raienteri igen, *Il sçait un peu l'affaire.*

Enhȣaten, *avoir pour neveu;* Aχienhȣ, *mes neveux;* Enhȣatensera, *népotisme.*

Ennajeton, non est in usu, sed
Ennajeta^c^kon, takȣa, tak, takȣe; *se moquer de q. c.* ou *de quelqu'un.* Est R.
Skȣannaietakȣa, *tu nous railles.*

Ennageraton, R. *aliquando habere aliquem vel aliquid pro lege, regula.*
Ennagaraton, neut. *se servir de q. c. pour règle.*
Naie honnennageraton hatiskenni, *Les anciens avoient cela pour règle.*
Atȣendageraton niongȣatetsins, *le songe est la reigle de nos vies.*

Ennaȣa, *langue.* Satennasonten, *tire la langue.*
Tȣatennokaraȣan, *tirer la langue par dérision.*
Tȣatennokaraȣenni, R. *tirer la langue contre quelq.*

Ennatsa, *fesses,* Ch. est 2^ae^.
Rannatsatske, *In clunibus.*
Gannatsajagon, R. *fustiger quelq.* v. Gannatsaregon.

Ennekȣannen, *avaler;* nha, nn, nhasere.
ȣahonne^c^kȣann, *il a avalé.*
Ennekȣanna^c^ton, *avaler tout d'un coup.*

Ennejon, Ch. *suer, faire suerie;* ons, on, onne.
Ennejontenni, R. *suer pour ou avec quelqu'un.*
Sneionθo agenneion, *faire chauffer les pierres que je sue.*

Ennejonskȣa, *suerie.*

Ennejon, S. *faire festin.*
Ennejonkon, *faire festin de q. c., donner à quelq. de quoi faire festin.*

Ennenron, Ch. *animal être en chaleur;* res, re, resere.
Onne ȣagiennenre ongnitsennen, *Nos chiens sont en chaleur.*

Tȣennenstren, Ch. *lier les bras à la façon des esclaves.*
Tȣatnenstren, *être ainsi lié.*
Tȣanneregȣaraon, Ch. *fulgurare.*

Ennt, R. *parler à quelqu'un ou de quelqu'un.*
ȣaongȣenhas, *me dit on.* ȣasagaȣenhas, *il leur dit.*

Enniaȣe, *cent :* huic proponitur partic. Te habet tantum plural.
Skat te jagȣenniaȣe, *nous sommes cent.*

Te skenniaȣe, Te honnenniaȣe, et sic conjungitur quando est sermo de re vivente.

Plusquam perf. Enniaȣennen, f. niaȣeg v. niaȣehag.

Quando vero est sermo de inanimatis, dices :

Skat te ȣenniaȣe, *un cent;* Tegni te ȣenniaȣe, 200; Enniaȣesera, *centaine;* Skat niȣenniaȣeserasen, *mille* seu *une dizaine de cent.*

Ojeri atejagȣenniaȣe asen tsiagȣenniaȣeserare, *nous sommes* 1300.

Ennihen, *præt.* & *fut.* sunt tantum in usu; *emprunter.*

Etiagonnihen, *on a déjà emprunté.*

ȣagonni, *je te preste.* Tagni, *prete moy.*

Ennihase inna, *emprunter de quelqu'un.*

Ennihason, *aller emprunter;* se, sa, sere.

Honnihaskon, *grand emprunteur.*

Egoñiennihas, *j'emprunterai de toy.*

Enniôt, *inviter au festin;* R. θa, ten, tanne.

Atenniot, Ch. *faire festin.*

Atenniotaken, Ch. *faire festin de.*

Atenniotasken, S. *faire souvent festin.*

Ennhonsa, *avoir pour gendre.* Raȣennhonsa, *son gendre.*

Ennet, R. *coucher un enfant dans son sein;* θa, t.

Hienneθa, *je le couche avec moy.*

Goñjennetakȣan, *dit l'Agnier à l'Onnejȣt.* Tȣennigatiagon.

Ennisegȣan v. **Enniskȣan**, S. gȣas, go, gohe; *différer.*

Enniskȣaton, *différer pour quelque chose.*

Ennisera, *échaffaut.* Enniserare, *il y a un échaffaut.*

Jontatenniseraren, *on met sur l'eschaffault.*

Ontetenniseraȣeron, *on le vuide, on renvoie les prisonniers.*

Ennisera, *jour.*

ȣennisera onȣe v. okti ȣenniseratéa, *un jour ouvrier.*

Jate ȣenniserâge, *tous les jours.*

Enniserokte, Ch. θa, ten, tanne; *passer le jour.*

V. Enniseriagon, *assumit plerumq.* notam localitatis.

Enniseroktakon, *le lieu ou la chose pourquoi on passe le jour.*

Enniseraronni, *avoir la fièvre tierce.*

Jȣenniserontie, *le lendemain.*

Ennisȣan, Ch. *passer le jour à faire quelque chose;* sȣas, so.

ȣagenniso ȣagnaarhon, *j'ai passé tout le jour à écrire.*

Ennisȣaton, *la chose qui fait passer le jour.*

Ennisne, *en haut.* Andichon.

Tȣennisiton, *aller et venir en un jour de quelque lieu.*

ȣatkennisat gannaȣage si ȣagennon, *Je suis allé et venu de Gannaȣage en un jour.*

Enniskotáon, *se mettre devant quelqu'un sur son derrière pour conférer avec luy, ou lui faire le rapport,* v. g. *d'un conseil tenu.*

Enniskotanni, R. *f.* θes.

Enniskotagȣan, *se retirer de devant ceux devant qui l'on estoit ainsi assis.* Enniskotagȣanni, R. *f.* gȣas.

Ennisnonsajen, Ch. *se reposer.*

Ennita, *lune.* Ennitehen, Sateȣenniten, *la pleine lune.*
Aten^c^nitokte, Ch. *la lune finir.* Jotennitonnia, *quartier de lune.*
Areko tsiotennitison, *nondum plena est.*

Ennitaien, Ch. *fianter;* ensken, enne.
Ennitajenton, *de pluribus.*
Jennitaientakȣa, *lieu où l'on f.*
Ennitennion, S. nies, ni; *pedere.*
Tȣennitose, R. *pedere alicui.*
ȣaθagennitos, *il m'a petté au nez.*

Ennitiagon, Ch. *mettre à son col quelq. ornement.* Ennitiasion, *l'oster.*
Tȣennitakaren, 2 *animaux accouplés.*
Ennitaskarenron, Ch. *chien branler le queue.*

Ennitsehȣa, *pance.* Ennitseho, *le ventre enflé.*
Kennihonnitsehȣagarate, *ventre gros comme celà.*

Ennitskȣah-re, *être assis sur quelque chose.*
Sennitskȣaren, *assis toy sur.*
Ennitskȣarakȣa, *ce sur quoy l'on s'asseoit.*

Eñon, *arriver*, S. ens, en, ensere; *a ql. accident bon ou mauvais.*
Hot iseñon hot isen? *Que t'est-il arrivera?*
In comp. usurpatur Jaȣeñon pro eñon.
Gaiataȣeñon, S. ens, en, ensere (*arriver à quelqu'un*).
Gaiataȣenseron, frequent.
Jotsannit sinni ȣagiataȣens, *chose étrange qui m'est arrivée.*
Θosnonte nahojataȣen, *il ne sait ce qui lui est arrivé.*
Θo gi ok neȣagiataȣen, *qu'il m'en arrive ce qui pourra.*
Jogenron sinni ȣagennigonraȣens, *Ce qui s'est passé dans mon esprit n'est pas à négliger.*

Eñon, in comp. ttum, *tomber;* ens, enne, ensere.
Gaiateñon, vide sup. in 2ª conj.
Ontahajatenne v. Eθojateñon, *il est tombé d'en haut.*
Extra comp. Aseñon, vide in 1ª conj. Sic
Enton, R. θa, θ, tanne; *faire tomber*, in comp.
Gaiatataten^c^ton, R. *faire tomber quelqu'un.*
Ontahoñsajatent, *on l'a fait tomber d'en haut.*
Asen^c^ton, extra comp.
Θosa tesasent, *Ne fais pas tomber cela.*

Ense, S. *f.* ens, *tomber à quelqu'un;* in comp.
Jaten te horihȣense, *Il ne s'oublie pas de l'affaire.*
Θosa tasarensens, *Ne laisse pas tomber ton chapelet.*
Extra com. Asense, S.
ȣagasense, *cela m'est tombé des mains.*

Ennon, *aller et venir.*
Ige v. iges, ese; v. Ises, ires, iȣes, &c. V. conj. *præt.* Iȣagennon, Jesennon, Ihaȣennon, Raȣennon.
Jejaȣenrion, *elle est allé.*

Ennoton, Ch. θa, t, tanne; *aller en quelque lieu.*
Sumit 2 ante personas, v. g.
Θo egeθa, *je vas là;* Neθo geneseθa, S. *vas en là.*
Jesȣs garonhiage jesaȣennonton, *Jésus est retourné au ciel.*

Ennonhȣeton, Ch. ts, t, θe; *coucher.*
Ennonhȣeθon, *aller coucher hors de sa cabane.*
Ennonhȣeti, R. *coucher chez quelq.;* sæpe in malam partem.
Ennonhȣeston, *le lieu où l'on couche.*
Ennonhȣetsion, S. *gister en voyage;* sions, si, sionhe.

Ennonna, *garder;* nakȣe, *imp.* ne, nanne.
Gnonsannonnakȣe, *je gardois la cabane.*
Garihȣannonna, Ch. *garder, attendre l'issue d'une affaire.*
Est R. Hinnonna rokskoña, *je parde le petit garçon.*
Gannonnanni, R. *f.* nhas; *garder à quelqu'un.*
Tagnonsannonnhas, *garde moy ma cabane.*

Ennonton, Ch. *perdre patience, attendre quelq.;* tons, tong.
Θo^c^sa tesennontong, *Ne t'impatiente pas.*

Ennontonnion, Ch. *penser, juger.*
Enhontonnion^c^kon, Ch. *penser à q. chose.*
Jennontonnion^c^kȣa, *le jugement, la pensée, l'esprit.*

Ennoȣen, S. *être menteur;* v. Ennoȣenton, S. θa, t, tanne.
Ennoȣentanni, *f.* ten; *faire mentir quelq., luy imputer ce qu'il n'a pas dit.*
Atennoȣenton, Ch. *desmentir.* Est etiam R.
Θosa teskȣatennoȣent, *Ne me donne pas un dementy.*
Ronnoȣentannion, *qui ment toujours.*

Enrhar, *canons de porcelaine.*

Enron, S. rons, re, ronne; *laisser, omettre, rester.*
Assumit notam reit. v. local.
Θo ne tsisenron? *Combien t'en est il resté?*
Naie tsagaȣenron, *Voilà ce qui est resté.*
Skarihȣat eθorihȣenre, *Il omet une chose.*
Atatenron, S. *être resté.*
Gaieri naonsaotatenre, *il en reste* 4.
Atatenron, neut. *rester à quelqu'un.*

Enta v. **Ennisera**, *jour.* Θaȣentenhaȣiton, *qui a emmené le jour.*
Θentenhaȣiθa, *il apporte le jour.*
Etiaȣentonti, *demain.*

Entagon, S. *estre à jeun.*
Entagatste, S. *endurer long temps le faim; jeuner long temps.*
Entaon, S. *jeuner, souffrir la faim;* tas, tanne, tasare.
Jagaȣentas, *la famine.*
Entaston, *jeuner à cause de quelque chose.*

Entaon, in comp. *finir, s'user;* tas, tanne, tasere.
Garihȣentaon, *l'affaire finir.*
Garihȣentaton v. Garihȣentaston, *l'affaire finir par quelque chose.*

Entonni, Ch. nisk, ni, nianne; *s'ennuyer.*

Entonniaton, *faire ennuyer.*

Jaȣentônniat, *O qu'il ennuye bien ici!*

Atentonni, *être anéanti.* V. 1 conj.

Entiek, *midy.*

Entoraon, Ch. rha, ren, ronne; *avoir de la peine à travailler, trouver difficile, n'être pas laborieux.*

Entora[e]kon, *avoir de la peine à cause de*

Atentora[e]kon, Ch. *se peiner en vain pour q. chose;* kȣá, kȣanne.

Entora[e]kȣanni, R. *f.* kȣen; *donner de la peine à quelq.*

Ensitaon, Ch. *brusler le poil de quelq. animal;* tas, taȣe.

Eȣe, *arriver.* V. conj.

Heren, Ahiren, *loin.*

Eren, Ch. *boire;* parum usitatum pro quo Gan[e]negíren, de quocumq. liquor portabili.

ȣagnegiren geñie, *j'ai bu de l'huyle.*

Gannegiráton, *boire q. c. ou avec q. c.*

Erhar, *chien.*

Erie, *cœur*, S. extra comp.

N. raȣeri, *N. est mon cœur, je l'aime.*

Eriasa, in comp. V. Erienta, quamquam istud signat potius *pensée, esprit.*

Eriasannonagon, S. *avoir mal au cœur;* ks, g, χe.

Eriasentaon, S. *faire tomber son cœur,* seu *remercier quelqu'un de qui l'on a receu quelque grâce.*

Skat ongneri v. ongneriasont, *Nous n'avons qu'un même cœur.*

Neθo nonȣe si jongȣeriasontaken, *à l'endroit de notre cœur.*

Eriaté, S. *avoir du cœur.*

Tȣateriatikon, Ch. *être en colère.*

Erientȣannen, S. *grand esprit.*

Erientakseñon, S. sens, sen, sensere; *être faché.*

Erientaksaton, S. *être faché pour q. c.;* θa, t, tanne. Est etiam R. *facher quelqu'un.*

Aterientaksaton, R. *gaster l'esprit de quelqu'un.*

Erientare, R. tarhe, taren; *tenir l'esprit de quelqu'un; suspendre, troubler quelqu'un, l'interrompre.*

Aterientáre, S. *juger, estimer.*

Aterientajenton, Ch. *penser, examiner;* tons, ton, tonne, est R.

Aterientojenton[e]kon, *ce par quoi l'on pense.* Inde Tȣaterientajentonkȣa, *notre esprit, notre pensée.*

Aterientatsenrion, Ch. *avoir trouvé quelque invention, être inventif.*

Aterientiagon, Ch. *perdre l'espérance de quelque chose.*

Onne joterientiagon ȣatȣenheie, *C'en est fait, nous sommes morts sans ressource.*

Aterientiagi, R. *ôter l'esprit à quelqu'un.*

Aterientokte, Ch. θa, ten; *perdre l'espérance, être à bout de ses pensées.*

Erientoriannon, R. *aller divertir, distraire quelqu'un.*

Sagaȣerientoriannon gajenθoge hejagaȣennon, *Il est aller desennuyer ceux qui travaillent aux champs.*

Eri, *merizier.*

Eron, igere, igerhakȣe, ȣageran, ȣagerhe, engerheg, *pensée, vouloir.*

Igere ahagitenre, *Je pense qu'il ayt pitie de moy.*

Es v. **Eson**, es, esonhag; *long*, in comp.

Garihȣes, *longue affaire.* Gannonses, *longue cabane.*

Gannateson^c^nen, *le village étoit long.*

Jons v. Jonsons, extra comp.

Θo najonsonhag, *De quelle longueur doit-il être?*

Ken nionsonsa, *un peu long.*

Esagon, Ch. ke, g, χe; *chercher.*

Gaiatisagon, R. *chercher quelqu'un.*

Esagi, R. acq. *chercher à quelqu'un.*

Tagȣesaks, *chercher moy*, v. g. *des poux.*

Eso, *beaucoup.* Esotsi, *multum nimis.*

Etage, *en bas.* Etageson, egatenti, *je marcherai par le chemin qui est dans le bois; j'iray par terre.*

VERBA 4^ae^ CONJUGATIONIS.

Genheion, Ch. hons, heie, heionsere; *mourir.*

Genheiaton, Ch. θa, t, tanne; *mourir pour q. c.*

Gaiatagenheion, Ch. *être flasque.*

Gaiatagenheiaton, *être flasque, foible par q. c.*

Genheiase, R. *mourir q. c. à quelqu'un.*

Honna^c^kȣagenheiase, *sa femme luy est morte.*

Genhejonta, *moribond.*

Genheiontannonna, *garder un moribond.*

Θo niȣenhejontȣten, *Comment se porte le moribond?*

Ontatenheiontenhaȣi, *On apporte un malade.*

Gengȣite, *le printemps.* Gengȣitetsi, *au petit printemps.*

Geñie, extra comp. Gaienna, in comp. *huile ou graisse liquide.*

Geñieȣaton, Ch. θa, t, tanne; *faire de l'huile.*

Gaiennogȣan, Ch. *lever l'huyle ou graisse.*

Raȣejennagate, *il a beaucoup d'huile.*

Jaȣejennat, *il y a de l'huyle.*

Gaiennaronnion, *sali de l'huyle.*

Gannaie, *l'été passé.*

Oia tsi tgennaie, *Il y a deux étés.*

Gennaieson, *tous les ans.*

Gennhongon, R. ks, g, kse; *appeler quelqu'un.*

Gennhonkton, R. *l'appeler pour ou par q. c.*

Gennhonkson, R. *aller querir, appeler quel.*

Genstokȣa, *un paquet de hardes ou d'autres choses,*

Gent, usitatius Genton, *parler de quelqu'un.*
I hagiton, *C'est de moy qu'il parle.*
N. gitakȣe, *Je parlois d'elle.*

Ota, in comp. Genta, extra comp., vel Ota additur omnibus fere verbis irrisionis vel contemptus; *fiante*, v. gennita.
Ihentaks, *il mange de la fiente.*
Aχetario, *Que je batte leur fiente.*
ȣagennitatsennonni, *je suis heureux.*
Gentannonhȣeon, R. *aimer une gueuserie.*
Gentare, *il y a de la fiante.*

Gentáon, S. *dormir;* task, tahȣe, tasere v. taseg.

Gentágre. Ch. grakȣe, grek, granne; *être gisant.*
Rentagre, *il est gisant.* Ronnitagrakȣe, *jacebant.*
Gentagre, R. gre, gren, grende; *mettre au lit de quelq.*
Ken θo hensitagren, *Mets le coucher là.*
Ken sennitagren, *hic jaceas.*
Gentagráon, Ch. *tomber;* gras, granne, grasere.
ȣagitagranne, *Me voilà tombé.*
Rentagraseronne, *Il va tombant et retombant.*

Gentare, *poil rouge que l'on mets autour de la teste ou au col.*
Gentien, S. *porter au col q. c.*
Gentjasion, *oster de son col;* est R.

Gentenron, R. *avoir pitié de quelq.;* rhe, re, ranne.
Sumitur neut. estq. Parad. S.
Taonχen ongitenre, *O la bonne rencontre pour moy!*
ȣesentenre, *Ca été ùn bon jour pour moi.*
Gentenraton, *avoir pitié à cause de q.*
Naie skitenraθa, *Ideo misereris mihi.*
Atanditenron, S. *être miséricordieux.*
Atatitenron, Ch. *déplorer sa misère.*
Atatitenraton, Ch. *se consoler par q. c.*

Gentio^c^kȣa, S. *troupe, assemblée.*
Gentio^c^kȣate, *il y a là une troupe.*
Gentio^c^kȣagohon, he, ha, hese; *aller querir une troupe.*
Ennitio^c^kȣison, sas, sa, saanne; *s'assembler.*
Onne honnenditio^c^kȣison, *on est assemblé.*
Ennitio^c^kȣaχasion, *l'assemblée se finir, séparer.*

Genteron, ron, rontag; *être en quelq. lieu.*
Jeteron, *il y a quelqu'un.*
Genteronta^c^kon, *être à quelqu'un.*
Genteron, R. *mettre q. c. animée en quel. lieu.*
Θo hetsiteron nhaksaa, *mets-la cet enfant.*
Genteronnon, R. *aller mener quelq.* ronne, ronna.
Tagiteronna, *viens moy mener.*
Genteronta^c^kon, R. *mener quelq. avec q. c.*

Gentskare, S. *natte, avoir une natte.*
Gentskaron, *estendre, mettre la natte.*
Gentskaranni, R. *f.* rhas; *mettre une natte à quelq.*
Gentskara^ckon, *avoir pour natte q. chose.*
Ennitskare, Ennitskara^ckon, *avoir pour natte q. c.*

Gentskôte, Ch. *impf.* takȣe, tag, tasere; *être en quelq. lieu.*
Θo siskotag, *Sois, demeure là.*
Gentskota^ckon, *être en q. lieu pour q. chose.*

Gentsion, S. *poisson.* Gentsiagon, Ch. *en manger.*
Gentsiagohon, Ch. *en aller chercher.*

Kentsion^ckon, Ch. *esternuer;* ka, g.
Te sentsionka, *tu esternues.*

Otsok, *blé qu'on groule dans les cendres;* extra comp.
Gentsokȣa, in comp.
Gentsokont, Ch. θa, ten, tanne; *en grouler.*
Gentsokontanni, R. *f.* θas; *en grouler à quelq.*
Tagitsokonθas, *groule moy de ce blé.*
Rentsokȣagatsθa, *le grand mangeur de blé groulé.*

Genθeon, S. θe; *être bête, sans esprit.*
Taonχenroθe, *O qu'il est beste!*
Genθeston, R. *rendre beste quelq.;* θa, ste.

Genθentéon, S. *être digne de compassion;* θa, te.
Ongiθente, *Je suis digne de compassion.*

I.

VERBA QUÆDAM IN I QUÆ ENTRANT IN COMPOSITIONEM, ET SUNT DIVERSÆ CONJUGATIONIS.

I, *moi, nous 2, nous 3 ou plusieurs.*
Te jagniase, *nous deux.* Vide conj.

I, compositum signat plenitudinem; J, Jg, Jsere.
Gannonsi, *la cabane est pleine.*
Egannonsig, *la cabane sera pleine.*
Garihȣi, *présent complet.*

I, compositum solitudinem exprimit:
Agonha ate giati, *moy seul.*
Jennaie okti agaonhȣa ontatiatis, *Ceux-là sont superbes qui ne parlent que d'eux en racontant,* v. g. *quelque histoire.*

Ise, neutr. S. *s'emplir à quelqu'un.*
ȣagetsetisa, *ma courage mihi impleta est.*

Ise, R. act. *f.* is, Tagnatsis; *remplis moi ma chaudière.*

Innigenhon, in comp. ens, enn, enhȣe; *mettre dehors.*
Gaiatinnigenhon, *mettre dehors quelqu'un.*
Innigenhonse, R. acq. Tagiatinnigensoha, *mets moi cette bette,* v. g. *ce chien dehors.*
Asongȣasirinnigeris, *Il nous a enlevé une couverte.*

Innigeñon, ens, enn, ensere; *sortir de quelque lieu où on étoit caché,* v. g. *un enfant du ventre de sa mère.*

Ontahajatinnigenne, *Il est sorti du.* Innigense, R. acq. S. *sortir à quelqu'un.*

Jaȣetȣanni nongiatinnigense onnerenha, *Quantité de vers luy sont sortis du corps.*

Innion, *entrer.*

Ongieson ontagarakȣinnion, *Le soleil entre dans la chambre.*

Arecko jorihȣinnion, *La nouvelle n'est pas encore venu.*

Innionton, θa, t, tanne; *faire entrer, admettre.*

ȣahannakȣinniont, *Il fit entrer une pique.*

Jagoiarinnionton, *On a porté le sac là dedans.*

Gaiatinnionton, R. *faire entrer quelq.*

Inniontanni, R. *f.* ten; *introduire à quelqu'un.*

Io, in comp. ttum, *beau, bon.*

Gaiatio, *être beau.* Garihȣio, *bonne affaire.*

Horihȣio, *esprit bien fait, bon.*

Raȣendio, *Dominus est, vox ejus est pulchra* seu *vim magnam habet.*

Ioston, sθa, ste, stanne, in comp.

Gaȣendioston, R. *reconnoitre quelq. pour maitre; θa,* t, tanne.

Gaȣendiostackon, R. *le reconnoitre maitre par q. c.*

Atȣendioston, Ch. *se faire maistre, seigneur de q. c.*

Atȣendiostackon, Ch. *se faire maître par q. c.*

Garihȣioston, Ch. *credere quasi magni facere rem auditam.*

Rorihȣioston, *un chrestien.*

Garihȣiostackon, Ch. *credere propter aliquid.*

Ionni, in comp. ttum, *s'advancer en pointe.*

Jongȣannenrionnihatie, *Nous allons comme en procession, les uns advancent devant les autres.*

Eθohajationni, *il est là gisant.*

Okti sajationni iaten satonrianneronsk, *Il est estendre tout de son long sans se remuer.*

Ionniaton, R. θa, t, tate; *estendre en long.*

Hetsiationniat, *Mets, étends-le de son long.*

Aetȣannenrionniat, *étendons, allongeons notre procession.*

Isen, in comp. ttum, *heurter.*

Gannhohȣisen, *frapper à la porte.*

ȣahogonretsisat, *Il a heurté sa main.*

Hannhohȣisonnionk, *Il ne fait qu'heurter à la porte.*

Itsaanni, R. *f.* isen; *piler à quelqu'un.*

Tagegakȣentisen, *pile-moy des poix.* Tagnogȣarisen.

It, R. in comp. *p.* & *f.* θa, taanne; *embarquer quelqu'un.*

Gaiatit, R. tagiatita, *embarque moy.*

Gaiatitackon, R. *embarquer dans quelq. vaisseau.* *pns.* kȣa, *f.* tak *n.* takȣanne.

Eskiatitak no sahoñeja, *Tu m'embarqueras dans ton canot.*

Gaiatitakȣan, R. kȣas, kȣa, kȣanne; *débarquer quelqu'un.*

It, neutr. in comp. *être embarqué.* It, activum.
Satakȣendita, *embarque ses hardes.*
Itaanni, R. *embarquer à quelq. ses.*
Atit, pass. *p.* & *f.* θa, *n.* taanne; *s'embarquer.*
Atita^c^kon, takȣa, tak, takȣanni; *s'embarquér en q. c.*
Atita^c^kȣan, kȣas, ko, kohe; *se débarquer.*
Atitakȣanni, R. *f.* kȣen; *se débarquer du canot du quelq.*

Itaχon, cum te divisionis in comp. *f.* tag.
ȣatȣagasinnitag, *J'ai froid aux pieds.*
ȣaθasinnitontago, *Il s'est gelé les pieds.*

Iton, inusit. pro quo Ioton, iot, iotonhag, iotonnen.
Neθo niot, *comme cela;* Θo niot, *pourquoy;* Hot gati niot, *cur;* Ok ken tiot, *comme cela;* Sate jot, *c'est tout de même.*
Ontajotonhatie si nahe, *Il va toujours de même depuis que.*

O.

O, inusitatum pro quo dic Iotó, *cela est enflé.* Eȣato, *cela s'est enflé.*
Atoose, S. *venir des enflures à quelqu'un.*
Ongȣátos, *il m'est venu une enflure.*

O, compositum. Sarasito, *tu as le pied enflé.*
ȣagatkonso, *j'ay le visage enflé.*

Oaȣie, *la rosée.* Ejoaȣiaθen egatenti, *Je partiray quand la rosée sera abbattue.*
Ongȣaȣiaks, *J'ay eu la rosée.*

Oge, *avoir des empoulles.* S.
Te ȣagasitoge, *J'ay des empoulles au pied.*

O, *y avoir ou mettre dans l'eau.*
Hinnon etkannego, *l'eau est bien basse.*
Garonto, *un arbre dans l'eau;* dela, *les canot de l'eau.*
Gahȣendo, *une isle.*
Igasco, de re vivente, *qui est dans l'eau.*

O signat etiam *être en un lieu humide.*
Gataro, *il y a de la terre.* Sic
Ganne^c^rio te hagakarent, *Il y a une taye dans ton œil.* V. Honnesio, *il a,* parad. S.

Ohon, hos, ho, hose; *mettre dans quelq. liqueur.*
Jagonnonkȣatserohon, *On a mis, jette un sort dans.*
Hotihoñjohon, *Ils ont mis le canot dans l'eau.*
Gannatsiatogetonge esnennisnonsok onne jensataȣiatonnonsatogeti, *Tu mettras ton doigt dans le bénitier en entrant dans l'église.*
Nota ȣahaaronne, *Il va tendre un rets.*

Ohose, R. *f.* θhos. Tageθeserohos, *Mets moy de la farine au pot.*

Oón, os, oha, ohe; *tomber dans l'eau.*
Jaóon, *Celà est tombé dans l'eau.*
Gaskóon, *faire naufrage.* V. Ose, neutr. acq. S. *f.* os.
Ongȣahonros, *Mon fusil est tombé dans l'eau.*

Nota ȣationgȣarakos, *Le soleil nous a fait mal aux yeux.* Quæ habent te dualitatis quia duo sunt oculi.

Gaskose, neut. acq. S. *Une chose vivante tomber dans l'eau à quelq.*

Ogȣan, gȣas, go, gohe; *retirer de l'eau.*

Sogo, *tire de l'eau.* Snegogo, *retire l'eau.*

Atogȣan, dep. *se retirer de l'eau,* cum nota reit.

Ogȣanni, R. *f.* ogȣas; *tirer de l'eau à quelqu'un.*

Ogen, *impers.* on, *f.* ka, *n.* gasere; *faire eau.*

Onne ȣaoka sontak, *Ta chaudière fait eau.*

Ogẹn, pers. S. Onne ȣaongioχa, *Voilà que notre canot fait eau.*

Jàten te jongiogasere, *Nous n'aurons point d'eau.*

Ogen, *chercher des fruits de terre, pommes de terre.*

Jonχa, *on en cherche.* Ogennion, freq.

Tiogen, cum te, dual. signat intervallum sive aliquid medium.

Te gannosógen, *entre 2 cabanes.*

Te jaógen, Te jaontarógen, *Où il y a deux rivières qui se croisent, qui se rencontrent.*

Te joθahogen, *Où il y a 2 chemins fourchus.*

Tiogen, compositum, fit aliquando personale, v. g.

Te ȣȣannonsogen ne tsiarase N. ȣahoñario, *N. fùt tûé entre ta cabane et celle de ton cousin.*

Ogennen (Huro), *dessous.* Garontogennen, *dessous un arbre.*

Ogerijon, *escailler, escosser fezoles, chataignes.* Ogeñjase, R. *f.* as.

Ogon, præpos. sub dessous. Gaskontorogon, *dessous l'écorce.*

Ogon, S. *être vuide, n'avoir rien.*

Raogon onsaraȣe, *Il est retourné à vide.*

Aogon iagȣaks, *Nous mangeons de la sagamité sans assaissonnement.*

Aagonge, *Il n'y a personne dans le village, dans la cabane.*

Ogoñaton, T. S. t, tanne; *racler, ôter le poil d'une peau.* Ch.

Kennihase gȣatserȣtakȣa jagogoñaθa, *Je viens emprunter le piquet sur lequel on racle la peau.*

Ohare, Ch. res, re, renne; *laver.*

Gaksohare, Ch. *laver un plat.* Extra comp. Gannohare, v. 1ae.

Oharese, R. *f.* res.

Ohárc, *emmancher.* Saserohären, *emmanche la hache.*

Sroñaroharen, *emmanche l'alesne.*

Okaon, R. kas, ka, kaȣe; *graisser, huiler.*

ȣagoñjoka, *que je te graisse.*

Atokaon, Ch. *se graisser, s'huiler.*

Okȣiráon, S. ras, ra, rahȣe; *faire bouillie de la viande que l'on réserve pour les affaires.*

On, *dònner,* R. Gatagon, *donne moy.*

Sagaon, *il leur a donné;* intrat etiam in comp.

Oñárate, *houe de bois.*

Ongie, *dans la cabane;* ongiason.

Ongóon, os, o, osere; *pénetrer, passer outre.*

Jaten te geȣennongos, *Ma voix ne pénetre pas, je parle en vain.*

Jaten te saȣennongos, *On n'entend plus sa voix; elle ne passe plus à travers*, v. g. *d'un enrouée.*

Ongoton, Ch. θa, t, tanne; *faire pénetrer.*

Ongotanni, R. *f.* ten; *faire pénetrer.*

Atongoton, Ch. θa, t, tanne; *passer outre, pénetrer.*

Ennonsongotannion, dep. *traverser les cabanes en les visitant.*

Atongotanni, R. *f.* ten; *passer outre devant quelq. en marchant.*

Atongotackon, *le lieu à travers lequel on passe.*

Tȣatiatongaton, S. *avoir le flus, aller du ventre.*

Te jagotiatongotackȣa onnonckȣat, *médecine purgative.*

Te jotiatongotanne ȣahorio, *le flus le tue.*

Ongoron, S. *avoir des soulèvemens de cœur, estre provoqué à vomir.*

Ongoriaton, S. *ce qui provoque à vomir.*

Ongȣe, *homme;* caret incrementis distinctivis temporum quæ supplentur per Igen.

Jaten songȣe tegen v. songȣesnon, *Comme si tu estois un homme, grand injure.*

Ongȣe, per antonomasion dicitur *d'une personne libérale, sage, irréprochable.*

Ongȣesera v. Ongȣeta, in compositione, *hommerie.*

J agongȣeta, *C'est ma créature, mon sujet.*

Hongȣeserio, *bel homme.* Hongȣetaksen, *laid homme.*

Hongȣetatsannit, *homme épouvantable.*

Ongȣetison, neutr. *être homme fait; p.* & *f.* sa.

Ongȣekȣannen, *estre homme fait depuis* 40 *à* 60 *ans.*

Onharon, Ch. rons, ron, ronne; *sarcler le blé.*

Onheȣen, Ch. *balier;* eȣas, eo. Jagonheȣaθa, *un balai.*

Tionharenron, *rendre malade.* Parum usitat pro quo Tȣatonharenron, S. *être en peine, en appréhension de quelque malheur;* ronsk, ron, ronne.

Tȣatonharenronckon, S. *être en crainte à cause de q. chose.*

Onhȣa, *seul*, S. Agonhȣa, sonhȣa.

Onhȣentsia, *terre*, S.

Diȣ raonhȣentison, *Dieu a fait la terre.*

Onhȣentsiannentágon, Ch. *Attacher son pays à un autre, demeurer ailleurs.*

Atonhȣentsiannentacsion, *Quitter son pays pour aller ailleurs demeurer, s'établir.*

Atonhȣentsionni, S. *Avoir besoin de q. c. de valeur qu'on a peine de trouver.*

Jotenhȣentsiohon najontenti, *On ne trouve personne pour partir.*

Onkaron, *ronfler;* ronsk, ron, ronne.

Onnegon, Ch. *retirer, éloigner q. chose.*

Atonnegon, Ch. kȣe, k, kse; *se retirer, s'éloigner.*

Satonnek, *retire toi.*

Ontereon v. **Onteron**, Ch. res, re, resere; *accorder, consentir.*

Onnha, *vie.* Onnhio, *vie qui est pour durer.*
Onhegatste, S. *avoir de la vie dure.*
Atonnhegatste, *être bon ménager.*
Onnhongennion, R. *surmonter la vie de quelq.;* nies, ni, nionhe.
Onnhe, Ch. *impf.* nhekȣe; *f.* nheg, *vivre.*
Diȣ songionnhekesie, *Dieu nous va donnant la vie.*
Onnhekon, *impf.* konnen; *vivre pour q. c. ou par q. c.*
Onnaie tionnhekon sirere Raȣendio ajongeȣennarakȣag, *La cause pour quoy nous vivons c'est que Dieu veut qu'on lui obéisse.*

Onnheson, sons, es; *avoir longue vie.*
Onnheston, *prolonger la vie.*
Naie jongionnhestonhatie, *hoc producit vitam nostram.*
Onnheton, R. ts, t, θe; *donner la vie.*
Onnheton, cum redup. *résusciter quelqu'un.*
Atonnheton, *avoir la vie.* Ch.
Jaten te agrihȣanderen si nahe etȣagasonnheton, *Non peccavi a nativitate mea.*
Atonheton, cum reit. *résusciter.* Atonnhatention, *mourir.*
Tȣatonnhakarien, Ch. rias, ri, rihe; *être misérable, souffrir.*
Tȣatonnhakariakton, R. θa, t, tanne.

Onnion, Ch. nisk, ni, nianne; *faire, être cause.*
Onnianni, R. *f.* nien; *faire à quelqu'un.*
Garihonnion, Ch. *être la cause.*
Naie ȣagarihonni, v. Naie ȣahonni, *C'est parceq.*
Garihonnianni, R. *f.* nien; *enseigner quelqu'un.*
Atrihonnianni, Ch. *s'instruire.*

Onnjon, fit rel. quando refertur ad 1am personam, v. g.
Jojandere ȣasongionni, *Il nous a mit à notre aise.*
Otkon esongionni, *Il nous rendra esprits.*
Songȣannaskoni, *Il nous a fait esclaves.*
Atonni, *être fait naître.*
Hotonnia, *petit enfant qui est né devant le temps.*
Atonni, S. *avoir des parents du côté de son père.*
Atonnisen, S. *imp.* takȣe, *f.* tak.
Atatonni, recip. Otkon hotatonni, *Il s'est fait démon.*
Otkon songȣatatonnianni, *Nobis factus est dœmon.*
Atatonnianni, recip.

Onniaton, *employer q. c. à en faire une autre.*
Onneja gannonsonniaton, *cabane faite de pierre.*
Item cum partic. Skati signat *tourner de l'autre côté.*
Skati sonniat, *Fais tourner de l'autre côté.*
Atonniaton, Ch. *Naître en un tel temps ou lieu.*

Onni, adverb. *aussi,* conjunc. Igere onni, *Je veux aussi.*

Oncnia, *pointe de terre.* Oncniate, *il y a une pointe.*
Ti oncnionni, *pointe qui advance sur la rivière.*
ȣahatonniatase, *il a fait le tour de la pointe.*

Onnison, Ch. *faire;* sas, sa, saanne.

Onnônni, S. nos, nonne, nosere; *iñonder, être gagné de l'eau.*

Onne ȣaongionne, *L'eau nous va gagner, entre chez nous.*

On^{c}dȣton, S. *avoir de l'eau, être profond.*

Honnendȣton, *L'eau entre dans la cabane.*

Θo niondȣtes, *De quelle profondeur est?*

Onneñon, *s'affaisser,* in comp.

Josiseronneñonhatie, S. ige; *La glace s'affaisse sous mes pieds.*

Gannonseñon, *cabane s'affaisser.*

Onnonhȣenha, *la fleur du blé.*

Onȣesaon, S. sas, sa, sasere; *être aisé, se rejouir.* Onȣesaseron, freq.

Jonȣesen garonhiage, *Il fait bon; on est bien content au ciel.*

Onȣeskȣanni, sumpt. neutr. est Parad. S. *f.* ken; *être content.*

Onȣeskȣaton, *agréer à cause de q. chose.*

Jaonȣeskȣat nontrendajensk, *Il y a du plaisir à prier.*

Onȣeskȣanni, *est* aliquando rel.

Jaten te hiatonȣeskȣanni, *Je ne l'agrée pas.* Atatonȣeskȣanni, recip.

Ajontatoneskȣen onne ȣagonniag, *Ceux qui se marient devroient s'entreaggréer.*

Onȣeskȣanniton, S. *p.* & *f.* θ, tanne; *agréer à cause de q. chose.*

Ongȣeton, R. *décourager quelq.* Vix in usu, θa, t, tanne.

Ongȣeta^{c}kon, R. kȣa, k, kȣanne; *faire perdre courage.*

Atongȣe^{c}ton, dep. *perdre courage.* Ch.

Atongȣetanni, R. *f.* ten; *perdre courage à l'occasion de q. chose.*

Onria, *haleine.*

Atonrion, Ch. ries, ri, rionne; *respirer.*

Atonrieton, θa, t, tanne; *respirer avec q. chose.*

Naie gatonrieθa Jesȣs ȣaθennonhȣeron, *Je ne respire point que pour invoquer Jésus.*

Atonnajen, *faire le hé, hé.*

Atonriajenni, R. *f.* enhas. V. in 1^{a} conj.

Onrisera, *haleine, souffle.*

Seg aesonriserannirha nange, *A fin que tu sois fort d'haleine.*

Ti onriserakȣan, cum te affirm. *N'en pouvoir plus.*

Usitatius Atonriserakȣan, cum te affir. *perdre haleine de foiblesse.*

Atonrisen, Ch. ens, en, enne; *se reposer.*

Atonrisenton, *se reposer souvent.*

Atonrisenta^{c}kon, Ch. *lieu où l'on se repose.*

Atonriserongoton, Ch. *respirer.*

Onsennon, S. *se plaindre* (d'un malade), nha, nn.

Ont, *être.* Semper postponitur vocabulis nec dicitur extra comp.

Gannhohont, *il y a une porte.* Te hasitont, *il a 2 pieds.*

Garihont, *avoir quelq. liaison, rapport.* Jaten te tsiorihant.

Ont, *faire être.* Tȣajatagȣegon songȣajatison Diȣ, agȣegen ȣasongȣagonsonten, ȣasongȣannentsonten, &c. *Dieu a fait tout notre corps, notre face, nos bras, &c.*

Sennhohonten, *faire une porte.*

Onta^{c}kon, postpositam voci signat *être de la forme morale* ou *physique d'un autre; impf.* konnen, *f.* kong, konhag.

Gannakȣa hondigonrontagon, *Il a l'esprit rempli de.*

Ganniegehage raȣennontagon, *Il parle la langue d'Agnier.*

Ongȣe gagonsonta^{c}kon gario, *Un animal qui a la face d'homme.*

Otkon gaiatontakon, *Il a la forme d'un démon.*

Garihȣa rajatontakon, *homme d'affaire.*

Ontakon, takȣa, tak, takȣanne; *donner à q. chose la forme morale ou physique; faire à q. chose par le motif d'un autre.*

θosa gannakȣa tesrihonta^{c}k neθo nensiere, *Quand tu feras ainsi, ne le fais pas par le motif du plaisir déshonnête.*

Gannakȣa harihontakȣa, *Il fait allusion en parlant aux choses sales.*

Atrendajent hoñandigon^{c}rontakon nonaieña, *Ses parents l'ont accoûtumé à prier.*

Ontakȣanni, R. acq.

Ongȣe songȣatiatontakȣanni notkon, *Le démon nous a paru en forme humaine.*

Ont, *mettre au feu;* θa, ten, tanne. Ontanni, R. *f.* θas.

Gannataront, S. θa, ten, tanne; *mettre du pain au four, au feu.*

Atnataront, S. *mettre du pain au feu pour soi.*

Tagnonkȣeñonθas, *Fais moi rôtir un épy.*

Onθon pro Onta^{c}kon, θosk, θo, θosere; *faire être dans le feu.*

Sonθo, *mets au feu.* Sientonθo, *mets du bois au feu.*

Onθanni, R. *f.* θas; *mettre cuire pour quelq.*

Ontak, S. *chaudière,* extra comp.

Ontak onȣe, *chaudière de terre.*

Ontak jotsogri, *chaudière ronde.*

Ontaȣeton, *trembler;* θa, t, tanne. Gaiatontaȣe^{c}ton, Ch. *frissonner.*

Garistontaȣe^{c}ton, Ch. *sonner une cloche.*

Jaontaȣeθa raondigonra, *Son esprit n'est pas rassurè; il tremble de peur.*

Ontarhéon, neut. *entrer, s'accrocher.*

ȣagatonkontarhenne rajatagon genha, *La flamme entra, s'attacha à son corps.*

Gaiatontarheon, *une chose vivante s'accrocher.*

Ontarheton, neut. S. *faire entrer.*

ȣahonnenstontarhet, *Il s'est fait entrer un grain de blé,* v. g. *dans le nez.*

Ontentáon, Ch. tas, taȣe, tasere; *brusler les champs.*

Onte^{c}ton, cum reitr. θa, t; *se trouver mieux.*

Jaten te tsiaonteθa, *On est très mal* (est R.).

Jaten te sȣagontetannen, *Je n'en pouvois plus.*

Oreñon, in comp. rens, renne, rensere; *trouver.*

Garihoreñon, Ch. *trouver l'affaire.*

Gaiatoreñon, *trouver quelqu'un.*

Tioren, *fendre;* ens, en, ensere. Tiorenseron, frequent.

Tȣatoren, pass. *être fendu;* utriusque parad.

Orianneron, ronsk, ron, ronne; *se mouvoir.*
Atorianneron, Ch. *se remuer, se deffendre.*
Atorianneron^{e}kon, Ch. *p.* & *f.* kȣa; *ce que fait mouvoir.*
Oron, *être sali de q. chose.*
Jaoronnion onnonkȣat, *Cela est infecté, sali par la médecine.*
Gaiataron, S. *Une chose vivante être sali.*
Orongȣan, Ch. *ramasser, recueillir.*
Osa, S. *robbe.* Osonni, Ch. *faire une robbe;* v. Osaon, Ch. sask, sa, saanne.
Tsiosat tsonnito, *Une robe de castor,* id est 6 *castors.*
Osera, *hyver.* Tioseriagon, S. ks, g, χe; *passer l'hyver.*
Ejongioserannoron, *Nous aurons peine de passer l'hyver.*
Tioserongoton, S. *idem.*
Iotoseratsannit, *hyver épouvantable.*
Oseraton, S. ts, t, θe; *l'hyver venir.*
Onne ongioserat, *Nous voilà dans l'hyver.* Oseraton, imperson.
Jaten te joserat garonhiage, *Il n'y a point d'hyver au ciel.*
Oseragi v. Koserhenne, *dans l'hyver.*
Atoseron, S. depon. rons, ron, ronne; *hyverner.*
Oserhon, rast, raȣe; *Mettre de l'eau dedans, inficere aliquem,* in comp.
Aetȣahoñoseraȣe, *Mettrons de l'eau dans le canot.*
Eskȣagenroseraȣe, *Tu me gâteras de cendres.*
Oseragеȣan, ȣas, ȣa, ȣahȣe; *nettoyer, laver quelq.*
Est R. Tagiatoseragеȣe, *lave, nettoye nous.*
Otarhon, Ch. hosk, ho, hosere; *accrocher.*
Garihȣtarhon, Ch. *l'affaire être accrochée.*
Otarhose, neutr. acq. S.
Ongȣaserotarhos, *Ma hache s'est accrochée.*
Atiatotarhon, *Se retirer pour occuper moins de place.*

www.ingramcontent.com/pod-product-compliance
Lightning Source LLC
LaVergne TN
LVHW021414110826
845150LV00007B/1917